# AP® PSYCHOLOGY
# CRASH COURSE®

I0109897

Nancy Fenton, M.A.
Jessica Flitter, M.A.

**Research & Education Association**
www.rea.com

## ABOUT REA

Founded in 1959, Research & Education Association (REA) is dedicated to publishing the finest and most effective educational materials—including study guides and test preps—for students of all ages.

Today, REA's wide-ranging catalog is a leading resource for students, teachers, and other professionals. Visit *www.rea.com* to see our complete catalog.

*Research & Education Association*
1325 Franklin Ave., Suite 250
Garden City, NY 11530
Email: info@rea.com

# AP® PSYCHOLOGY CRASH COURSE, 4th Edition

Printed in the United States of America

Library of Congress Control Number 2024952505

ISBN-13: 978-0-7386-1285-0
ISBN-10: 0-7386-1285-5

# AP® Psychology
# Crash Course
# TABLE OF CONTENTS

**PART I**

## INTRODUCTION

**PART II**

## CONTENT REVIEW

### UNIT 1: Biological Bases of Behavior

### UNIT 2: Cognition

### UNIT 3: Development and Learning

## REA ACKNOWLEDGMENTS

REA thanks the following for bringing this book to life: Pam Weston, publisher; Larry B. Kling, editorial director; Joe Kraynak, copy editor; Caroline Shupe, technical editor; Sally Fay, proofreader; Caragraphics, composition services; Jennifer Calhoun, book file prep; and Heidi Gagnon, digital content prep.

## ABOUT OUR BOOK

REA's *AP® Psychology Crash Course* is designed for the last-minute studier who wants a quick refresher before the AP® exam or the student who wants access to review materials to help prepare for exams in their AP® Psychology class. This *Crash Course* is based on the latest AP® Psychology course and exam description and focuses on the key information you need to make the best use of your study time. Its comprehensive coverage and user-friendly format make it an invaluable tool for reinforcing your understanding of class material and achieving success.

Written by veteran AP® Psychology teachers, our *Crash Course* gives you a concise review of the major concepts and important topics tested on the AP® Psychology digital exam.

- Part I gives you **Keys to Success** to tackle the exam confidently.

- Part II gives you a comprehensive **Content Review**, which covers every critical aspect of today's exam.

- Part III gives you specific **Test-Taking Strategies** to conquer the multiple-choice and free-response questions, along with AP®-style **Practice Questions** to prepare you for what you will see on exam day.

## ABOUT OUR ONLINE PRACTICE EXAM

How ready are you for the AP® Psychology exam? Find out by taking **REA's online practice exam** available at *www.rea.com/studycenter*. This test features automatic scoring, detailed explanations of all answers, and diagnostic score reporting that will help you identify your strengths and weaknesses so you can be ready on exam day.

Whether you use this book throughout the school year or as a refresher in the final weeks before the exam, REA's *Crash Course* will show you how to study efficiently and strategically so you can boost your score.

*Good luck on your AP® Psychology exam!*

## ABOUT OUR AUTHORS

**Jessica Flitter, M.A.**, teaches AP® Psychology at West Bend East High School in West Bend, Wisconsin. She has taught the course since 2004 and has participated in the AP® Reading as a Reader, Table Leader, and Question Leader. Ms. Flitter is a College Board Consultant. In addition, she has served on textbook content advisory boards, worked on assessment banks, and recorded AP® Daily videos. Ms. Flitter also contributes to the *Books for Psychology Class Blog.*

**Nancy Fenton, M.A.**, teaches AP® Psychology at Adlai E. Stevenson High School in Lincolnshire, Illinois, and psychology online for the Center for Talent Development at Northwestern University. Ms. Fenton has been an AP® Psychology instructor since 2006 and participated in the AP® Psychology exam reading since 2008 as a Reader and Table Leader and became a College Board Consultant in 2014. She has written questions for AP® Classroom and recorded AP® Daily videos. She holds a B.A. in History and Secondary Education and two M.A. degrees, in Psychology and Curriculum & Instruction. Ms. Fenton also contributes to the *Books for Psychology Class Blog* and is a co-author of the *AP® United States Government and Politics Crash Course* review book.

## ABOUT OUR TECHNICAL EDITOR

**Caroline Shupe** is an AP® Psychology teacher with more than 16 years of experience teaching psychology and AP® Psychology at Adlai E. Stevenson High School in Lincolnshire, Illinois. Ms. Shupe is passionate about making psychology engaging and accessible for high school students. She is a team leader for the Psychology team at Stevenson High and is a co-sponsor of Stevenson's Psychology Club. In addition to teaching, she has also presented at local and national education conferences on topics related to psychology education, innovative teaching strategies, and student engagement. Ms. Shupe holds a bachelor's degree from Illinois State University and a master's degree from Northwestern University.

## AUTHORS' ACKNOWLEDGMENTS

The authors, Nancy and Jessica, would like to thank their husbands for their continuous support. Many events and weekends were sacrificed to make this project possible. Sigmund the pug will forever be at our feet as we write about psychology.

We also extend our appreciation to Pam Weston, Larry B. Kling, Jennifer Calhoun, Heidi Gagnon, Sally Fay, Joe Kraynak, and Caroline Shupe.

# PART I
## INTRODUCTION

# Five Keys for Success on the AP® Psychology Exam

The AP® Psychology course explores the scientific study of human behavior and mental processes. In the course, you will apply psychological perspectives, theories, concepts, and research findings. The course is structured within a framework consisting of the five pillars of psychology: biological bases of behavior; cognition; development and learning; social psychology and personality; and mental and physical health. This book covers all the essential content of AP® Psychology and will help you understand the science practices crucial for success on the exam.

## 1. Understand the Exam Structure and Scoring

The AP® Psychology exam is delivered digitally; it is 2 hours and 40 minutes long and contains two sections. Section I includes 75 multiple-choice questions. Section II includes 2 free-response questions, each weighted equally. There is a short break between the two sections. This *Crash Course* offers a number of test-taking strategies for all the types of multiple-choice and free-response exam questions.

| Section | Question Type | Number of Questions | Exam Weighting | Timing |
|---------|---------------|---------------------|----------------|--------|
| I | Multiple-Choice Questions | 75 | 66.7% | 90 minutes |
| II | Free-Response Questions | 2 | 33.3% | 70 minutes |
|  | FRQ 1: Article Analysis | 1 | 16.65% | |
|  | FRQ 2: Evidence-Based | 1 | 16.65% | |

The multiple-choice section awards points for each correct answer. No points are lost for skipped or incorrect answers. Experienced high school teachers and college instructors grade the free-response questions. The

College Board combines the multiple-choice and free-response scores to yield a total exam score using this 5-point scale:

| AP® Score | Recommendation |
|---|---|
| 5 | Extremely well qualified |
| 4 | Well qualified |
| 3 | Qualified |
| 2 | Possibly qualified |
| 1 | No recommendation |

## 2. Review the Five Units

The course is organized into five content units, all covered clearly and concisely in this *Crash Course* book. Each of the five units is equally weighted on the exam. It is thus important to distribute your study time accordingly.

As test day approaches, use this *Crash Course* to review the content you are uncertain about. Pay special attention to the *Test Tips* and *Science Tips* that highlight difficult topics and help you make important distinctions that will give you the edge you need on exam day.

| Units of Instruction | Exam Weighting |
|---|---|
| Unit 1: Biological Bases of Behavior | 15%–25% |
| Unit 2: Cognition | 15%–25% |
| Unit 3: Development and Learning | 15%–25% |
| Unit 4: Social Psychology and Personality | 15%–25% |
| Unit 5: Mental and Physical Health | 15%–25% |

## 3. Apply the Four Science Practices

While reviewing each of the five units, focus on the four key science practices foundational to success on the AP® Psychology exam. The science practices will be found on the multiple-choice and free-response sections.

| Science Practices | Exam Weighting |
|---|---|
| Practice 1: Concept Application | 65% |
| Practice 2: Research Methods and Design | 25% |
| Practice 3: Data Interpretation | 10% |
| Practice 4: Argumentation | Only on FRQs |

### Science Practice 1: Concept Application

- Apply psychological perspectives, theories, concepts, and research findings to a scenario, explaining their application, comparing and contrasting how they explain behavior and mental processes, and drawing logical and objective conclusions.

- The psychological perspectives covered in the course include: psychodynamic, behavioral, humanistic, cognitive, social-cognitive, biological, evolutionary, sociocultural, and biopsychosocial.

- The course requires you to understand how cultural factors and cognitive biases impact behavior and mental processes.

### Science Practice 2: Research Methods and Design

- The course requires you to be able to differentiate types of research methods and designs.

- You will need to evaluate the elements of experimental and non-experimental methodologies.

- Non-experimental methodologies covered in the course include: case study, correlation, meta-analysis, and naturalistic observation.

- Explain how research conclusions have evolved through the scientific process.

- Be able to identify appropriate ethical procedures.

### Science Practice 3: Data Interpretation

- The course requires you to identify and interpret statistical and psychological concepts represented in tables, graphs, charts, figures, or diagrams.

- Be able to calculate and interpret the measures of central tendency, variation, and percentile rank.

- Be able to interpret inferential data.

### Science Practice 4: Argumentation (EBQ only)

- The course requires you to propose defensible claims grounded in reasoning and supported by scientific evidence.

- Be able to effectively cite sources of evidence.

**Test Tip**

**Keyboard Shortcuts:** Save time while navigating the exam by learning the keyboard shortcuts for the College Board's Bluebook digital testing application.

## 4. Build a Plan for Success

Start studying early, divide material into manageable sections, and set realistic goals. Identify challenging topics, review regularly, and stay flexible to make adjustments as needed. Remember, slow and steady. Getting adequate rest is important for optimal performance.

Come ready to shine on test day! Remember that you have trained and prepared; don't worry too much about your score. It is just one moment in time! Data supports that even students who don't earn college credit on AP® exams are more prepared and successful in college.

Feel confident in your preparation, while having the appropriate amount of stress; remember that Yerkes-Dodson arousal theory!

## 5. Practice! Practice! Practice!

**Test Tip** **Get to Know the Exam's Digital Tools:** Download the College Board's Bluebook digital testing application today to familiarize yourself with valuable tools to help you build confidence and master the clock when it matters the most. Your exam-day toolbox lets you highlight, underline, and make notes as well as use a strikethrough feature that will help you keep track of the response options as you eliminate them from consideration on multiple-choice questions. The strikethrough tool is a real timesaver when reviewing flagged MCQs!

Utilize retrieval techniques, such as distributed practice and the testing effect, which you learn in this course, to help effectively prepare for the AP® Psychology exam. You'll build deeper understanding and long-term retention of key concepts, resulting in higher exam performance.

**Test Tip** **Practice in the Bluebook app:** Complete the untimed test preview and full-length practice exam in the College Board's Bluebook application before exam day to become completely comfortable with the format and navigation.

After completing the online practice exam that comes with this book, review the detailed answer explanations to deepen your connection with the material. The practice exam is timed and reflects the real test in the number and type of questions.

This *Crash Course* has everything you need to succeed on the exam. However, the College Board's AP® Classroom website (*https://apcentral.collegeboard.org*) is also a valuable resource. The site provides information about the test structure, question types, review videos, FAQs, and, most importantly, additional study materials and sample questions. Some of these materials need to be assigned by your instructor, but others are automatically available.

**Test Tip**

**Watch the Timer:** The exam has a running timer that turns red with 5 minutes left. Keep in mind that no proctor warnings will be given, so monitor your time carefully.

# PART II

## CONTENT REVIEW

# Scientific Foundations

## I. PSYCHOLOGY AS A SCIENCE

### A. PSYCHOLOGY AS A DISCIPLINE

1. **Psychology:** The scientific study of the behavior and mental processes of humans and other animals.

   a. **Behavior:** Any action that may be observed and measured.

   b. **Mental processes:** Any cognition, sensation, perception, or emotion.

2. Psychology uses empirical methods to observe, measure, predict, explain, and positively influence behavior.

### B. PERSPECTIVES

1. Perspectives are used to understand the causes of human behavior and mental processes.

2. These perspectives are also known as schools of thought or approaches.

| Perspective | Definition | Example |
| --- | --- | --- |
| Evolutionary | Behavior and mental processes exist today because they were naturally selected for a survival or reproductive advantage. | Test anxiety is a type of thinking that comes from anxiety in general. Anxiety was naturally selected because it helped humans survive by making them more careful and keeping them away from danger. |
| Biological | Behavior and mental processes result from physiological or genetic causes. | Test anxiety results from brain activity or an imbalance of specific neurotransmitters related to anxiety. |

*(continued)*

| Perspective | Definition | Example |
|---|---|---|
| **Cognitive** | Behavior and mental processes result from thought processes (e.g., memory, attention, problem-solving, perception, language). | Test anxiety results from negative or irrational thoughts about failure. |
| **Humanistic** | Behavior and mental processes result from striving to reach one's full potential. | Test anxiety results from a lack of unconditional positive regard or being unable to reach one's full potential. |
| **Psychoanalytic/ Psychodynamic** | Behavior and mental processes result from unconscious forces and early childhood experiences. | Test anxiety results from unresolved unconscious conflict. |
| **Behavioral** | Behavior and mental processes result from learning and can be identified through observable behavior. | Test anxiety results from observing and imitating siblings who also experienced test anxiety. |
| **Sociocultural** | Behavior and mental processes result from norms associated with culture and societal groups (e.g., gender, nationality, socioeconomic status [SES], religion). | Test anxiety results from cultural norms (e.g., individualist or collectivist cultures) related to success in school and achievement. |
| **Biopsychosocial** | Behavior and mental processes result from a combination of three influences: biological (evolutionary and biological), psychological (psychodynamic, behavioral, cognitive, and humanistic), and sociocultural (sociocultural). | Test anxiety results from a combination of biological influences (e.g., genetic vulnerability), psychological influences (e.g., irrational thoughts), and sociocultural influences (e.g., cultural norms related to success). |

Remember to distinguish between similar perspectives. The biological perspective deals with the brain (organ in the body), and the cognitive perspective focuses on the mind (what the brain does). The biological perspective explains that a person's behavior is influenced by the inheritance of specific genes (genetic predisposition) from the individual's biological parents. The evolutionary perspective explains behavior as a gradual change, allowing for species-level survival.

## C. CULTURAL BIASES

1. **Cultural bias:** The tendency to interpret and judge the behaviors and beliefs of others in terms of one's own cultural norms, values, and perspectives.

2. Cultural biases may include display rules, halo effect, gender bias, implicit attitudes, just-world phenomenon, out-group homogeneity bias, in-group bias, ethnocentrism, and stereotype threat.

3. Cultural bias is often addressed in research, psychometrics, health psychology, social psychology, and clinical psychology.

4. Cultural bias can lead to prejudice, including stereotyping and discrimination.

5. You must explain how cultural norms, expectations, and circumstances apply to behavior and mental processes.

## D. COGNITIVE BIASES

1. **Cognitive bias:** A type of error in thinking caused by the desire to simplify the world. These biases can influence beliefs about behavior and mental processes.

2. **Confirmation bias:** The tendency to pay attention to information consistent with one's existing viewpoint and ignore or minimize information that challenges that belief.

3. **Hindsight bias:** The tendency to think the outcome is obvious after it is known.

4. **Overconfidence:** The tendency to overestimate the accuracy of one's prediction or belief.

5. Cognitive biases may include actor/observer bias, availability heuristic, attribution theory, belief perseverance, change

blindness, confirmation bias, cognitive dissonance, egocentrism, experimenter bias, false-consensus effect, framing, functional fixedness, fundamental attribution error, gambler's fallacy, groupthink, halo effect, inattentional blindness, in-group bias, mere-exposure effect, misinformation effect, source amnesia, imagination inflation, overconfidence, placebo effect, primacy effect, priming, representativeness heuristic, self-serving bias, serial position effect, social desirability bias, imaginary audience, and just-world phenomenon.

### E. RESEARCH DESIGNS

1. **Experimental research:** An empirical method that uses random assignment to groups, manipulates the independent variable, and controls other variables to explain cause-and-effect relationships.

   a. Research question—studying whether the independent variable (manipulated by the researcher) causes the dependent variable (outcome) to change

   b. Method used—random assignment, controlled conditions

   c. Appropriate conclusion—explanation of findings that indicate a likely cause-and-effect relationship

   d. Advantages—can infer cause-and-effect

   e. Disadvantages—confounding variables weaken cause-and-effect explanations, results cannot always be applied to the real world, manipulation of a variable may be impossible or unethical, and obtaining a representative sample may be difficult

2. **Non-experimental research:** An empirical method, including observational and descriptive studies, that does not involve manipulation of variables or random assignment. Instead, it focuses on describing, correlating, or analyzing phenomena as they naturally occur.

   a. Research question—studying a single variable or how two or more variables relate

   b. Method used—case study, correlation, meta-analysis, naturalistic observation

   c. Appropriate conclusion—broad picture of a phenomenon and predictions about the strength and direction of the relationship between two variables

    d. Advantages—use observations or data to find patterns for future research, generate predictions for further experimental research, useful when manipulating a variable is impossible or unethical, allows for real-world observations, useful for rare behaviors

    e. Disadvantages—cannot infer cause-and-effect, potential third-variable problem, experimenter presence may alter participant behaviors

**Science Tip**

To have a true experiment, random assignment to a control and experimental group must occur, which can establish cause and effect.

## F. SCIENTIFIC METHOD

1. **Empirical evidence:** Knowledge gathered by careful observation, experimentation, and measurement essential to the scientific method.

2. **Theory:** A broad, organized explanation for data gained through empirical processes.

## II. EXPERIMENTAL METHODOLOGY

### A. RESEARCH DESIGN ELEMENTS

1. **Hypothesis:** A specific and testable prediction of the relationship between variables.

    a. **Falsifiable hypothesis:** A prediction that can be disproven through observation or experimentation.

    b. For example, the statement that a study technique can increase recall can be tested and disproven, making it falsifiable.

2. **Operational definition of a variable:** An explanation that states as precisely as possible what a variable means, including how it will be measured.

    a. It allows for replication.

    b. Variables are expressed quantitatively.

3. **Replication:** The process of repeating the study (directly or conceptually) to increase confidence in the accuracy of the results.

   a. It may lead to inconsistent results, which is to be expected with the scientific process.

   b. To address inconsistencies, researchers use meta-analysis to estimate the size and consistency of a variable's effect.

4. **Population:** The larger group from which a sample is drawn and to which the results apply.

   a. For example, all employees working in the technology industry.

5. **Sample:** A small subset of individuals in the study who represent the population.

   a. For example, a subset of 300 employees from various technology companies chosen to be in the study.

6. **Representative sample:** A sample that matches the population according to specific characteristics.

   a. It allows researchers to generalize the results to the population.

   b. Researchers select participants who represent the diversity of the population and use cross-cultural research.

7. **Random sample:** A group of people who had an equal chance of being chosen for participation in the study.

   a. If it is representative, then researchers can generalize the results to the population.

   b. For example, fifty students from Wundt High School were chosen by chance to be in the study.

8. **Random selection:** The method for choosing a random sample.

   a. It allows researchers to generalize the results to the specific intended population.

   b. For example, the process of choosing fifty students from Wundt High School to be in the study by pulling their names by chance from a hat.

9. **Convenience sample:** A subset of the population chosen based on individuals who are easily available.

   a. No strategy was used, but selection was based on convenience.

   b. For example, a professor researching the social media habits of all college students uses only students from the professor's classes in the study.

10. **Sampling bias:** An error caused by a non-representative sample.

   a. The results cannot be generalized to the population.

   b. For example, a small sample size or convenience sample does not indicate that the results would apply to the larger population.

11. **Generalizability:** The degree to which findings from a specific sample can be extended to the larger population.

   a. For the findings of a study to be generalizable, researchers must use a representative sample.

   b. Random sampling and an appropriate sample size help to create a sample that is representative of the population.

**Science Tip**

For questions asking about generalizability, remember that smaller samples are less likely to be representative, making findings less reliable. Larger samples are more desirable and more likely to provide representative samples that accurately reflect the population.

## B. VARIABLES

1. **Independent variable (IV):** The factor being manipulated (cause) by the researcher in an experiment.

   a. It is located on the *x*-axis and should be operationally defined.

   b. Given to the experimental group but not the control group.

2. **Dependent variable (DV):** The factor being observed and measured (effect) by the researcher in an experiment.

   a. It is located on the *y*-axis and should be operationally defined.

   b. Must be measured for both the experimental and control groups.

3. **Confounding variable:** Any factor in an experiment other than the IV that impacted the DV.

   a. Random assignment reduces confounding variables.

   b. Holding all variables constant except for the IV also reduces confounding variables.

**Experimental Group vs. Control Group**

- ▮ Age
- ▮ Amount of sleep
- ▯ Time of day
- ☐ Gender

Independent Variable → IV

Experimental Group          Control Group

---

**Science Tip**

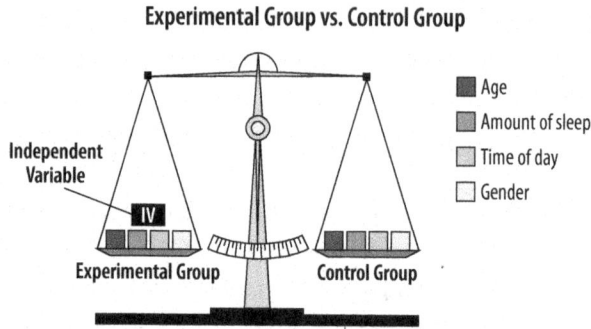

Keep in mind the difference between controlling for confounding variables (e.g., random assignment) and using a control group in an experiment.

## C. GROUPS

1. **Experimental group:** The part of the sample that includes the participants who receive the IV.

2. **Control group:** The part of the sample that includes the participants who are not exposed to the IV and functions as a comparison.

   a. **Placebo:** An inert substance (e.g., sugar pill) or treatment that has no effect and is given to the control group.

   b. **Placebo effect:** A response to a treatment with no active ingredient that results from believing it will produce a response.

3. **Random assignment:** The method of placing participants by chance into either the experimental or control group.

   a. The process is required to determine cause-and-effect conclusions.

   b. The purpose is to minimize confounding variables and individual differences of the participants in the groups.

---

**Science Tip**

When you see the word "random," you need to distinguish between the procedures for choosing participants (sampling) and placing them into groups (assignment).

| Technique | Definition |
|---|---|
| **Random selection** | The process of choosing by chance participants for the sample. |
| **Random sample** | The participants who were chosen by chance to be in the study. |
| **Random assignment** | The process of placing participants from the sample into either the experimental or control group (condition) by chance. |

### D. BIAS AND PROCEDURES FOR CONTROL

1. **Experimenter bias:** Any unintentional influence of the researcher that impacts participant responses.

   a. For example, the researcher unintentionally gives a cue that enables participants to guess what the researcher is studying and causes them to change their reactions.

   b. The double-blind procedure controls for experimenter bias.

2. **Participant bias:** The tendency for participants to respond to a study based on their beliefs, expectations, or desires rather than the conditions presented in the study.

   a. **Social desirability bias:** The tendency for participants to depict themselves positively or provide favorable answers to the researcher.

   b. The single-blind and double-blind procedures control for social desirability bias.

3. **Single-blind procedure:** A research procedure in which participants are unaware of whether they are in the control or experimental group.

   a. It controls for the placebo effect and participant bias.

   b. It does not control for experimenter bias.

4. **Double-blind procedure:** A research procedure in which both the experimenter and the participants are unaware of who is in the control or experimental group.

   a. A third party interprets the results.

   b. It controls for both experimenter and participant bias.

### E. MEASUREMENT INSTRUMENTS

1. **Qualitative:** The measurement instrument used for gathering descriptive (non-numerical) data to seek meaning and context.

   a. **Structured interview:** A qualitative measurement instrument that ensures each interviewee is asked the same predetermined questions in the same order. It may also collect scores on a rating scale, making it also quantitative.

2. **Quantitative:** The measurement instrument used for gathering numerical data to seek objective knowledge.

   a. **Likert scale:** A quantitative measurement instrument that involves having participants rate statements from negative to positive, often using five-point scales.

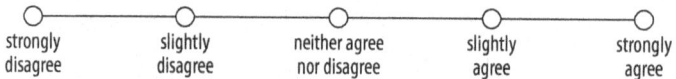

| strongly disagree | slightly disagree | neither agree nor disagree | slightly agree | strongly agree |

### F. CONCLUSIONS

1. Appropriate participant representation in a study enhances the reliability, validity, and generalizability of findings.

   a. A representative sample ensures that study results can be applied to the broader population.

   b. Diverse demographics enable researchers to draw more meaningful conclusions about human behaviors and mental processes across cultures.

2. Scientific processes lead to evolving conclusions about behavior and mental processes.

   a. **Peer review:** The process in which experts examine research studies before publication to ensure quality (e.g., research questions, methodology, analysis, and significance to the field) of psychology research by filtering out substandard work, which leads to evolving conclusions in the field.

   b. **Replication:** The process of repeating studies to confirm findings, which leads to evolving conclusions in the field.

      i. Exact replication involves procedures similar to those used in the original study.

      ii. Modified replication adds new elements to the study.

## III. NON-EXPERIMENTAL METHODOLOGIES

### A. TYPES

1. **Case study:** An in-depth investigation of an individual or group.

   a. Different types of data (psychological, physiological, biographical, environmental) are compiled through several methods, including observation, interviews, surveys, and testing.

   b. For example, in-depth research on Phineas Gage, Patient H.M., Little Albert, and Genie.

2. **Correlation:** A type of study that examines the strength and direction of the relationships between observed variables without the researcher manipulating a variable.

   a. **Variables of interest:** Factors or characteristics in a correlational study that are examined for potential relationships.

   b. **Positive (direct) correlation:** A relationship in which both variables move in the same direction. ↑↑ or ↓↓

   c. **Negative (inverse) correlation:** A relationship in which the two variables move in opposite directions. ↑↓

3. **Meta-analysis:** The statistical technique for combining effect size estimates (results) from numerous studies on the same topic into a single effect size.

   a. In a meta-analysis, researchers convert the findings of each study to a standardized statistic known as effect size.

   b. For example, researcher John Hattie found the effect size for student achievement using Cohen's D. A small effect is 0.2, a medium effect is 0.5, and a large effect is 0.8.

4. **Naturalistic observation:** The systematic recording of data by watching participants in a real (natural) or artificial (lab) setting without manipulation of variables.

   a. Researchers should not interfere while watching.

   b. For example, studies conducted by Jane Goodall (chimpanzee studies) and Jean Piaget (cognitive development).

## B. DESIGN ELEMENTS

1. **Hypothesis:** A specific, testable, and falsifiable prediction of the relationship between variables.

   a. **Falsifiable hypothesis**: A prediction that can be disproven through observation or experimentation.

   b. For example, the statement that a relationship exists between the number of hours of sleep and a self-reported level of alertness can be tested and disproven, making it falsifiable.

2. **Operational definition of a variable:** An explanation that states as precisely as possible what a variable means, including how it will be measured.

   a. It allows for replication.

   b. Variables are expressed quantitatively.

3. **Replication:** The process of repeating the study to increase confidence in the accuracy of the results.

   a. It may lead to inconsistent results, which is to be expected with the scientific process.

   b. To address inconsistencies, researchers use meta-analysis to estimate the size and consistency of a variable's effects.

4. Correlation does not equal causation!

   a. **Directionality problem:** The inability to determine which variable is the cause and which is the effect in a correlation.

   b. **Third-variable problem:** The inability to determine cause and effect because a hidden variable is the cause of the two other variables in a correlation.

## C. MEASUREMENT INSTRUMENTS

1. **Qualitative:** The measurement instrument used for gathering descriptive (non-numerical) data to seek meaning and context.

   a. **Structured interview:** A qualitative measurement instrument that ensures each interviewee is asked the same predetermined questions in the same order. It may also collect scores on a rating scale, making it also quantitative.

2. **Quantitative:** The measurement instrument for gathering numerical data to seek objective knowledge.

   a. **Likert scale:** A quantitative measurement instrument that involves having participants rate statements from negative to positive, often using five-point scales.

### D. SURVEY TECHNIQUE

1. **Survey technique:** The measurement of attitudes and behaviors of a group of participants by using a structured interview or self-report questionnaire.

   a. Results are summarized but do not identify relationships or causal statements.

   b. For example, large-scale data is collected for the World Happiness Report and the United States Census.

2. **Wording effect:** Inaccuracies based on the phrasing of survey questions.

   a. **Self-report bias:** A problem that happens when researchers rely on individuals to describe their thoughts or behaviors instead of measuring them directly.

      i. Responses may be inaccurate due to incomplete information or a desire to present oneself favorably (social desirability bias).

      ii. **Social desirability bias:** The tendency for participants to depict themselves positively or provide favorable answers to the researcher.

### E. CONCLUSIONS

1. Appropriate participant representation in a study enhances the reliability, validity, and generalizability of findings.

2. Scientific processes, including peer review and replication, lead to evolving conclusions about behavior and mental processes.

## IV. STATISTICS

### A. DESCRIPTIVE STATISTICS

1. **Descriptive statistics:** The methods for organizing and summarizing data without generalizing to the population.

2. Tables and graphs are often used to display data.

    a. **Frequency distributions:** Tables that organize information about how often certain scores occur.

    b. **Frequency histograms:** A graph that displays continuous data on the *x*-axis and frequency on the *y*-axis.

3. **Normal curve:** A graph of a frequency distribution in which the mean, median, and mode are all equal and located at the center. It forms a symmetrical bell curve.

    a. **Empirical rule:** A statistical rule for a normal distribution that indicates how data will predictably fall within three standard deviations.

        i. 68% within one standard deviation

        ii. 95% within two standard deviations

        iii. 99.7% within three standard deviations

    b. **Percentile rank:** A statistic representing the percentage of scores equal to or below a specific score in a distribution.

        i. For example, if scoring 100 on an intelligence assessment places an individual in the 50th percentile, then 50% of the other individuals tested must have scored 100 or below.

4. **Skewed distribution:** A graph of a frequency distribution with a few extreme scores that forms an asymmetrical curve.

    a. **Positive (right) skewed distribution:** A graph with more low scores in which the tail of the distribution points toward the right.

    b. **Negative (left) skewed distribution:** A graph with more high scores in which the tail of the distribution points to the left.

    c. Frequency will always be identified on the *y*-axis.

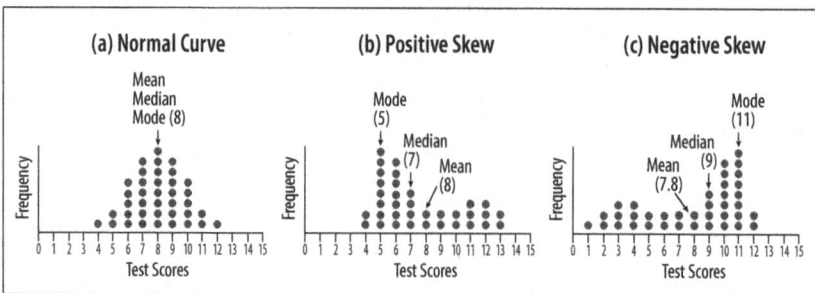

| (a) Normal Curve | (b) Positive Skew | (c) Negative Skew |

5. **Measures of central tendency:** A group of three descriptive statistics that summarize the data with one typical value.

   a. **Mean:** The arithmetic average. It is the most commonly used measure of central tendency but is also the most affected by outliers.

   b. **Median:** The score in the exact middle of the distribution when the scores are listed in order. The main advantage of the median is that it is not sensitive to outliers.

   c. **Mode:** The most frequently occurring score in a distribution.

      i. **Bimodal:** Two separate scores that occur most often.

      ii. The mode is the most useful for categorical data.

6. **Measures of variability (variation):** A group of descriptive statistics that depict the spread of the data.

   a. **Range:** The difference between the highest and lowest scores.

   b. **Standard deviation:** The average distance of each score from the mean.

7. Correlational data is analyzed to interpret the results.

   a. Correlation coefficients quantify the strength (−1 to +1) and direction (positive or negative) of the relationship.

   b. Scatterplots indicate the slope and scatter for a correlation in a graph.

8. **Regression toward the mean:** A tendency for extremely high or low scores to move closer to the average upon retesting.

   a. This may happen because the same mix of chance factors that caused the extreme finding to occur the first time is not present the second time.

   b. For example, in a driving test study, participants who perform exceptionally well or poorly initially might show more average driving skills when retested later.

9. **Correlation coefficient:** A number that describes the strength and direction of the relationship between variables and is represented by an r value.

   a. Stronger relationships are closer to −1.0 and to +1.0.

   b. Weaker relationships are closer to 0.

   c. Positive (direct) relationships are indicated with a positive number.

  d. Negative (inverse) relationships are indicated with a negative number.

**10. Scatterplot:** A graph that depicts the strength and direction of the correlation often between two variables.

  a. **Variables of interest:** Factors or characteristics in a correlational study that are examined for potential relationships.

  b. A perfect correlation will make a straight line.

  c. The stronger the correlation, the less scatter.

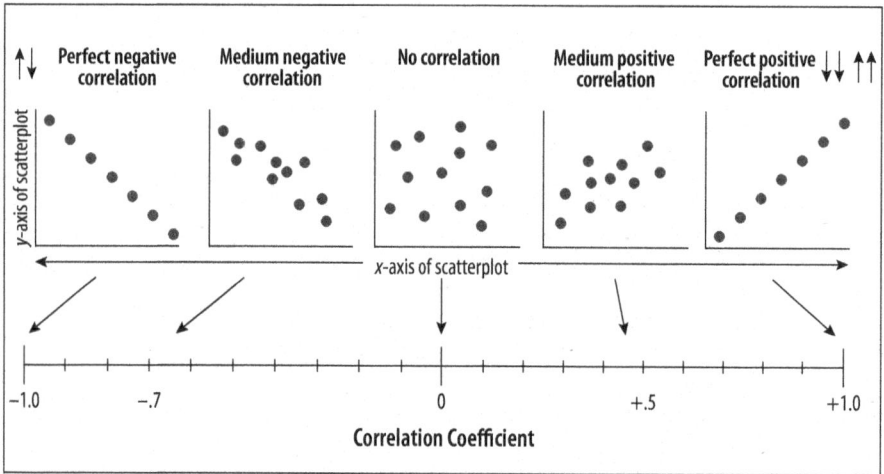

## B. INFERENTIAL STATISTICS

1. **Inferential statistics:** The methods for generalizing the results from the sample to the population and identifying the degree of error.

  a. They evaluate the size and quality of the sample.

  b. They evaluate the size of the difference found in the results.

2. **Statistical significance:** The degree to which the results are not likely due to chance.

  a. If the findings are statistically significant ($p \leq .05$), then the results are likely not due to chance.

b. The IV likely caused the difference in the DV, allowing the researcher to reject the null hypothesis.

c. If the findings were not statistically significant ($p > .05$), then the results are likely due to chance.

3. **Effect size:** The meaningfulness of a relationship between variables. It often indicates the practical significance of the findings.

a. The larger the effect size, the stronger the relationship between the two variables.

b. **Meta-analysis:** The statistical technique for combining effect size estimates (results) from numerous studies on the same topic into a single effect size.

c. In a meta-analysis, researchers convert the findings of each study to a standardized statistic known as effect size.

d. For example, researcher John Hattie found the effect size for student achievement using Cohen's D. A small effect is 0.2, a medium effect is 0.5, and a large effect is 0.8.

## V. ETHICS IN RESEARCH

### A. HUMAN PARTICIPANTS

1. **Institutional Review Board (IRB):** A group of professionals who evaluate and approve research studies to ensure participants are protected and ethical guidelines are followed.

2. Many professional organizations, including the American Psychological Association (APA), have created ethical guidelines for the protection of participants.

3. The ethical considerations required are based on the decision of the IRB and the type of study used.

a. For example, naturalistic observation studies often do not require informed consent.

4. **Confederate:** An assistant of the researcher who pretends to be part of the experiment.

| Ethical Procedure | Explanation | Researcher Responsibilities and Participant Rights |
|---|---|---|
| **Informed consent**<br><br>*Informed assent* | Before the study, researchers must explain the details, and participants must voluntarily agree to participate.<br><br>Informed assent is needed in cases involving minors. | Participants typically sign a document stating that they have been told about the purpose, time commitment, compensation, procedures, and potential benefits and risks associated with the study. They must be told that they can withdraw at any time. |
| **Confidentiality** | Participants are known to researchers, but have their privacy protected. | Researchers must not disclose the identity of the participants. |
| **Anonymity** | Participants' identity is not known. | Researchers do not collect personal information on the participants. |
| **Protection from harm** | Participants cannot be exposed to severe physical or emotional harm. | Researchers take steps to protect participants from harm.<br><br>1. Studies involving even minimal harm must be approved by the IRB.<br><br>2. Participants must be informed prior to the start of the study if there will be exposure to harm. |
| **Approved deception** | Researchers withhold information or lie to participants potentially using confederates. | Researchers can deceive participants if the IRB determines that the potential research value justifies the deception. |
| **Debrief** | After the study, researchers must fully explain the details of the research and inform participants if deception was involved. | Researchers tell participants about the results of the study and whom to contact if they have questions.<br><br>Researchers tell the participants about any deception used and why it was necessary. |

**Test Tip**

You will need to know ethical guidelines for the AAQ part D. Remember them with the mnemonic: **I Do Care About Research Participants.**

**I**nformed consent/assent

**D**ebriefing (Correct deception)

**C**onfidentiality

**A**nonymity

**R**eview Board (IRB) and Institutional Animal Care and Use Committee (IACUC)

**P**rotection from harm (physical and psychological)

### B. NONHUMAN ANIMALS

1. Colleges, universities, and research institutions must have an Institutional Animal Care and Use Committee (IACUC) and follow federal, state, and local laws.

2. The American Psychological Association (APA) provides guidelines for pain, surgery, stress, deprivation, and termination.

3. Animal research should be **A**ppropriate, **B**eneficial, and **C**aring (ABC model).

**Science Tip**

Remember that elements of research design are not ethical requirements. Random sampling, random assignment, and blind techniques are aspects of research design and not ethical requirements.

# Heredity, Environment, and the Nervous System

## I. HEREDITY AND ENVIRONMENT

### A. NATURE AND NURTURE

1. **Nature or heredity:** The influence of genetics or predisposed characteristics that influence physical traits, behavior, and mental processes.

2. **Nurture or environment:** The influence of external environmental factors on behavior and mental processes.

3. Genes interact with environmental factors in complex ways, making it difficult to measure the relative influence of biological and environmental factors.

**Test Tip**

Remember to distinguish common terms associated with nature and nurture. Nature: heredity, biological, predisposition, innate, and native. Nurture: family, peers, culture, interactions with others, education, and wealth or socioeconomic status (SES).

**Exclusion Statement:** Specific information about genetics (genotype, phenotype, DNA, chromosomes, and recessive and dominant gene expression) is beyond the scope of the AP® Psychology exam.

### B. EVOLUTIONARY PSYCHOLOGY

1. **Evolutionary psychology:** A field of study that applies evolutionary theory to human behavior and mental processes.

2. **Evolutionary perspective:** The psychological approach that explores how natural selection affects the expression of behavior

and mental processes to increase survival and reproductive success.

3. **Natural selection:** The idea that heritable characteristics that aid survival and reproduction are more likely to be selected over time. This term applies to populations rather than individuals.

4. **Eugenics:** A discredited and scientifically flawed philosophy that sought to improve human populations through selective breeding based on the ideas of "superior" and "inferior" beings. It promoted reproduction by those deemed superior and discouraged it by those deemed to have undesirable traits.

   a. Eugenics led to unethical policies such as sterilizing people with intellectual disabilities.

   b. Scientifically flawed because genetic conditions are often inherited unpredictably.

## C. EPIGENETICS

1. Genes can either be active (expressed) or inactive. Genes can be activated for short or long periods and sometimes never at all.

2. **Epigenetics:** The study of changes in gene expression that do not involve modifying the sequence of DNA—genes can be "turned on or off" by environmental influences.

3. Environmental influences (e.g., diet, stress, and adverse childhood experiences [ACEs]) cannot change genetic makeup but can impact gene expression and lead to psychological disorders, health problems, or health benefits.

## D. HERITABILITY

1. **Heritability:** A mathematical measure (0 to 1) of the variation among individuals related to genes. Estimates of heritability are determined from the results of twin studies. It applies only to the population and not to individuals.

2. If heritability for a trait is 0.6, that suggests 60% of the variation among individuals within a population for that trait is caused by genetics, and 40% of the differences are related to environmental factors.

## II. RESEARCH ON HEREDITY AND ENVIRONMENTAL FACTORS

### A. FAMILY STUDIES

1. Family studies compare biological relatives (e.g., siblings, parents, grandparents, cousins) to identify the genetic component for a specific trait.

2. They may overlook environmental influences shared within families, which makes it difficult to distinguish between genetic and environmental factors.

### B. TWIN STUDIES

1. **Identical (monozygotic) twins:** A set of twins who share 100% of their genes.

2. **Fraternal (dizygotic) twins:** A set of twins who share 50% of their genes.

3. The strongest evidence for a genetic influence on a trait are trait similarities between identical twins raised apart.

### C. ADOPTION STUDIES

1. Adoption studies compare individuals with their biological and adoptive parents to identify the genetic and environmental influences for a specific trait.

   a. Traits that adopted children share with their biological parents are considered higher in heritability. These traits include intelligence, personality, and susceptibility to specific psychological disorders.

   b. Traits that adopted children share with their adoptive parents are considered more influenced by environmental factors. These traits include morals, religious beliefs, and attitudes.

2. Biases in the adoption process, such as selective placement (e.g., parental traits, geographic location, SES), can confound results.

## III. NERVOUS SYSTEM

### A. MAIN BRANCHES OF THE NERVOUS SYSTEM

1. **Central nervous system (CNS):** The neurons and glial cells in the brain and spinal cord.

2. **Peripheral nervous system (PNS):** The nerves outside of the brain and spinal cord.

### B. PERIPHERAL NERVOUS SYSTEM

1. **Somatic nervous system:** The nerves that control the voluntary movement of skeletal muscles and transmit sensory input to the brain.

2. **Autonomic nervous system:** The nerves controlling the involuntary activity of glands, organs, and involuntary muscles.

   a. **Sympathetic nervous system:** The branch of the autonomic nervous system that coordinates arousal during stress.

      i. When the fight-or-flight response is activated, bodily changes include increased breathing, increased heart rate, dilated pupils, and inhibited digestion.

   b. **Parasympathetic nervous system:** The branch of the autonomic nervous system that calms and restores after a time of stress.

      i. This branch is associated with rest, repair, and energy storage. Bodily changes include decreased breathing, decreased heart rate, constricted pupils, and increased digestion.

**The Human Nervous System**

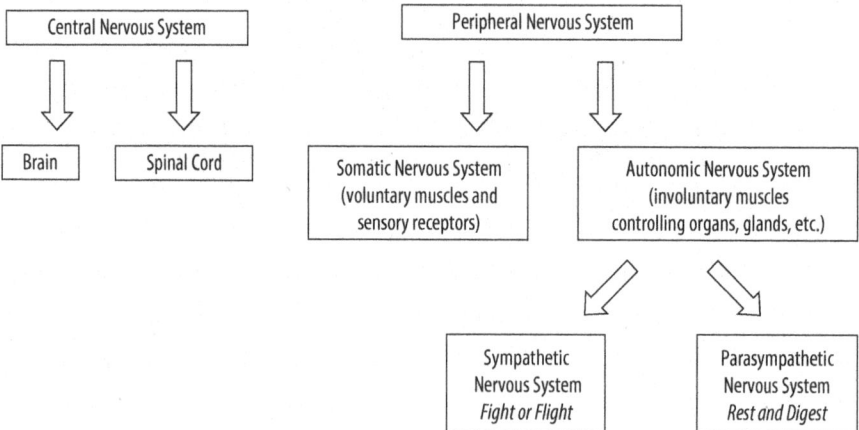

## IV. NEURAL CELLS

### A. GLIAL CELL

1. **Glial cell:** A cell within the nervous system that provides structure, insulation, communication, and waste removal. There are various types of glia with specific purposes, such as producing myelin sheaths for neurons.

2. **Multiple sclerosis (MS):** A neurological disorder characterized by the deterioration of the myelin sheath that leads to the loss of muscle control and eventual paralysis.

3. **Myasthenia gravis (MG):** An autoimmune disorder in which the body generates antibodies against acetylcholine receptors, disrupting nerve impulse transmission at neuromuscular junctions.

   a. It weakens voluntary muscles and leads to rapid fatigue due to breakdowns in nerve-to-muscle communication.

   b. This condition progresses over time, eventually impacting muscles throughout the body. There is no cure, but treatment can reduce symptoms.

**Test Tip**

Remember to explain how disruptions in the neural process can lead to disorders (e.g., multiple sclerosis or myasthenia gravis).

- Multiple Sclerosis (**MS**) involves the loss of the myelin sheath (**ms**), which slows nerve signals on the axon.

- Myasthenia Gravis (**MG**) involves the loss of muscle grip (**mg**), and the communication of acetylcholine with muscles is hindered.

### B. NEURON

1. **Neuron:** A neural cell that transmits information and forms the building blocks of all behavior and mental processes.

2. There are three main types of neurons in the nervous system.

   a. **Sensory neuron:** A type of neuron located in the peripheral nervous system that transfers information from the environment to the central nervous system.

      b. **Motor neuron:** A type of neuron located in the peripheral nervous system that transfers information from the central nervous system to the muscles, organs, and glands of the body.

      c. **Interneuron:** A type of neuron located in the central nervous system that connects sensory and motor neurons. It is the most abundant of the three major neuron types.

  3. **Reflex arc:** A quick circuit involving three types of neurons that work together to respond to stimuli.

      a. The reflex arc can happen quickly because the brain is not involved until after the movement has happened.

      b. The reflex arc process includes three steps.

         i. Sensory neurons send a message to the spinal cord.

        ii. Interneurons (in the spinal cord) communicate to motor neurons.

        iii. Motor neurons send the message to muscles that produce a movement.

## C. PARTS OF A NEURON

  1. **Dendrites:** The branch-like extensions that receive neurotransmitters from other neurons and transport the message to the cell body.

      a. **Receptor sites:** The location on the dendrite (postsynaptic neuron), which receives neurotransmitters.

  2. **Cell body (soma):** The part of the neuron that contains the nucleus and which initiates an action potential.

  3. **Axon:** The long extension that sends the electrical message (action potential) away from the cell body.

  4. **Myelin sheath:** A fatty substance produced by a specific type of glial cell that provides insulation and increases the speed of the electrical message (action potential).

  5. **Nodes of Ranvier:** The regularly spaced gaps in the myelin sheath along the axon that enable ion exchange.

  6. **Terminal button:** The knob at the end of each axon branch that contains neurotransmitters in vesicles (sacs) to be released across the synapse.

  7. **Synapse:** The narrow space between neurons where neurotransmission occurs.

**Parts of a Neuron**

DENDRITES

NUCLEUS

CELL BODY

MYELIN SHEATH

DIRECTION OF NERVE IMPULSE

AXON

AXON TERMINALS

SYNAPSE

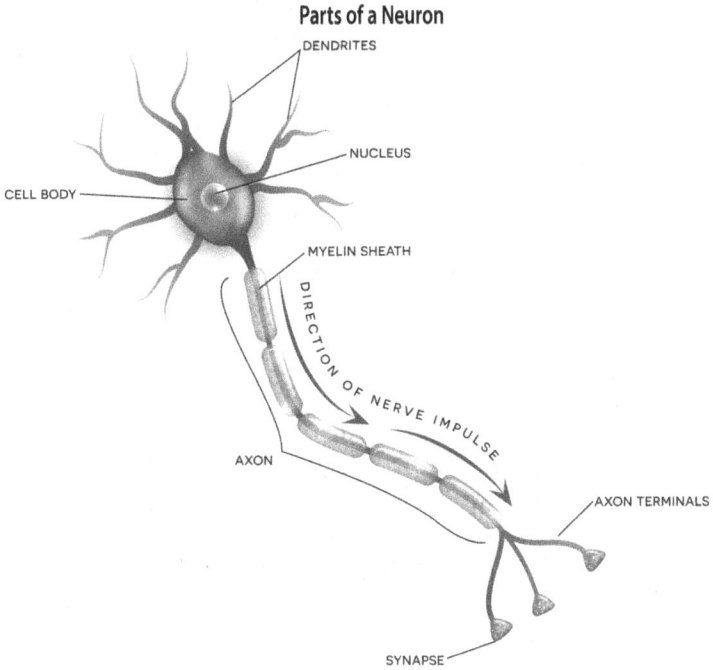

*Source: iStockphoto.com/TefiM*

## V. NEURAL FIRING

### A. RESTING POTENTIAL

1. **Resting potential:** The state while the neuron is waiting for a message, in which the fluid-filled interior of the axon has a negative charge (−70 millivolts), and the fluid exterior has a positive charge.

2. Charged particles, or ions, are located inside or outside the axon membrane.

   a. At rest, sodium ($Na^+$) ions outside the axon create a positive charge.

   b. At rest, potassium ($K^+$) ions and other negative ions inside the axon create a negative charge.

### B. THRESHOLD

1. Neurotransmitters either communicate excitatory or inhibitory messages.

   a. **Excitatory message:** A neurotransmitter's message that makes an action potential more likely.

b. **Inhibitory message:** A neurotransmitter's message that makes an action potential less likely.

c. The total amount of excitatory messages must be greater than the inhibitory messages for the neuron to reach threshold.

2. **Threshold:** The minimal level of stimulation needed to fire an action potential in a neuron. The firing of the action potential works on the all-or-nothing principle.

3. **All-or-nothing principle:** The firing of an action potential at 100% strength or not at all.

## C. DEPOLARIZATION

1. **Depolarization:** The change in the electrical charge of an axon, during the action potential, when the interior of the axon changes to a less negative or slightly positive charge.

a. This process begins when the axon allows certain ions through its semi-permeable membrane, making the interior of the axon more positive.

b. Sodium ($Na^+$) ions pass into the axon, resulting in a less negative or slightly positive charge.

## D. END OF THE ACTION POTENTIAL

1. The cell resets and returns to its resting potential, and the electrical charge inside the axon is more negative than the outside.

2. **Refractory period:** A brief period after a neuron fires, when it cannot generate another action potential or respond to a stimulus.

---

**Exclusion Statement:** The sodium-potassium pump is outside the scope of the AP® Psychology exam.

---

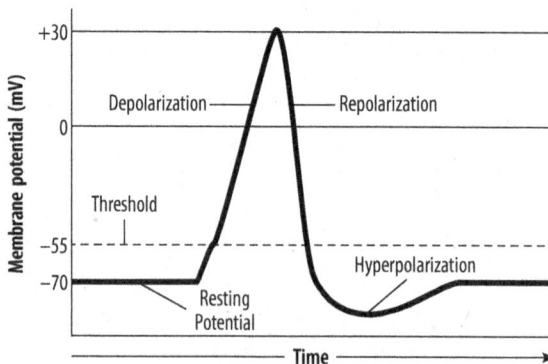

### E. CLEARING THE SYNAPSE

1. **Reuptake:** The process of the presynaptic neuron reabsorbing the neurotransmitters it has released into the synapse.

2. Enzyme deactivation is the process of breaking down neurotransmitters in the synapse.

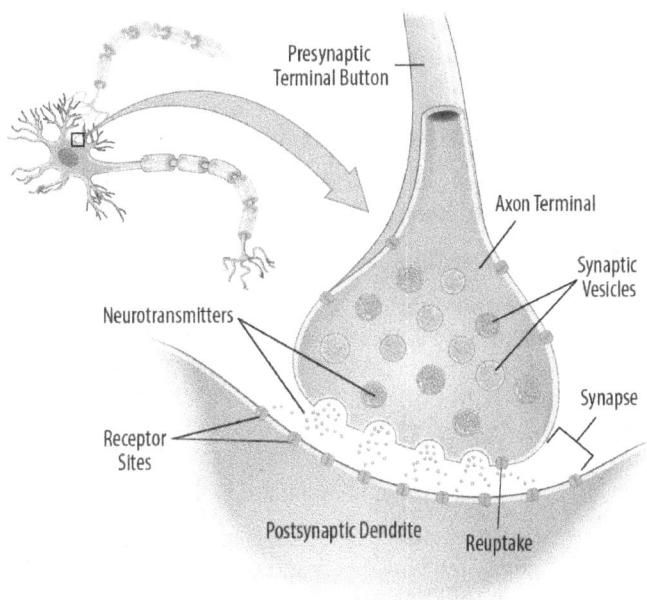

Presynaptic
Terminal Button

Axon Terminal

Synaptic
Vesicles

Neurotransmitters

Synapse

Receptor
Sites

Postsynaptic Dendrite

Reuptake

*Source: Wikimedia Commons*

## VI. CHEMICALS

### A. NEUROTRANSMITTERS

1. **Neurotransmitters:** Chemicals in the nervous system that work like a uniquely shaped "key" fitting into a specific "lock," which are the receptor sites on dendrites.

2. **Acetylcholine:** A chemical released in the central nervous system associated with memory formation and learning. It is also released in the peripheral nervous system at the neuromuscular junction and is associated with muscle contraction.

a. Undersupply is associated with Alzheimer's disease and paralysis.

b. Oversupply is associated with muscle convulsions.

3. **Dopamine:** A chemical released in the hypothalamus and nucleus accumbens associated with the pleasure and reward system. It is also released in the basal ganglia and associated with movement.

a. Undersupply is associated with Parkinson's disease.

b. Oversupply is associated with schizophrenia.

4. **Serotonin:** A chemical released in the central nervous system associated with mood, appetite, sleep, and aggression.

a. Undersupply is associated with depression, sleep-wake disorders, and increased aggression.

b. Oversupply is associated with anxiety.

5. **Norepinephrine:** A chemical created in the central nervous system associated with alertness and arousal. In the endocrine system, it is a hormone produced in the adrenal glands and is associated with the fight-or-flight response.

a. Undersupply is associated with depression.

b. Oversupply is associated with anxiety and mania.

6. **GABA:** A chemical released in the central nervous system associated with sleep and calming effects. It is the most abundant inhibitory neurotransmitter.

a. Undersupply is associated with anxiety disorders, insomnia, and seizures.

b. Oversupply is associated with sleep disturbances.

7. **Glutamate:** A chemical released in the central nervous system associated with memory and learning, including long-term potentiation. It is the most abundant excitatory neurotransmitter.

a. Undersupply is associated with seizures and insomnia.

b. Oversupply is associated with strokes and various neurological disorders. Overactivity is also associated with migraines, seizures, and the destruction of nerve cells.

8. **Endorphins:** A chemical released in the pituitary gland and hypothalamus that is associated with pain reduction.

a. Undersupply is created by the abuse of heroin and other opioids.

b. Oversupply is associated with runner's high.

9. **Substance P:** A neurotransmitter in both the central and peripheral nervous systems that is responsible for signaling pain.

   a. Undersupply is associated with less pain.

   b. Oversupply is associated with more pain.

**Test Tip** Remember that psychoactive drugs as a biomedical therapy intervention are used to influence neurotransmitter levels.

### B. HORMONES

1. **Hormones:** Chemicals secreted by endocrine glands and released into the blood that affect tissues throughout the body.

2. **Adrenaline:** A hormone released by the adrenal glands in large amounts when aroused by fear, anxiety, or stress. It is also called epinephrine.

3. **Leptin:** A hormone produced and secreted by fat cells that assists in decreasing food intake and reducing hunger (increasing satiation).

4. **Ghrelin:** A hormone secreted by the stomach to arouse hunger.

5. **Melatonin:** A hormone produced by the pineal gland that assists in falling asleep and regulates the sleep-wake cycle.

6. **Oxytocin:** A hormone released by the pituitary gland that assists in social bonding and is also involved in sexual arousal, labor contractions, and lactation.

**Exclusion Statement:** The AP® Psychology exam will only address the listed hormones. Specific information about the glands of the endocrine system (with the exception of the pituitary gland) is outside the scope of the AP® Psychology exam.

### C. COMPARE AND CONTRAST CHEMICAL MESSENGERS

1. Neurotransmitters and hormones are both chemical messengers.

2. Neurotransmitters are located in the nervous system, while hormones are located in the endocrine system.

Neurotransmitters vs. Hormones

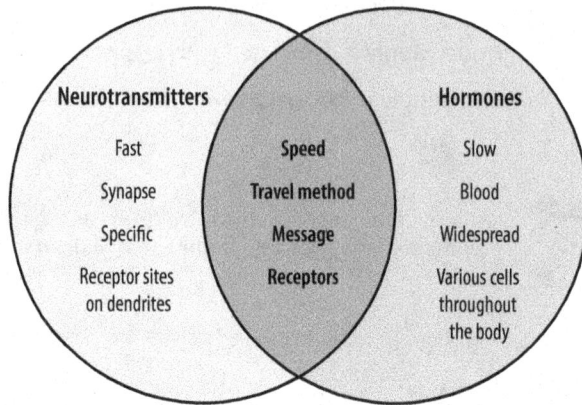

## VII. PSYCHOACTIVE DRUGS

### A. AGONIST VERSUS ANTAGONIST DRUGS

1. **Agonist**: A drug that increases neurotransmission either by mimicking the natural neurotransmitter or blocking reuptake.

   a. Antianxiety medications mimic GABA and increase neurotransmission.

2. **Reuptake inhibitor:** A drug that blocks the reabsorption of neurotransmitters released by the presynaptic neuron, thereby raising the quantity of neurotransmitters accessible to bind to postsynaptic receptors.

   a. **Selective serotonin reuptake inhibitors (SSRIs):** An antidepressant drug that works by blocking the reuptake of serotonin, thereby increasing neurotransmission.

   b. Cocaine blocks the reuptake of dopamine and increases neurotransmission.

3. **Antagonist:** A drug that decreases neurotransmission by occupying the receptor sites on the postsynaptic neuron.

   a. Antipsychotic medications block the receptor sites for dopamine and decrease neurotransmission.

   b. Naloxone (brand name Narcan) blocks opioid receptors and decreases neurotransmission.

**Test Tip**

Think of neurotransmitters as "keys" that fit specific "locks" on receptor sites of dendrites.

- **Agonists** are **"counterfeit keys"** that mimic neurotransmitters, thereby enhancing neural firing.

- **Antagonists "block the lock"** by blocking neurotransmitters at the receptor site, thereby decreasing neural firing.

- **Reuptake inhibitors "extend the stay of the key"** by blocking the key from returning to the owner's pocket (presynaptic neuron), thereby keeping the neurotransmitters in the synapse and enhancing neural firing.

### B. CLASSIFICATION OF PSYCHOACTIVE DRUGS

1. Psychoactive drugs have psychological and physiological effects.

2. Addictive drugs stimulate the brain's pleasure centers that are sensitive to dopamine.

| Category | Description | Example | Neurotransmitter(s) |
|---|---|---|---|
| **Depressants** | Decrease nervous system activity causing muscle relaxation, sleep, and inhibition of the cognitive centers in the brain. | Alcohol | GABA |
| **Opioids** | Produce pain reduction. | Heroin | Endorphins |
| **Stimulants** | Increase nervous system activity, mood, and alertness. | Caffeine  Cocaine | Dopamine  Norepinephrine  Acetylcholine |
| **Hallucinogens** | Alter thoughts and perceptions. | Marijuana (Cannabis) | Serotonin  Glutamate |

### C. ADDICTION

1. **Addiction:** A condition in which an individual is in a state of psychological and/or physical dependence on the use of drugs.

    a.  It is often used as an equivalent term for substance use disorder or substance dependence.

    b.  The term can also be applied to non-substance-related behavioral addictions, such as sex, exercise, and gambling.

2.  **Tolerance:** The need to take greater amounts or stronger versions of a drug to achieve the same psychotropic effect.

3.  **Withdrawal:** The unpleasant physical symptoms resulting from stopping prolonged and heavy psychotropic drug use.

    a.  Symptoms may include cold sweats, vomiting, convulsions, hallucinations, depressed mood, and anxiety.

    b.  Often, the physical effect of withdrawal is the opposite of the drug's effect.

# The Brain

## I. BRAIN PARTS

### A. HINDBRAIN AND MIDBRAIN

1. **Brainstem:** A collection of brain parts that control automatic bodily functions, including breathing, heart rate, salivation, and digestion.

2. **Cerebellum:** The hindbrain structure responsible for balance, coordination of muscle movement, fine motor movements, and procedural learning.

3. **Medulla:** The hindbrain structure responsible for critical survival functions (e.g., heart rate, breathing).

4. **Reticular activating system (RAS):** A system that is generally involved in arousal to stimuli, alertness, and the sleep-wake cycle. The RAS and the brain's reward system generally control some voluntary movement, eye movement, and some types of learning, cognition, and emotion.

### B. FOREBRAIN

1. **Cerebral cortex:** The approximately quarter-inch-thick, wrinkled outer layer of the brain that is divided into two hemispheres linked with advanced thinking abilities, such as language, learning, perception, and planning.

2. **Hemispheres:** The term used for the roughly symmetrical left and right halves of the brain.

   a. The two hemispheres are divided by a deep longitudinal fissure but connected by the corpus callosum.

   b. This connection allows each side of the brain to control functions on both sides of the body, known as cortex specialization or lateralization.

3. **Limbic system:** A group of brain parts involved in learning, memory, motivation, and emotion.

   a. **Thalamus:** The forebrain structure located at the top of the brainstem that relays sensory information, except for smell, to the appropriate parts of the cerebral cortex.

   b. **Hypothalamus:** A limbic system structure located below the thalamus responsible for maintenance functions (e.g., eating, drinking, body temperature, sex), controlling the autonomic nervous system, and controlling the endocrine system by influencing the pituitary gland.

   c. **Pituitary gland:** The endocrine gland located at the base of the brain responsible for numerous functions, including growth, stress response, reproduction, and metabolic rate.

      i. It coordinates the release of hormones from other glands and is often referred to as the "master gland."

   d. **Hippocampus:** A limbic system structure responsible for explicit memory formation and learning.

   e. **Amygdala:** A limbic system structure responsible for strong emotions (e.g., fear, aggression), the perception of threats, fear learning, and the processing of emotional memories.

4. **Corpus callosum:** A large collection of nerve fibers that connects the two hemispheres.

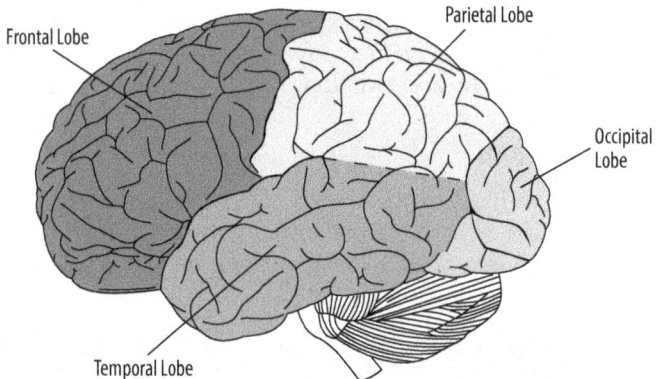

*Source: Henry Vandyke Carter via Wikimedia Commons*

5. **Occipital lobes:** The areas of the cerebral cortex (left and right hemispheres) located in the rear of the brain responsible for visual processing.

6. **Temporal lobes:** The areas of the cerebral cortex (left and right hemispheres) located on the sides of the brain responsible for auditory (hearing) and linguistic processing.

   a. **Auditory cortex:** The area of each temporal lobe devoted to the processing of sound input from the thalamus.

   b. **Wernicke's area:** A key association area responsible for language comprehension usually located in the left temporal lobe.

7. **Parietal lobes:** The areas of the cerebral cortex (left and right hemispheres) located in the upper central area of the brain responsible for the processing of sensory information related to the touch senses (e.g., pain, pressure, temperature) and spatial abilities.

   a. **Parietal association areas:** An area of the parietal lobe that processes and organizes information.

   b. **Somatosensory cortex:** The strip of cerebral cortex found at the front of the parietal lobes responsible for processing touch sensitivity for the opposite side of the body.

8. **Frontal lobes:** The area of the cerebral cortex (left and right hemispheres) located just behind the forehead that controls higher-level thinking (e.g., reasoning, planning, judgment, impulse control, memory), executive functioning, motor movement, and linguistic processing.

   a. **Prefrontal cortex:** The most forward portion of the frontal lobes responsible for higher-level thinking and executive functioning.

   b. **Motor cortex:** The strip of cerebral cortex found at the back of the frontal lobes responsible for voluntary skeletal movements for the opposite side of the body.

   c. **Broca's area:** A key association area responsible for speech production usually located in the left frontal lobe.

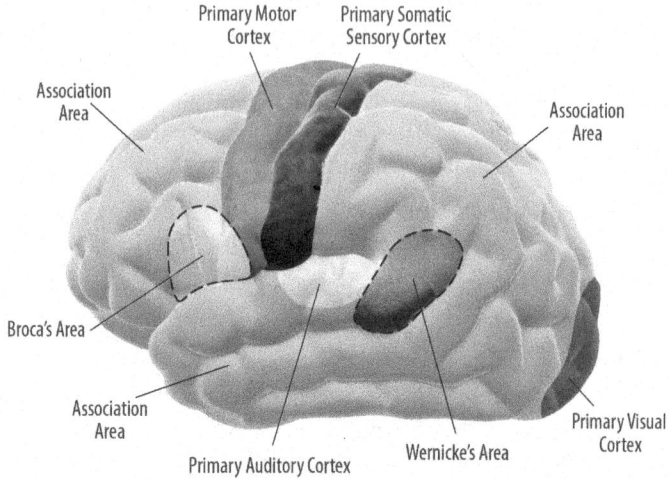

Source: WikiJournal of Medicine via Wikimedia Commons

9. **Association areas:** All the areas of the cerebral cortex that are not devoted to sensory or motor functions but are instead involved in higher-order functions, such as language, cognition, and reasoning.

## II. SPECIALIZATION

### A. SPLIT BRAIN RESEARCH

1. **Split brain patients:** Individuals whose corpus callosum was often cut to treat severe epilepsy.

2. **Aphasia:** A neurological condition caused by disease or injury to the portions of the brain responsible for language that produces difficulties in communication.

   a. **Broca's aphasia:** A disruption in speech production due to damage in Broca's area in the left frontal lobe.

   b. **Wernicke's aphasia:** A disruption in speech comprehension due to damage in Wernicke's area in the left temporal lobe.

3. **Contralateral control:** The organization of the central nervous system in which each hemisphere is responsible for the motor movements and sensory perceptions of the opposite side of the body.

4. **Lateralization or cortex specialization:** The tendency for certain cognitive functions to be controlled by one hemisphere of the brain more than the other.

   a. Much of what is known about cortex specialization was discovered through work with split-brain patients.

   b. If a word is flashed to the right visual field, it is received by the left hemisphere, and the split-brain patient says the word. This is possible because speech is associated with the left hemisphere.

   c. If a word is flashed to the left visual field, it is sent to the right hemisphere, which cannot produce speech. However, the patient can point with the left hand to identify the object.

   d. The right half of the cortex is primarily involved in spatial ability and recognizing faces.

**Test Tip**

Remember that for split-brain patients, in order to say what they saw on the screen, the information needs to be presented to the right visual field. Information from the right visual field **(RVF)** goes to the left hemisphere **(LHemi),** which commonly controls language.

**Right Visual Field . . . Left Hemisphere . . . Right Hand**

**Left Visual Field . . . Right Hemisphere . . . Left Hand**

B. **BRAIN PLASTICITY AND NEUROGENESIS**

   1. **Brain plasticity:** The ability of the brain to modify itself to recover from injury or as a result of learning.

   2. **Neurogenesis:** The growth of new neurons during the development of the nervous system and throughout the lifespan.

**Test Tip**

Some common real-world examples of brain plasticity include learning a new language or skill (reorganization) and recovering from a stroke through rehabilitation (compensating for damage).

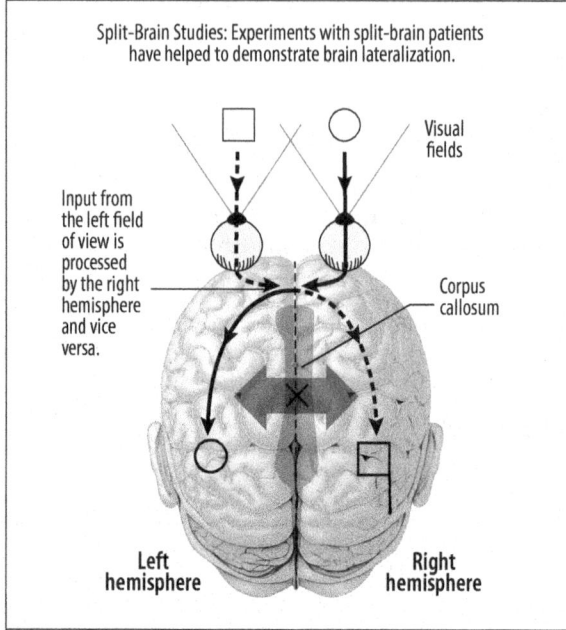

Split-Brain Studies: Experiments with split-brain patients have helped to demonstrate brain lateralization.

Visual fields

Input from the left field of view is processed by the right hemisphere and vice versa.

Corpus callosum

**Left hemisphere**

**Right hemisphere**

A word is flashed briefly to the right field of view, and the patient is asked what he saw.

*Face*

Because the left hemisphere is dominant for verbal processing, the patient's answer matches the word.

Now a word is flashed to the left field of view, and the patient is asked what he saw.

*Nothing*

The right hemisphere cannot share information with the left, so the patient is unable to say what he saw, but he can draw it.

## III. RESEARCH ON THE BRAIN

### A. CASE STUDIES

1. Many important findings have been made through observing behavioral changes in individuals who have experienced a brain injury (e.g., accidents, stroke, brain disease).

2. For example, Phineas Gage had a metal rod forced through his head while working on the railroad. He survived, but his personality was impacted because his frontal lobe association areas were disconnected from his limbic system.

**Science Tip** The non-experimental methodology of the case study is often used to better understand how the structure and function of the brain apply to behavior and mental processes.

### B. SURGICAL PROCEDURES

1. **Lesioning:** The removal or destruction of a portion of an organism's brain to determine the function of specific areas.

2. Direct stimulation is the process of delivering an electrical current to the surface of the brain and is used to help map the brain for specific functions.

### C. BRAIN SCANS

1. **Electroencephalogram (EEG):** A method for studying the brain that amplifies and records electrical activity (function) using electrodes placed in different locations on the scalp.

   a. Used to examine brain wave patterns during sleep stages and seizures.

   b. A disadvantage includes lack of brain localization due to measuring activity on only the surface of the brain.

2. **Functional magnetic resonance imaging (fMRI) scan:** A method for studying the brain that uses the MRI (structure) and tracks brain activity by measuring blood flow (function) carrying oxygen to active brain areas.

   a. Advantages include identifying structure and function without exposure to radiation.

   b. A disadvantage is that it indirectly measures activity via blood flow.

# Sleep and Sensation

## I. LEVELS OF CONSCIOUSNESS

### A. CONSCIOUSNESS

1. **Consciousness:** The state of being responsive to events and stimuli in the environment and being mindful of internal cognitions, such as feelings, memories, and beliefs.

2. Consciousness is unique to each individual and continually fluctuates.

### B. SLEEP

1. **Sleep:** A biological rhythm and state of consciousness marked by muscle relaxation and decreased responsiveness to stimuli.

2. Unique EEG patterns distinguish natural sleep from unconsciousness due to brain injury, illness, or drugs.

## II. BIOLOGICAL RHYTHM

### A. CIRCADIAN RHYTHM

1. **Circadian rhythm:** A biological rhythm involving a predictable pattern in the fluctuations of hormones, eating habits and digestion, blood pressure, body temperature, and wakefulness over a 24-hour period.

2. Humans would naturally prefer a 25-hour circadian rhythm.

### B. DISRUPTION AND RESET

1. **Jet lag:** A disruption to the circadian rhythm when individuals travel across different time zones. Jet lag is influenced by the

direction of travel, time difference across zones traveled, age, and individual differences.

2. **Social jet lag:** A disruption to the circadian rhythm when individuals stay awake longer on weekends for social obligations, such as school, family, or friends.

3. Shift work and shift rotation are also disruptive.

4. Disruption of the circadian rhythm can lead to problems with metabolism, weight, immune system functioning, mood, concentration, problem-solving, creativity, and memory.

5. Circadian rhythm can be reset with light, consistent sleep-wake times, sleep hygiene, exercise, caffeine avoidance, reduced exposure to blue light, and melatonin.

## C. BIOLOGICAL AND ENVIRONMENTAL CONTROLS

1. Biological factors influence the circadian rhythm.

   a. **Suprachiasmatic nucleus (SCN):** A region of the hypothalamus that influences the sleep-wake cycle by receiving input about the amount of light from the retina and then sending a message to the pineal gland to stop producing melatonin.

   b. **Pineal gland:** An endocrine gland in the brain that produces melatonin.

   c. **Melatonin:** A hormone that results in drowsiness when released from the pineal gland.

2. Environmental factors, including alarm clocks, blue light, seasonal changes, disease, and aging, can impact the circadian rhythm.

## III. SLEEP

## A. NON-REM (NREM)

1. **NREM:** All the stages of sleep, with the exception of REM, during which dreams are uncommon. NREM decreases in duration throughout the sleep cycle.

2. **Stage 1 NREM:** A type of light sleep identified by the presence of theta waves.

a. **Hypnagogic sensations:** A brief dreamlike hallucination or sudden movement (hypnic jerks) as an individual enters the initial Stage 1 sleep.

b. Individuals can be easily awakened.

3. **Stage 2 NREM:** A type of light sleep identified by the presence of sleep spindles and K-complexes in the theta waves.

**Stage 2 NREM**

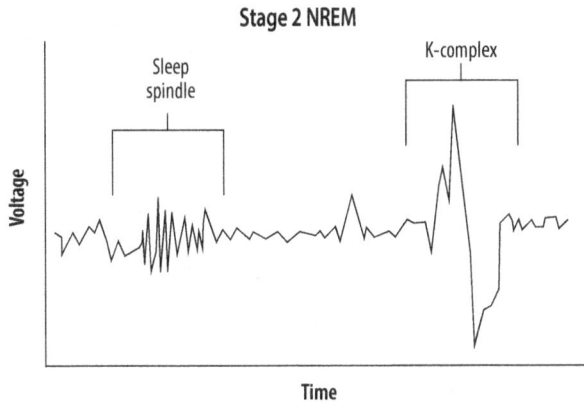

*Source: OpenStax*

4. **Stage 3 NREM:** A type of deep sleep identified by the presence of delta waves.

a. Individuals are difficult to awaken.

b. This stage is associated with body restoration, the release of growth hormone, and memory consolidation.

## B. RAPID EYE MOVEMENT (REM)

1. **REM (paradoxical sleep):** The stage of sleep in which eyes move behind closed eyelids and most dreams occur.

a. Identified by sawtooth-like waves that look similar to the beta waves predominant when an individual is awake.

b. The physiological changes during this stage involve increased heart rate, breathing, and blood pressure.

c. The frequency of REM typically increases as the cycle progresses.

      d. It represents a paradox (contradiction) because it produces waves similar to wakefulness, but the body is at its most relaxed.

  2. **REM rebound:** An increase in REM after being deprived of REM that illustrates the importance of this sleep stage.

### C. SLEEP PATTERNS

  1. **Sleep cycle:** A recurring pattern that involves three stages of NREM and one stage of REM.

      a. Approximately every 90 minutes individuals pass through the entire cycle. The entire cycle repeats four to six times during a typical eight-hour period of sleep.

      b. The stages are identified by their specific EEG patterns.

      c. The length of each sleep stage varies within the sleep cycle. As each cycle of sleep repeats, the REM stage becomes longer, and deep sleep becomes shorter.

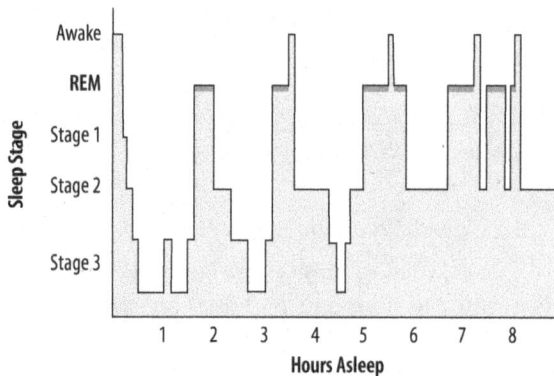

*Source: OpenStax*

  2. There may be variations in sleep patterns based on age, gender, and individual differences.

      a. Infants spend more time than anyone in REM sleep and require more sleep overall than any other group.

      b. As an individual ages, the overall need for sleep declines gradually.

**Test Tip** Remember that biological clocks have different times. The circadian rhythm, or sleep-wake cycle, is 24 hours. One sleep cycle lasts about 90 minutes in humans.

## IV. PURPOSES OF SLEEP

### A. MEMORY CONSOLIDATION

1. Sleep may be necessary for the brain to form long-term memories.

2. Sleep deprivation leads to poor memory performance.

### B. RESTORATION

1. Sleep restores resources that have been depleted during the day.

2. Provides the body with a chance to rest, repair muscles, grow tissue, and clear away any potentially toxic products that accumulate while awake.

3. For example, marathon runners sleep longer on the night after the race.

## V. PURPOSES OF DREAMS

### A. BIOLOGICAL

1. **Activation-synthesis model:** A biological theory which proposes that dreams are the result of the frontal lobe trying to interpret the stimulation it receives from the brainstem during sleep.

2. Dreams occur because some activation during sleep is needed to create and maintain neural connections.

### B. COGNITIVE

1. Dreams allow individuals to work through emotional concerns and everyday preoccupations.

2. Dreams are involved in the memory consolidation process.

**Exclusion Statement:** The psychoanalytic theory of dreams is outside the scope of the AP® Psychology exam.

## VI. SLEEP SCHEDULE

### A. SLEEP HYGIENE

1. Healthy sleep patterns can improve performance and overall well-being.

2. Good sleep habits may include a consistent routine, environmental considerations (e.g., quiet, lighting, temperature, limited electronics), and healthy daily habits (e.g., diet, exercise, reduced alcohol or caffeine consumption).

### B. SLEEP DISRUPTIONS

1. Sleep deprivation is linked to numerous adverse effects, including reduced immunity, health issues, weight gain, accidents, slowed reaction time, reduced attention, memory problems, and mood disturbances.

2. Long-term sleep deprivation has been associated with psychosis, including hallucinations and delusions in some individuals.

## VII. SLEEP-WAKE DISORDERS

### A. INSOMNIA DISORDER

1. **Insomnia disorder:** A disorder involving the chronic inability to fall asleep or stay asleep.

2. Treatments include regular sleep patterns, relaxation techniques, diet and exercise changes, and medications.

3. Relying on sleep medications or using alcohol is ineffective for managing insomnia disorder.

### B. SLEEP APNEA

1. **Sleep apnea:** A disorder involving repeated awakenings due to momentary cessations in breathing that lead to reflexive gasping for air.

2. Because individuals often wake up multiple times a night, they are tired the next day.

3. Treatments include weight management, medications, surgery, and using a continuous positive airway pressure (CPAP) machine.

## C. NARCOLEPSY

1. **Narcolepsy:** A disorder that involves the presence of sudden involuntary sleep attacks and excessive daytime sleepiness.

2. Individuals may present with or without cataplexy.

   a. **Cataplexy:** The sudden muscle weakness that ranges from mild (e.g., slurred speech, loss of grasp, or head nodding) to severe (e.g., total collapse).

      i. Strong emotions, such as laughter or surprise, often trigger it.

      ii. Episodes can last seconds to minutes, and the person stays conscious and aware.

3. Treatments include medications (e.g., stimulants and antidepressants) and controlled naps.

## D. NON-REM SLEEP AROUSAL DISORDERS

1. **Somnambulism (sleepwalking):** Repeated episodes of walking about while asleep. Individuals often have a blank stare and are unresponsive and difficult to awaken.

2. Sleep terrors are recurrent episodes of intense fear and autonomic arousal. Individuals are often unresponsive, cannot be comforted, and do not remember the event.

## E. REM SLEEP BEHAVIOR DISORDER

1. **REM sleep behavior disorder (RBD):** A disorder that involves movement during REM sleep, such as kicking, punching, flailing, and vocalizations, which are characteristic of dream reenactment (the acting out of dreams).

   a. These movements are unusual because the body is normally paralyzed during REM sleep.

   b. RBD is relatively rare, but prevalence is highest in older adults, especially men over 50.

2. Dream reenactment can be dangerous and lead to injury to the individual or the individual's bed partner.

**Exclusion Statement:** The AP® Psychology exam will only address the listed disorders.

## VIII. SENSATION

### A. PSYCHOPHYSICS

1. **Psychophysics:** A branch of psychology that studies how physical stimuli (sensations) translate to psychological experiences (perceptions).

2. **Sensation:** The process of detecting information from the environment via the sensory organs.

3. **Perception:** The complementary process to sensation, which involves the cognitive processes of organizing and interpreting sensations in the brain.

## IX. STIMULUS DETECTION

### A. TRANSDUCTION

1. **Transduction:** The conversion of stimuli received from the environment by specialized cells in sensory organs into neural messages.

2. For vision, light waves are converted into neural messages that are sent to the brain.

3. For smell, chemicals are converted into neural messages that are sent to the brain.

**Test Tip**

Be able to describe the process of transduction, beginning in the specialized receptor cells in each of the sensory organs and the specific pathway that the information takes to the brain.

### B. ABSOLUTE THRESHOLD

1. **Absolute threshold:** The minimum intensity of stimulation needed for detection 50% of the time.

2. For example, for sound, the faintest sound of a chirping bird that can be detected 50% of the time.

3. For example, for vision, the smallest font of a letter that can be detected 50% of the time.

## C. DIFFERENCE THRESHOLD (JUST-NOTICEABLE DIFFERENCE)

1. **Just-noticeable difference (JND):** The smallest amount of change in or between stimuli that can be detected 50% of the time.

2. For example, a student would establish the JND for weight after removing enough books from a backpack to notice that it became lighter. The JND can also be detected when a student notices that the backpack is heavier than a friend's backpack.

**Test Tip**

Remember to distinguish between the absolute threshold and just-noticeable difference (JND). The absolute threshold involves detecting a single stimulus, while the JND involves detecting a change and will therefore include a comparison—for example, something becomes more (e.g., saltier, heavier, brighter, louder).

## D. WEBER'S LAW

1. **Weber's law:** The minimum change needed to create a JND is a constant percentage of the original stimulus.

2. Larger stimuli require greater increases in intensity for a difference to be noticed. The formula does not work as well for extremes.

3. For example, the JND for a 50-pound backpack is 1 pound. Any weight added or removed that is greater than 1 pound will be detected by the subject. However, any weight below 1 pound will not be recognized.

## E. SENSORY ADAPTATION

1. **Sensory adaptation:** The reduced responsiveness in sensory receptor cells due to constant or prolonged exposure to a stimulus.

2. Evolutionary psychologists explain that sensory adaptation was naturally selected because ignoring repetitive stimuli makes it easier to focus attention on potentially more important novel stimuli in the environment.

3. For example, the constant pressure of a cellphone in a pocket may lead to the individual not feeling it anymore.

## X. MULTIPLE SENSES

### A. SENSORY INTERACTION

1. **Sensory interaction:** The sensory systems working together to influence how we perceive the world.

2. For example, flavor is the combination of smell, taste, vision, etc. This interaction is evident when an individual has a cold and struggles to taste food.

3. For example, balance is the combination of vision, kinesthetic, and vestibular senses.

### B. SYNESTHESIA

1. **Synesthesia:** A condition in which one sensory system generates automatic and consistent sensations in another sensory system.

2. For example, hearing colors or tasting shapes.

## XI. VISION

### A. LIGHT WAVES

1. Light waves are described in terms of their physical and psychological properties.

2. **Wavelength:** The physical property of a light wave that determines color (e.g., red is long, green is medium, blue is short).

3. **Amplitude (intensity):** The physical property of a light wave that determines brightness (e.g., tall is bright, short is dull).

### B. VISUAL PATHWAY

1. Light enters the eye through the cornea and then passes through the pupil, which is surrounded by the iris.

2. The lens then focuses light on the retina, where transduction occurs.

3. **Retina:** A photosensitive layer located at the back of the eye containing two types of photoreceptor cells.

   a. **Cones:** Photoreceptors mainly located in the retina's center responsible for detecting stimuli under bright light conditions and providing information about color and detail.

      i.   **Fovea:** A small central region of the retina where visual acuity is the sharpest because it has the most cones.

   b.  **Rods:** Photoreceptors mainly located on the outer edge or periphery of the retina that are responsible for detecting stimuli under low light conditions.

4.  Rods and cones are connected by bipolar cells to the ganglion cells.

   a.  **Bipolar cell:** A retinal cell that connects a photoreceptor and a ganglion cell.

   b.  **Ganglion cell:** A retinal cell that receives information from bipolar cells. The axons of the ganglion cells combine to form the optic nerve.

5.  **Blind spot:** The gap within the visual field created by the lack of photoreceptor cells in the optic disc, which is the area on the retina where the optic nerve exits the eye.

6.  A part of the optic nerve from each eye crosses at the optic chiasm to the opposite hemisphere of the brain. The message is then transmitted to the thalamus, which relays it to the visual cortex in the occipital lobes to be processed.

7.  Feature detectors are the specialized neurons in the brain that respond to particular elements of an image including straight lines, edges, curves, angles, or direction.

## C. VISUAL PROCESSES

1.  Visual transduction is the process of converting light waves received by sensory receptor cells (rods and cones) into neural messages that can be interpreted by the brain.

2.  **Accommodation:** The process in which the lens in the eye bends to direct light waves onto the retina.

3.  There are two main processes for the eye to adapt to light.

   a.  **Light adaptation:** The processes that occur in the eye that make it easier to see under bright conditions. These include pupil constriction and changes in the photoreceptors that decrease the sensitivity to light.

   b.  **Dark adaptation:** The processes that occur in the eye that make it easier to see under low light conditions. These include pupil expansion and changes in the photoreceptors that increase the sensitivity to light.

## D. COLOR VISION THEORIES

1. **Trichromatic theory:** The theory that the brain perceives color based on information from three types of cones in the retina.

   a. All colors are a combination of red (long), green (medium), or blue (short) wavelengths of light.

   b. For example, the perception of yellow is created in the brain when cones sensitive to red and green wavelengths are stimulated.

2. **Opponent-process theory:** The theory that the brain perceives color based on information from three pairs of opponent neurons that work together. One half of the opponent pair is inhibited by the other half, which is activated.

   a. The complementary pairs are red-green, blue-yellow, and white-black.

   b. For example, when the red-green opponent neuron is excited by red, green will be inhibited for that neuron.

   c. This theory explains afterimages.

      i. Negative afterimages: An opposite image in color or brightness that remains after the stimulus has been removed.

      ii. For example, if a person stares at an image of a green, black, and yellow flag for an extended time and then looks at a white piece of paper, a lingering image of a red, white, and blue flag will remain.

## E. VISUAL DIFFICULTIES

1. **Color vision deficiency:** A genetic condition on the X chromosome related to damaged or missing cones. It is more common in males.

   a. **Dichromatism:** A type of color vision deficiency that results when there are only two types of cones instead of three.

      i. The most common type is red-green.

      ii. The blue-green type is less common.

   b. **Monochromatism:** A type of color vision deficiency that results when there is only one type of cone instead of three.

      i. The result is that everything is perceived as different shades of a single color.

2. **Nearsightedness:** A condition that occurs when the eyeball is longer than normal, and the lens focuses the image in front of the retina resulting in reduced sharpness of vision for far-away objects.

3. **Farsightedness:** A condition that occurs when the eyeball is shorter than normal, and the lens focuses the image behind the retina resulting in decreased sharpness of vision for close objects.

4. **Prosopagnosia (face blindness):** A condition that makes recognizing and perceiving faces difficult.

5. **Blindsight:** A condition in which individuals with damage to their visual cortex can still sense and sometimes locate visual stimuli in their blind visual field.

## XII. HEARING (AUDITION)

### A. SOUND WAVES

1. Sound waves are described in terms of their physical and psychological properties.

2. **Wavelength:** The physical property of a sound wave that determines pitch (e.g., low pitches are long, high pitches are short). Pitch is measured in hertz.

3. **Amplitude:** The physical property of a sound wave that determines loudness (e.g., loud sounds are tall, soft sounds are short). Loudness is measured in decibels.

### B. AUDITORY PROCESS

1. Sound waves enter the outer ear through the pinna and are funneled to the auditory canal. The sound then passes through the eardrum (tympanic membrane) into the middle ear. The vibration is amplified by the ossicles (hammer, anvil, and stirrup) and sent to the oval window, a membrane covering the opening to the inner ear. The inner ear consists of the cochlea, which is a fluid-filled tube. Waves of fluid in the cochlea move the cilia along the basilar membrane, which runs down the center of the cochlea.

2. Transduction occurs in the cochlea. The sound waves cause the cilia (hair cells) located on the basilar membrane to bend, initiating a message.

   a. **Cochlea:** A snail-shaped inner ear part, lined by the basilar membrane, where auditory transduction occurs.

b. **Basilar membrane:** A membrane within the cochlea that vibrates leading to the stimulation of auditory receptor cells.

3. The auditory nerve sends the message to the thalamus, which relays it to the auditory cortex in the temporal lobes to be processed.

## C. PITCH THEORIES AND SOUND LOCALIZATION

1. **Place theory:** The theory that the brain perceives pitch based on where the message originates on the basilar membrane.

   a. High-frequency sounds activate the cilia at the beginning of the cochlea, while low-frequency sounds activate the cilia at the end of the cochlea.

   b. Best for explaining high-pitch sounds.

2. **Frequency theory:** The theory that the brain perceives pitch based on the rate of the neural impulse coming from the basilar membrane.

   a. A sound wave of 200 hertz is converted into a neural message that travels to the brain at the same rate as the sound wave.

   b. Best for explaining low-pitched sounds.

3. **Volley theory:** A theory that the brain perceives very high-pitched sounds by having multiple neurons work together, firing in rapid succession, to send a message.

   a. Neurons cannot fire more than 1,000 times per second; therefore, any sounds above 1,000 hertz require the activity of multiple neurons working together.

   b. Best for explaining very high-pitched sounds.

4. **Sound localization:** The process the brain uses to perceive where a sound is coming from.

   a. The brain determines the location of the sound based on which ear receives the sound wave faster.

   b. Sounds that originate from directly above, below, or behind a person are the most difficult to locate.

## D. HEARING DIFFICULTIES

1. **Conduction hearing loss:** A type of deafness resulting from problems with funneling and amplifying sound waves to the inner ear.

a. Causes include damage to structures (e.g., eardrum, bones of the middle ear) that transmit sound waves.

b. Treatments may include medication, a hearing aid, or surgery.

2. **Sensorineural hearing loss:** A type of deafness resulting from problems related to the transduction of sound waves or the transmission of neural messages.

a. Causes include damage to the structures (e.g., cochlea, basilar membrane, cilia, auditory nerve) that transduce or relay the message. Prolonged exposure to loud noise, aging, or disease can damage the cilia resulting in hearing loss.

b. Treatments may include a hearing aid or a cochlear implant.

## XIII. CHEMICAL SENSES

### A. SMELL PROCESS

1. Chemicals in the air (odorants) enter the nostrils and dissolve in mucous membranes containing olfactory receptor cells. There are thousands of different types of olfactory receptor cells (cilia).

2. Transduction occurs at the olfactory receptor cells. The axons of the olfactory receptor cells travel to the olfactory bulb, located below the frontal lobe.

a. **Olfactory receptor cells:** The cilia located in the upper region of the nasal passages where transduction occurs.

b. **Olfactory bulb:** The end of the olfactory nerve that is part of each cerebral hemisphere that receives the message from the cilia in the nose.

3. Unlike other senses, olfaction does not travel through the thalamus; instead, information passes to the olfactory cortex that connects to the limbic system.

4. **Pheromones:** A chemical signal released by animals that influences the behavior of others of the same species. It can attract mates or signal danger.

a. Whether humans have true pheromones is debated, but scents such as body odors may affect sexual attraction.

### B. OLFACTION (SMELL)

1. Olfactory messages interact with the limbic system structures, including the hippocampus and amygdala, to create strong emotional responses and memories associated with smell.

2. Olfactory receptor cells are continually being replaced.

3. Overall responsiveness to smell declines with age and can be impacted by environmental factors.

### C. TASTE PROCESS

1. Chemical molecules mix with saliva or fluid in the mouth. The specialized receptor cells are mostly located within taste buds and are not visible to the human eye. Transduction occurs at the taste receptor cells.

   a. **Taste receptor cells:** Specialized hair-like extensions within the taste buds where transduction occurs.

   b. **Taste bud:** A structure that contains taste receptor cells found on the insides of the cheeks, the roof of the mouth, and within papillae on the tongue.

2. The cranial nerve sends messages through the thalamus to the gustatory cortex.

### D. GUSTATION (TASTE)

1. Researchers have identified basic tastes (e.g., sweet, sour, bitter, salty, umami, oleogustus) and are investigating others.

   a. **Umami:** A primary taste that is found in protein-rich foods like meats, fish, vegetables, and cheeses described as "savory."

      i. Umami is exemplified by monosodium glutamate (MSG), which enhances other flavors.

      ii. The word "umami" is Japanese, and translates to "delicious."

   b. **Oleogustus:** A primary taste that refers to the sensation of fat that helps humans perceive the flavor and richness of fatty foods.

2. Researchers from the evolutionary perspective examine the potential reasons various human taste preferences were naturally selected.

    a.  Taste preferences for sweet and salty helped humans identify nutritious foods.

    b.  The avoidance of sour and bitter helped humans identify rotten or poisonous foods.

3.  Variation exists in terms of how sensitive (e.g., supertaster, medium taster, nontaster) individuals are to various tastes, which is mostly determined by genetics.

    a.  **Supertaster:** An individual with unusually sensitive taste buds, leading to strong reactions to moderate concentrations of taste stimuli.

    b.  They often have lower gustatory thresholds compared to others, making them highly responsive to tastes.

4.  Damaged taste receptors can regenerate every one or two weeks.

5.  Overall responsiveness to taste declines with age or may be reduced due to activities like smoking or drinking alcohol.

### E.  CHEMICAL SENSORY INTERACTION

1.  Chemical senses interact to create the sensation of flavor.

2.  For example, a reduced sense of smell (e.g., due to cold or infection) weakens or eliminates the sense of taste.

## XIV.  TOUCH SENSE

### A.  TOUCH PROCESS

1.  Transduction for the sensation of touch occurs when specialized receptor cells located in the skin respond to pressure, temperature, and/or pain.

    a.  Many touch sensations are a combination of different types of receptor cells activating.

    b.  For example, the sensation of hot is due to the activation of warm and cold receptors in the skin.

2.  A greater surface area along the somatosensory cortex represents areas of the body that are more sensitive to touch.

### B. PAIN PROCESS

1. Pain is processed both in the body and the brain.

2. From the biopsychosocial perspective, the perception of pain involves biological (e.g., genetics, brain, spinal cord), psychological (e.g., attention, expectations), and social (e.g., norms, the presence of others) factors.

3. Pain receptors are located throughout the body and follow two pathways.

   a. The fast pathway involves small nerves that carry sharp pain messages.

   b. The slow pathway involves large nerves that carry dull pain messages that persist after the initial injury.

4. **Gate-control theory:** The theory that pain signals traveling to the brain via the spinal cord pass through a series of invisible gates.

   a. The brain must receive the message for pain to occur.

   b. The gates can be closed in various ways, including sensory information, endorphins, distraction, meditation, emotion, visual input, or medication.

5. **Phantom limb sensation:** The presence, discomfort, or pain in an amputated limb. Phantom limb pain can be treated with mirror therapy—having the patient perform exercises with their intact limb in front of a mirror, which causes the illusion that the missing limb is moving, to reduce the discomfort.

## XV. BODY POSITION SENSES

### A. VESTIBULAR

1. **Vestibular sense:** The sense responsible for maintaining balance and equilibrium by monitoring the overall position of the body in relation to the position of the head.

2. Transduction for the vestibular sense occurs in specialized receptor cells called cilia. Information from the cilia regarding balance is sent to the brain via the auditory nerve.

   a. **Semicircular canals:** A group of loop-shaped fluid-filled tubes in the inner ear that contains cilia where transduction occurs by monitoring the position of the head.

b.  The cerebellum is the brain part that receives messages from the cilia involved in the vestibular sense.

3.  Overstimulation of the vestibular system can cause dizziness.

## B. KINESTHESIS

1.  **Kinesthetic sense:** The sense responsible for the awareness of the relative position of the parts of the body that are used to control and coordinate movement, gestures, and posture.

2.  Transduction for the kinesthetic sense takes place in the proprioceptors.

    a.  Proprioceptors are the specialized receptor cells sensitive to body movement and position and are located in the joints and muscles of the body where transduction occurs.

    b.  The cerebellum is the brain part that receives messages involved in the kinesthetic sense.

# Perception and Thinking

## I. PERCEPTION

### A. PROCESSING

1. **Bottom-up processing:** The method by which the brain builds a perception based on external sensory information.

   a. Bottom-up processing relies on external factors.

   b. For example, numerous feature detectors fire simultaneously (parallel processing) to provide information about shape, angle, and movement.

2. **Top-down processing:** The method by which the brain builds a perception based on internal prior expectations.

   a. Top-down processing relies on internal factors.

   b. For example, if a sentence is presented with a word missing, your brain will fill in the missing word based on your expectations and understanding of language.

### B. INTERNAL FACTORS FOR PERCEPTION

1. **Schema:** A mental framework that organizes experiences to make faster or more accurate perceptions.

   a. For example, a schema for a horror movie includes fear, suspenseful music, and a scary character.

2. **Perceptual set:** The expectation that an event or stimulus will happen in a particular way based on beliefs, emotions, or previous experiences.

   a. For example, after watching a horror movie, you are more likely to interpret an unusual noise in your house as an intruder, when under other circumstances you might ignore the same noise.

## C. EXTERNAL FACTORS FOR PERCEPTION

1. Context, experiences, and cultural experiences and expectations are external influences that impact perception.

2. Cultures have unique values, beliefs, and norms that shape how individuals perceive and interpret the world.

   a. For example, in some cultures, direct eye contact is perceived as a sign of respect, while in others, it may be seen as disrespectful.

   b. The Müller-Lyer illusion involves two equal-length lines, but the one with outward-pointing arrows seems longer. Cultural factors influence this perception. People from environments with right angles misjudge the lines' lengths, while those in settings without right angles are less affected by the illusion.

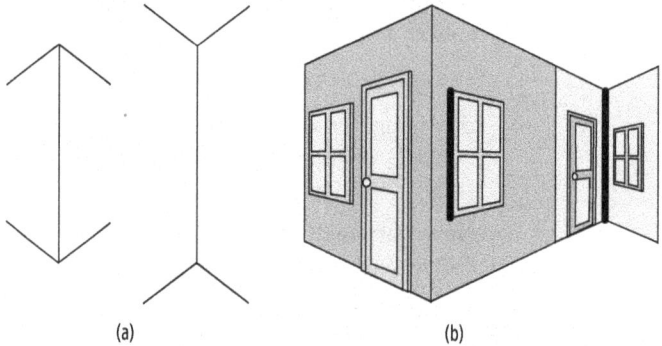

(a)                              (b)

*Source: OpenStax*

3. The media we watch (e.g., television, movies, and the internet) can shape our perceptions of various issues and influence our attitudes.

   a. For instance, biased or sensationalized news coverage can distort perceptions of reality.

**Science Tip**

Cultural factors influence perception. Remember, one of the science practices requires that you explain how cultural norms, expectations, and circumstances, as well as cognitive biases, apply to behavior and mental processes.

## II. GESTALT

### A. GESTALT PSYCHOLOGY

1. **Gestalt psychology:** An approach to psychology that focuses on the perception of whole patterns or forms. It emphasizes the idea that the whole is greater than the sum of its parts.

2. Gestalt psychologists began much of the perception research, which is continued today in cognitive psychology.

### B. FIGURE-GROUND

1. **Figure:** The part of the stimulus that is perceived as being important and separate from the ground.

2. **Ground:** The part of the stimulus that surrounds the figure.

3. Figure and ground work together to form a perception.

   a. For example, at a halftime show, the figure is the band members who are important and stand out in their uniforms.

   b. For example, at a halftime show, the ground is the surrounding area including the field and bleachers in the distance.

| Grouping Cue | Definition | Example |
|---|---|---|
| Proximity | Stimuli that are physically close to each other are perceived as a group. | Band members are perceived to be a group because they are standing close together. |
| Similarity | Stimuli that are alike are perceived as a group. | Drummers are perceived to be a group because they have the same type of instrument. |
| Closure | Stimuli are perceived as a group by filling in the gaps. | Band members create a whole shape because your brain fills in the gaps. |

## III. ATTENTION

### A. DIVIDED ATTENTION

1. **Divided attention:** The ability to focus attention on two or more streams of information simultaneously. It is possible only if the combined tasks do not exceed the cognitive load capacity.

a. For example, task switching and multitasking divide your attention and can be problematic.

## B. SELECTIVE ATTENTION

1. **Selective attention:** The process of choosing which stimuli to focus on and which to ignore.

2. **Cocktail party effect:** An example of selective attention that involves the ability to focus attention on one voice while ignoring other noises in a loud or distracting environment. However, information of special interest (e.g., your name or favorite song) will likely be noticed.

   a. In the crowded cafeteria, you can focus on your friend's voice while ignoring the noise around you. However, if a teacher calls your name, you will notice it.

   b. This has been studied using the dichotic listening test (having a subject repeat aloud a message presented to one ear while ignoring a message presented to the other ear).

## C. INATTENTIONAL BLINDNESS

1. **Inattentional blindness:** The failure to perceive a particular stimulus in the field of vision because attention is being focused elsewhere.

   a. For example, if you are concentrating on following another car, you may fail to notice that the light turned yellow even though it was in your field of vision.

## D. CHANGE BLINDNESS

1. **Change blindness:** The failure to perceive a difference in a particular stimulus that has occurred after a disruption in the field of vision.

   a. For example, if you look down at your cellphone after seeing a green light, you may fail to notice that the light turned red when you return your eyes to the road.

## IV. BINOCULAR CUES FOR DEPTH PERCEPTION

### A. RETINAL DISPARITY

1. An object is close if there is a larger difference between what each eye sees.

2. An object is far if there is a smaller difference between what each eye sees.

## B. CONVERGENCE

1. An object is close if there is more muscle strain associated with the inward turn of the eyeballs.

2. An object is far if there is less muscle strain associated with the inward turn of the eyeballs.

# V. MONOCULAR CUES FOR DEPTH PERCEPTION

## A. RELATIVE SIZE

1. An object is close if it is larger compared to others.

2. An object is far if it is smaller compared to others.

3. Must consider size constancy.

## B. INTERPOSITION

1. An object is close if it is blocking the view of another object.

2. An object is far if it is blocked by another object.

## C. RELATIVE CLARITY

1. An object is close if it appears clear within the atmosphere.

2. An object is far if it appears blurry within the atmosphere.

3. Atmospheric changes may include dust, fog, clouds, and precipitation.

## D. TEXTURE GRADIENT

1. An object is close if it has a more detailed and distinct surface.

2. An object is far if it has a less detailed and indistinct surface.

## E. LINEAR PERSPECTIVE

1. An object is close if it is located away from where two parallel lines seem to meet in the distance.

2. An object is far if it is located near where two parallel lines seem to meet in the distance.

Remember to distinguish between similar depth perception cues. Convergence is a binocular cue involving both eyes turning inward. Linear perspective is a monocular cue involving two lines that seem to meet in the distance. Relative clarity involves atmospheric changes, while texture gradient involves the surface of an object.

## VI. VISUAL PERCEPTUAL CONSTANCIES

| Constancy | Definition | Example(s) |
|---|---|---|
| **Perceptual constancy** | The ability to hold onto the perception of an object despite continuous change. | Size<br><br>Shape<br><br>Color |
| **Size constancy** | Objects are perceived as the same size even if the image on the retina increases or decreases. | A dog is perceived as remaining the same size despite the distance it is away from you. The farther away the dog is, the smaller the image on your retina will be, but you realize the dog did not shrink. |
| **Shape constancy** | Objects are perceived as the same shape even if the image on the retina involves a change in angle or orientation. | Bracelets are perceived as keeping their circular shape despite the angle they are viewed from when placed on a table. |
| **Color constancy** | Objects are perceived as the same color even if the amount of reflection changes. | A red stop sign is perceived as red, despite different amounts of light being reflected off the object, such as on a cloudy or sunny day. |

## VII. APPARENT MOVEMENT

| Term | Definition | Example(s) |
|------|-----------|-----------|
| Apparent movement | An illusion of motion | Stroboscopic movement<br><br>Phi phenomenon |
| Stroboscopic movement | The perception of movement by the brain when a series of images that change slightly are presented in rapid sequence. | The perception of movement is created when a flipbook quickly presents a series of still images. |
| Phi phenomenon | The perception of movement by the brain when a group of stationary lights placed in a row turn on and off in a rapid sequence. | The perception of movement is created when holiday lights flash on and off in a rapid sequence. |

## VIII. THINKING

### A. SCHEMAS

1. **Schemas:** A mental framework that organizes past experiences and aids in perception, memory, cognition, and problem-solving.

    a. For example, a dorm room schema would include a desk, bed, computer, and mini-fridge, but not likely a full-size oven, piano, or car.

2. **Assimilation:** The process of taking in new information without changing the schema.

3. **Accommodation:** The process of taking in new information and changing the schema or creating a new schema.

### B. CONCEPTS

1. **Concept:** A mental category within a schema for objects or experiences that share common traits.

    a. For example, the concept of flower would include roses, lilies, and tulips.

### C. PROTOTYPES

1. **Prototype:** The best example and the corresponding mental image of a particular category, which includes all the typical features of that concept.

   a. For example, the prototypical fruit would be an apple as opposed to an avocado, tomato, or olive.

   b. Prototypes vary among individuals and are impacted by age, location, and culture. For example, the prototype of a tree for one person might be an oak tree and another an apple tree. However, someone living in a tropical region might think of a palm tree.

## IX. PROBLEM-SOLVING

### A. ALGORITHM

1. **Algorithm:** A problem-solving strategy that involves using a set of rules that, if followed correctly, guarantees a correct solution, but can be time-consuming.

   a. For example, following a specific step-by-step recipe to bake a cake.

### B. HEURISTIC

1. **Heuristic:** A problem-solving strategy that involves using a shortcut that is likely to produce a solution quickly but does not guarantee a correct answer. While heuristics are faster and more efficient, they are also more prone to errors than algorithms.

   a. For example, using experiences to estimate ingredients while baking a cake.

2. **Representativeness heuristic:** A problem-solving shortcut that involves judging the likelihood of an event regarding how well it seems to match a particular prototype, which can result in either a correct or incorrect decision.

   a. For example, correctly assuming that hiking enthusiasts you meet are also environmentally conscious because it matches your prototype of an environmentally conscious person.

   b. For example, incorrectly assuming that a person with tattoos and long hair must be a rock star instead of a doctor solely based on how closely the individual matches the prototype of a rock star.

3. **Availability heuristic:** A problem-solving shortcut that involves judging the likelihood of an event in terms of how readily it comes to mind, which can result in either a correct or incorrect decision.

   a. For example, incorrectly assuming sharks are the deadliest animals to humans because frequent media coverage causes that answer to quickly come to mind.

   b. For example, correctly assuming that mosquitos are the deadliest animals because you recently read an article about how they spread disease, and this is the first thing that comes to mind.

**Test Tip**

Remember that heuristics are shortcuts, and therefore can lead to both correct and incorrect conclusions.

## C. CONFIRMATION BIAS

1. **Confirmation bias:** A problem-solving barrier that involves selectively attending to information consistent with one's viewpoint and ignoring or minimizing information that challenges one's beliefs.

   a. For example, when you are in love and notice only the positive qualities of your partner, and ignore any negatives, such as the fact that you have nothing in common.

## D. OVERCONFIDENCE

1. **Overconfidence:** A problem-solving barrier that involves overestimating how correct one's predictions and beliefs about ideas are.

   a. For example, when you think you will get your homework done in one hour, but it takes two.

**Science Tip**

Remember, one of the science practices requires that you explain how biases such as confirmation bias, hindsight bias, and overconfidence apply to a scenario.

### E. BELIEF PERSEVERANCE

1. **Belief perseverance:** A cognitive bias that involves holding onto an assumption or belief after it has been disproven.

   a. For example, after reading several articles proving that driving while texting is dangerous, you still believe you can drive safely while texting.

### F. PRIOR EXPERIENCES AND CIRCUMSTANCES

1. **Mental set:** The tendency for an individual to cling to an old method of problem-solving that was previously successful.

2. **Priming:** A retrieval cue that helps or prevents individuals from processing information if they have been exposed to a stimulus previously. This prior exposure will make it more likely that they will recall that same or a similar stimulus later.

3. **Framing:** A problem-solving barrier that involves making a decision based on how a problem is worded.

   a. For example, you are more likely to attend a college that states 75% of its graduates find a job in their field than if it states 25% of graduates did not find a job, even though both statements convey the same fact.

### G. COGNITIVE PROCESSES THAT HINDER DECISION-MAKING

1. **Gambler's fallacy:** A cognitive bias that involves incorrectly believing a chance event can be predicted based on past chance events. Falsely thinking the odds of a chance event increase if it has not happened recently. However, the probability remains the same.

   a. For example, if you flip a coin and get heads five times in a row, you may think that the next flip has a greater chance of being tails. But there is always a fifty percent chance of heads or tails.

   b. The gambler's fallacy reflects the representativeness heuristic because we predict future results matching the prototype of a random process.

2. **Sunk-cost fallacy:** A cognitive bias in which individuals continue investing resources (e.g., time, money, effort) into a situation because they have already invested a great deal and hope to recover the investment.

    a. For example, staying on a sports team that no longer brings enjoyment because you have already invested in expensive equipment.

    b. This term reflects loss aversion and our dread of losing what we have already put into a venture if we give up. It involves continuing to invest even when it is irrational or detrimental.

## X. COGNITIVE CONTROL

### A. EXECUTIVE FUNCTIONING

1. **Executive functioning:** A set of cognitive skills, including working memory, task switching, and inhibition, that allow for creating, planning, and executing goal-oriented behaviors.

    a. It is processed in the prefrontal cortex.

    b. For example, when you plan your night of attending practice and completing homework while continually thinking about how your actions impact your goals.

2. Working memory, a component of executive functioning, serves as a temporary, easily accessible memory system that helps update plans when distractions occur.

3. Task switching is a type of executive functioning that involves the process of moving back and forth between two cognitive activities. This allows you to focus on your homework and monitor your environment for cues, such as your parents calling you for dinner, so you can move between tasks.

4. Inhibition, related to executive functioning, involves restraining behaviors or impulses. This allows you to focus on homework (the task at hand) and not think about what happened during practice (unwanted information).

## XI. CREATIVITY

### A. FACTORS THAT INFLUENCE CREATIVITY

1. **Creativity:** The ability to generate novel and useful products or solutions to problems. Creativity tests are often scored in terms of the number of original ideas that are generated.

      a. Can be enhanced by knowledge of the topic, imaginative thinking skills, a risk-taking personality, intrinsic motivation, and a creative environment.

  2. **Divergent thinking:** A type of cognition that produces a variety of solutions to a particular problem and is associated with creativity.

      a. For example, writing, playing chess, creating pottery, or entertaining children all require divergent thinking because they require the generation of many possibilities.

## B. FACTORS THAT HINDER CREATIVITY

  1. **Convergent thinking:** A type of cognition that determines one correct answer by applying consistent rules and categorizing events.

      a. For example, simple arithmetic is solved by convergent thinking.

  2. **Functional fixedness:** A problem-solving barrier that involves thinking about objects only as working in their typical or normal way.

      a. For example, if you have ever sat in a room with a can and no can opener, you know the difficulties involved in trying to find another object that can be used as a can opener.

# Memory

## I. INTRODUCTION TO MEMORY

### A. MODELS OF MEMORY

1. Memory is often separated into three main processes.

   a. **Encoding:** The process of getting information into memory.

   b. **Storage:** The process of keeping or holding information in memory.

   c. **Retrieval:** The process of pulling information out of memory.

2. The multi-store model proposes that information can be stored in different interacting memory systems.

   a. **Sensory memory:** The first stage of storage involves a very short-lived recording of information perceived by the senses.

   b. **Short-term memory (STM):** The second stage of storage involves storing a limited amount of information for a short time.

   c. **Long-term memory (LTM):** The third stage of memory involves the permanent storage of a limitless amount of information.

**Multi-Store Model of Memory**

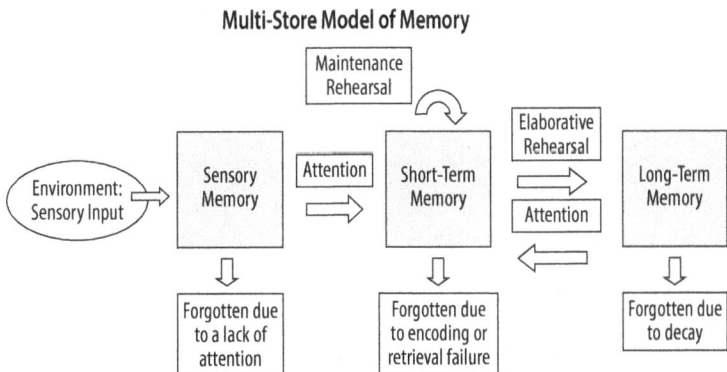

3. Working memory is a more detailed understanding of short-term memory storage.

   a. **Working memory model:** A detailed explanation for how short-term memory is now understood to be an active process that holds and manipulates information within several subsystems.

      i. **Central executive:** The aspect of working memory that manipulates rather than maintains the information from the two content-specific stores. It does this by adding or deleting information and coordinating the transfer between short-term and long-term memory.

      ii. **Phonological loop:** The aspect of working memory that holds internal speech.

      iii. **Visuospatial sketchpad:** The aspect of working memory that holds a mental picture of objects and their location in space.

**Science Tip**

Cultural factors influence memory. For example, culture shapes how people rehearse and recall information. However, some aspects of memory such as STM capacity, working memory, and the structure of LTM appear to be more consistent across cultures.

## B. BRAIN AND MEMORY

1. **Consolidation:** The gradual biological process of long-term memory storage in the brain.

2. Memory is not located in only one area of the brain. However, some regions are specialized for certain aspects of memory that relate to encoding, storage, and retrieval.

   a. **Hippocampus**—formation of explicit memories

   b. **Cerebellum**—formation of implicit memories

   c. **Amygdala**—formation of strong emotional memories and learning of fears

   d. **Prefrontal cortex**—using working memory and executive functioning

3. Many neurotransmitters are involved in memory.

   a. **Acetylcholine (ACh)**—The neurotransmitter important to memory formation. Deterioration of ACh has been linked to Alzheimer's disease.

   b. **Glutamate**—The neurotransmitter that is linked to long-term potentiation.

4. **Long-term potentiation (LTP):** A biological process that involves the repeated stimulation of neural networks that strengthens the synaptic connections between neurons and results in learning and memory creation.

## II. ENCODING MEMORIES

### A. PROCESSING

1. **Automatic processing:** The unconscious process of encoding material quickly and effortlessly for familiar information or information about space, time, and frequency.

2. **Effortful processing:** The conscious process of encoding material that involves attention.

### B. REHEARSAL

1. **Maintenance rehearsal:** The deliberate process of encoding through conscious repetition of information.

   a. For example, studying by stating a fact over and over until the start of the test.

   b. This process maintains information in short-term memory.

2. **Elaborative rehearsal:** The deliberate process of encoding through the use of connections to previously learned material that provides better retention rates than maintenance rehearsal.

   a. For example, studying by explaining the vocabulary to yourself in your own words and creating original examples (deep processing).

   b. Personally relevant information is easier to retrieve.

### C. LEVELS OF PROCESSING MODEL OF MEMORY

1. **Levels of processing model of memory:** Attention given to the process of encoding will impact future recall.

a. **Structural encoding:** A type of encoding that involves shallow processing by looking at the stimulus.

   i. For example, how many letters are in the word "brain"?

   ii. For example, looking at your notes leads to low recall.

b. **Phonemic encoding:** A type of encoding that involves intermediate processing by paying attention to the sound of the stimulus.

   i. For example, what words rhyme with "brain"?

   ii. For example, repeating your notes aloud leads to better recall.

c. **Semantic encoding:** A type of encoding that involves deep processing by providing meaning for the stimulus.

   i. For example, the brain is an organ of the body.

   ii. For example, rephrasing your notes into your own words with examples leads to the best recall.

**Levels of Processing Model of Memory**

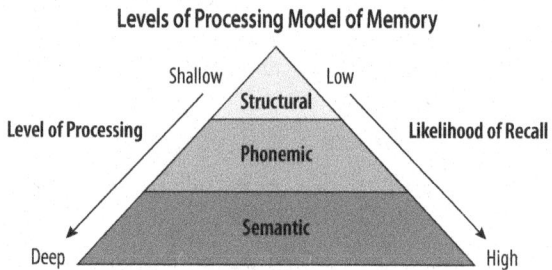

Shallow — Low

Structural

Phonemic

Semantic

Level of Processing — Likelihood of Recall

Deep — High

## D. MEMORY IMPROVEMENT

1. **Mnemonic devices:** Various techniques designed to improve memory that often include elaboration and connections with other material.

2. **Imagery:** The process of creating a mental picture for items or events to be memorized is especially helpful and is particularly effective if the mental picture is dramatic or unusual.

3. **Method of loci:** A mnemonic that involves associating the information that needs to be memorized with a series of locations, typically in a familiar place, through vivid imagery.

4. **Chunking:** The process of grouping related items into meaningful units.

a. Chunking can increase the amount of material that can be held in short-term memory.

b. For example, combining a phone number into three chunks, such as 414-555-1272.

5. **Categories:** Groups formed by clustering items with similar properties that enhance encoding by providing a structured framework for organizing information.

6. **Hierarchies:** A structured system that enhances encoding by categorizing items into broader groups and then subdividing them into smaller categories moving from general to specific.

7. **Spacing effect (distributed practice):** A practice strategy that involves spreading out studying into a series of shorter sessions with long periods of rest in between.

a. It is more effective than massed practice (cramming for learning).

b. For example, studying for the AP® Psychology exam in several shorter review sessions, as opposed to studying in one long cram session.

## III. STORING MEMORIES

### A. SENSORY MEMORY

1. **Sensory memory:** The first stage of storage involves a very short-lived recording of information perceived by the senses. The purpose is to collect data about the world and hold onto the material briefly for processing to take place. If attention is provided it will transfer to STM; if not, it will be forgotten.

a. **Iconic memory:** The retention of a brief visual image for a fraction of a second.

b. **Echoic memory:** The retention of a brief sound for a few seconds.

### B. SHORT-TERM VERSUS LONG-TERM

1. These two memory stores are distinct in terms of duration and capacity and are demonstrated through the serial position effect.

2. **Serial position effect:** The ability to remember items at the beginning and end of a list better than items in the middle. There are two aspects to the serial position effect.

   a. **Primacy effect:** The ability to remember items at the beginning of the list best. It occurs because rehearsal moves the information into LTM.

   b. **Recency effect:** The ability to remember items at the end of the list best. It occurs because the information is still stored in STM.

   c. The recency effect, but not the primacy effect, disappears if recall is delayed.

Types of Memory

| Stage | Duration | Capacity | Content |
|-------|----------|----------|---------|
| **Sensory** | Fractions of seconds or less | Large | Iconic, echoic |
| **Working** | 10–30 seconds | Limited: Seven, plus or minus two and as few as four | Central executive<br>Phonological loop<br>Visuospatial sketchpad |
| **Long-term** | Minutes to forever | Limitless | Implicit, explicit |

## C. EXPLICIT AND IMPLICIT LONG-TERM MEMORY

1. **Explicit memory:** A long-term memory that can be recalled consciously. This type of memory includes conversations, facts and events, and everything we normally think of as memory.

   a. **Semantic memory:** An explicit LTM consisting of general knowledge (e.g., facts, words, dates, theories).

   b. **Episodic memory:** An explicit LTM consisting of personal experiences and events tied to particular times and places.

2. **Implicit memory:** A long-term memory created indirectly and without awareness.

   a. **Procedural memory:** The most well-known category of implicit LTM consisting of skills, habits, and processes for how to perform a particular task.

**Different Kinds of Long-Term Memory**

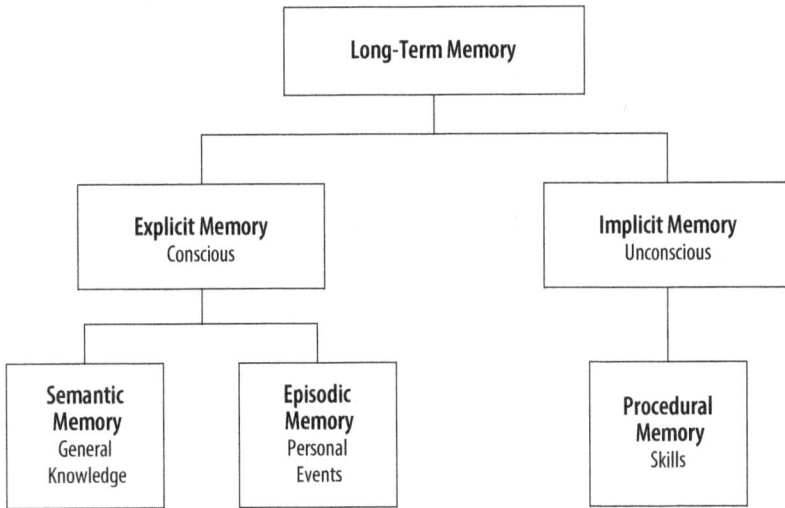

```
                    ┌─────────────────────────┐
                    │    Long-Term Memory      │
                    └─────────────────────────┘
                  ┌──────────────┴──────────────┐
        ┌───────────────────┐         ┌───────────────────┐
        │  Explicit Memory  │         │  Implicit Memory  │
        │     Conscious     │         │    Unconscious    │
        └───────────────────┘         └───────────────────┘
          ┌───────┴───────┐                    │
  ┌──────────────┐ ┌──────────────┐   ┌──────────────┐
  │   Semantic   │ │   Episodic   │   │  Procedural  │
  │    Memory    │ │    Memory    │   │    Memory    │
  │   General    │ │   Personal   │   │    Skills    │
  │  Knowledge   │ │    Events    │   │              │
  └──────────────┘ └──────────────┘   └──────────────┘
```

| LTM | Test Tip | Example |
|---|---|---|
| **Semantic** (Explicit) | "I remember that . . . | . . . Paris is the capital of France." <br> . . . my middle name is Diana." |
| **Episodic** (Explicit) | "I remember this time when . . . | . . . I won first place in an art contest." <br> . . . I first drove a car." |
| **Procedural** (Implicit) | "I remember how to . . . | . . . snowboard." <br> . . . change a tire." |

3. **Prospective memory:** The ability to remember to do something in the future.

   a. For example, remembering to turn in assignments by their deadlines or remembering to meet friends to study after school.

### D. HIGHLY SUPERIOR AUTOBIOGRAPHICAL MEMORY

1. **Highly superior autobiographical memory (HSAM):** A rare ability in which individuals can recall detailed personal experiences from their past with exceptional clarity. This includes specific events, such as what they did, wore, and heard on specific dates.

2. Case studies on HSAM may provide insight into biological processes for enhanced memory storage.

## IV. RETRIEVING MEMORIES

### A. RETRIEVAL METHODS

1. **Recall:** The retrieval of information learned earlier with little to no hints.

    a. For example, the free-response question (FRQ) requires recall.

    b. For example, providing a description of a suspect to a sketch artist.

2. **Recognition:** The retrieval of information by identifying the correct response from a list of choices.

    a. For example, the multiple-choice section uses recognition.

    b. For example, identifying a suspect from a police lineup.

### B. RETRIEVAL CUES

| Cue | Definition | Example |
|-----|------------|---------|
| **Context-dependent** (External cue) | Retrieval is aided if an individual is in an external environment similar to the one in which the material was originally encoded. | You remember a project that was due when walking into the classroom where it was assigned. |
| **State-dependent** (Internal cue) | Retrieval is aided if an individual is in the same physical and mental state (e.g., hunger, pain, mood, exercise) as when the information was encoded. | Being caffeinated when you take your test will improve your recall if you were caffeinated while studying. |
| **Mood-congruent** (Internal cue) | Retrieval is influenced by one's current emotional state. | After losing a game, you are in a bad mood, so you recall more negative events from the game. However, after a victory, you are in a good mood, so you recall more positive moments. |

### C. SUCCESSFUL RETRIEVAL PRACTICE PROCESSES

1. **Testing effect:** The finding that using practice assessments to study previously learned information leads to better retrieval than restudying material for the same amount of time.

   a. While testing is an assessment tool, it is also a learning tool.

   b. For example, use the practice questions in this book and others from your textbook or the College Board's AP® Classroom online platform to effectively prepare you for the AP® Psychology exam.

2. **Metacognition:** A strategy that involves the deliberate and conscious process of examining and trying to control cognitive processes.

   a. For example, after receiving test feedback, the process of reflecting on how you studied and what you could do to improve in the future.

## V. FORGETTING AND OTHER MEMORY CHALLENGES

### A. PROCESSING FAILURE

1. **Encoding failure:** Forgetting that occurs when information is not attended to and therefore will not move into storage. Insufficient encoding impairs retrieval due to the shallow processing of information.

   a. Both the amount of time spent on rehearsal and the depth of processing impact how rapidly information is forgotten.

   b. For example, inattentional blindness prevents the encoding of a memory due to selective attention to only some aspects of a scene.

2. **Inadequate retrieval:** Forgetting that involves the inability to extract information that has been successfully stored in long-term memory.

   a. **Tip-of-the-tongue:** The phenomenon in which you cannot locate the desired word in your memory even though you are sure you know it and it is just beyond your reach.

   b. For example, prospective memory failure involves forgetting to do something in the future. Remember that prospective memory focuses more on when to remember something than the content of the memory.

## B. DECAY

1. **Decay**: The fading of the physical memory trace in the brain over time due to normal brain processes, especially if it is not used regularly.

    a. Sensory memories and short-term memories are limited in capacity and quickly fade.

    b. Long-term memories, both explicit and implicit, may disappear over time if they are not retrieved and used.

2. **Forgetting curve**: The graphed representation of how much information was lost over time due to decay.

    a. According to early memory research by Hermann Ebbinghaus, the greatest amount of forgetting occurs within the first day after learning.

    b. After the initial steep drop-off in recall, forgetting levels off and no more learning is lost.

**The Forgetting Curve**

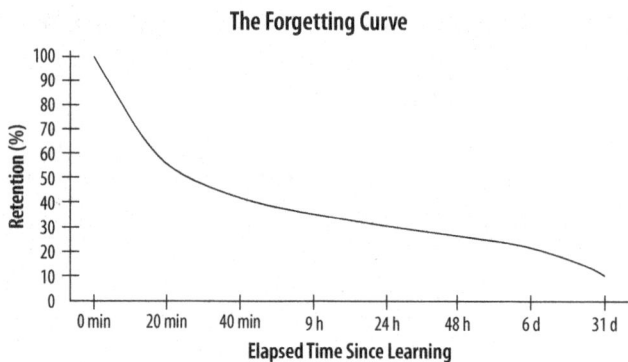

Source: OpenStax

## C. REPRESSION

1. **Repression**: The unconscious motivated forgetting of upsetting memories or unacceptable urges and desires.

2. According to Sigmund Freud, repression is an important defense mechanism or unconscious method for reducing stress and anxiety.

## D. AMNESIA

1. **Amnesia:** A condition that involves partial or complete memory loss that results from injury, illness, or psychological factors. It can be mild or severe and either temporary or permanent.

2. **Retrograde amnesia:** The inability to retrieve memories that were stored before the injury or illness that resulted in amnesia.

   a. For example, an athlete has a concussion and does not remember the events before getting hurt.

   b. It is a potential side effect of electroconvulsive therapy (ECT).

3. **Anterograde amnesia:** The inability to form new memories after the injury or illness that resulted in amnesia.

   a. For example, an athlete has a concussion and does not remember being examined after the injury but remembers everything that happened before it.

   b. Patient H.M. developed anterograde amnesia as a result of surgery to treat his epilepsy that destroyed his hippocampus.

4. **Infantile amnesia:** The inability to remember events before the approximate age of three due to immature brain development and cognitive abilities.

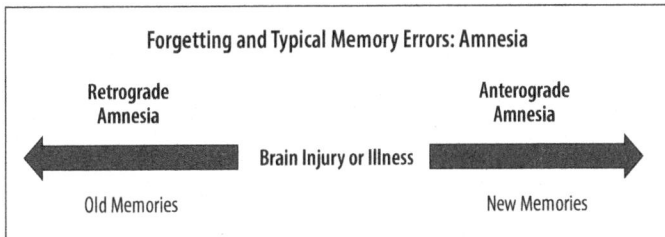

Forgetting and Typical Memory Errors: Amnesia

Retrograde Amnesia — Brain Injury or Illness — Anterograde Amnesia

Old Memories — New Memories

## E. INTERFERENCE

1. **Interference theory:** The hypothesis that forgetting occurs because two memories conflict with one another.

2. **Proactive interference:** A retrieval error that occurs when previously learned information interferes with the ability to recall a new memory.

   a. For example, old high school basketball plays block the recall of newly learned college basketball plays.

3. **Retroactive interference:** A retrieval error that occurs when recently learned information prevents the recall of old memories.

   a. For example, the current World Series champion team blocks recall of who won last year.

**Test Tip**

Remember to differentiate between similar types of memory or memory problems with similar words: proactive/retroactive interference, retrograde/anterograde amnesia, and prospective/retrospective memory.

### F. PHYSICAL IMPAIRMENTS

1. Serious problems with memory encoding and retrieval can result from damage to the brain due to degenerative diseases, physical injury, infection, or tumor growth.

2. **Alzheimer's disease:** A progressive neurocognitive disorder that causes memory loss and other widespread impairments.

3. **Traumatic brain injury (TBI):** Injury to the brain caused by an external impact.

### G. MEMORY CONSTRUCTION

1. **Memory consolidation:** The neurological process of creating a permanent memory.

   a. For example, the neurological process by which short-term memories are transformed into long-term memories, making them more stable and enduring over time.

2. **Constructive memory:** The active process of building recollections of events or experiences using stored information, such as schemas, to modify or add to the memory.

3. **Misinformation effect:** The tendency for individuals who have been provided with subtle misleading information to alter their memories by adding false information to their recollections.

   a. For example, a witness to a car accident may initially remember seeing a blue car involved in the collision. However, after hearing news reports or discussing the incident with others who mention a red car, the individual may unintentionally incorporate this into memory and recall the car as red when asked later about the accident.

4. **Imagination inflation:** A type of memory distortion that occurs when imagining an event that did not happen increases the likelihood of recording it as a memory of an event that did happen. This process involves creating a mental image of the event, which may later be mistaken for a real memory.

   a. For example, before testifying in court a witness mentally constructs the events, imagining or amplifying certain details in the process. The witness may later misinterpret these details as genuine memories during testimony.

5. **Source amnesia:** The inability to recall the origin (source) of how, when, or where a particular memory was acquired despite having a strong recollection of the memory.

   a. For example, you remember hearing a rumor about a new school rule but do not know where you heard it.

**Science Tip**

Practice applying Science Practices 2 and 3 to the Elizabeth Loftus "car crash" study by analyzing her research design and interpreting representations of her data in tables, graphs, and charts.

# Intelligence and Achievement

## I. INTELLIGENCE

### A. DEFINITION

1. **Intelligence:** Broadly defined, intelligence involves the capacity to acquire knowledge, reason effectively, and adapt to one's surroundings by using a combination of inherited abilities (nature) and learned experiences (nurture).

2. **Intelligence quotient (IQ):** A specific score on an intelligence test, that may or may not be an accurate measure of cognitive capabilities.

3. Early intelligence tests determined IQ using the ratio formula.

   a. **Ratio IQ:** An IQ score determined by dividing an individual's mental age by the person's chronological age and then multiplying the result by 100. If mental and chronological ages are equivalent, the individual is said to have an average IQ, which is 100.

      i. **Mental age:** The average age at which an individual can obtain a particular score on a test. This result is not helpful after the age of 14.

      ii. **Chronological age:** The biological age of an individual.

   b. The major flaw in the traditional IQ formula is that the mental age is not accurate for older individuals.

4. Modern intelligence tests determine IQ using deviation scores based on norms.

   a. **Deviation IQ:** Dividing an individual's score on the IQ test by the average test score of individuals the same age in a pretested group and then multiplying that result by 100.

b. Modern intelligence tests identify students for educational services and now use test norms.

    i. They are individually administered, designed for various age groups, include verbal and nonverbal measures, and provide both an overall score and subscores.

    ii. Examples include the Stanford-Binet Intelligence Scales and Wechsler Intelligence Scales.

---

**Exclusion Statement:** Labeling or describing cognitive abilities and disabilities are outside the scope of the AP® Psychology exam.

---

## B. THEORIES OF INTELLIGENCE

1. A variety of theories have been proposed to explain how intelligence can be defined and measured.

2. Some theories describe intelligence as one type of general ability (g) and others describe intelligence as being made up of several different abilities (multi-factor).

## C. GENERAL ABILITY THEORIES

1. **General ability (g):** A single factor that represents an individual's overall ability.

    a. General ability can be measured on IQ tests and can be used as a predictor of academic success.

    b. However, the overall score focuses on cognitive abilities and may not measure other important types of abilities.

2. General ability can be divided into fluid and crystallized intelligence.

    a. **Fluid intelligence:** The rapid processing of information and memory span used to solve novel problems and make new associations with existing knowledge.

    b. **Crystallized intelligence:** The knowledge gained over the lifespan, including facts, vocabulary, verbal skills, and cultural knowledge.

    c. Fluid and crystallized intelligence are positively correlated, and individuals with high fluid intelligence also have high crystallized intelligence, providing evidence for a general overall intelligence.

    d. Despite their similarity, the two intelligences become more distinct with age. Crystallized intelligence remains stable with age, but fluid intelligence peaks in adulthood and then declines.

## D. MULTIPLE ABILITY THEORIES

1. **Multiple abilities:** Multiple factors that represent an individual's abilities.

2. Intelligence can be divided into eight multiple intelligences: verbal-linguistic, spatial, logical-mathematical, musical, bodily-kinesthetic, interpersonal, intrapersonal, and naturalistic.

    a. Although these intelligences are distinct, they are used together to solve complicated problems.

    b. Researchers gathered evidence beyond traditional IQ test data using multiple sources, including individuals with brain injuries, prodigies, and savants, to support the existence of multiple intelligences.

    c. It is difficult to identify how many specialized intelligences exist and devise an accurate method of measuring them. It has also been questioned how some of the intelligences are different from talents or skills.

3. Intelligence can also be divided into three broad areas that work together—practical, analytical, and creative.

    a. This theory differentiates between what is commonly called "book smarts" (analytic) and "street smarts" (practical).

    b. It is difficult to determine whether these are distinct or they work together as part of general intelligence.

## II. PSYCHOMETRIC PRINCIPLES OF TEST CONSTRUCTION

### A. PSYCHOMETRICS

1. **Psychometrics:** The scientific study of using mathematical or numerical methods to measure psychological variables by creating reliable and valid tests.

2. Psychometrics includes the creation and interpretation of intelligence, personality, and psychological tests.

## B. STANDARDIZATION

1. **Standardization:** A type of control in which procedures are kept the same to eliminate potential confounding variables and ensure that all test-takers have an equal experience.

2. For example, the AP® Psychology exam uses the same directions, time frames, and scoring rubrics for everyone taking the exam.

## C. DISTRIBUTION OF SCORES

1. Once norms have been established, they often form normal curves, which are bell-shaped curves in which the mean, median, and mode are equal and located at the center of the distribution. The normal curve has a predictable distribution of scores.

   a. **Empirical rule:** Approximately 68% of scores fall within one standard deviation of the mean. A total of 95% of scores fall within two standard deviations of the mean, and 99.7% of scores fall within three standard deviations of the mean.

   b. **Percentile rank:** A statistic representing the percentage of scores equal to or below a specific score in a distribution. If an individual scored 100 on an intelligence assessment, they would be at the 50th percentile, which means that 50% of the tested sample scored at or below their test score of 100.

**Normal Distribution**

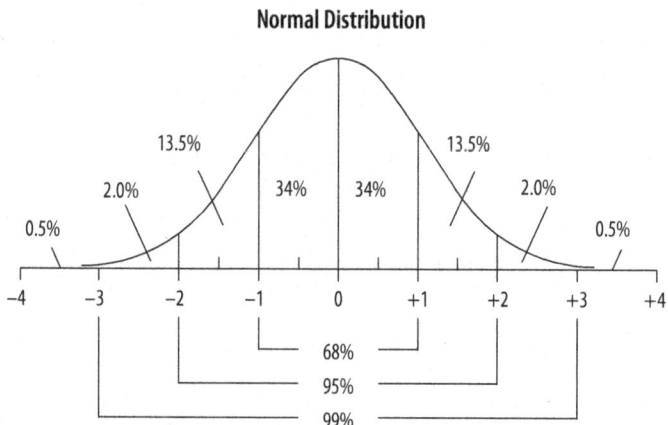

**Science Tip**

Be prepared to interpret mean, median, mode, range, standard deviation, and percentile rank from a set of data. In intelligence testing, percentile rank compares an individual's performance with a group, which helps understand an individual's cognitive abilities relative to others and informs decisions about education and career opportunities.

## D. VALIDITY

1. **Validity:** The accuracy of an assessment and whether it measures what it is designed to measure.

2. **Construct validity:** The extent to which a test accurately measures a particular theoretical idea (construct), such as intelligence, assertiveness, or aggression.

   a. Constructs should be operationalized to prevent threats to validity.

   b. For example, the Wechsler Adult Intelligence Scale (WAIS) has construct validity if it measures cognitive abilities and not a different theoretical idea (construct), such as language ability or cultural knowledge.

3. **Predictive validity:** The extent to which a test is accurate based on how well scores correlate with scores on an established test or criterion that measures the same topic given in the future.

   a. For example, the Stanford-Binet (SB-5) has predictive criterion validity if high scores are strongly positively correlated with future academic success or high GPA (established criterion).

## E. RELIABILITY

1. **Reliability:** The consistency or repeatability of the results of an assessment across administrations.

   a. A test can be reliable but not valid, meaning that individuals may receive the same inaccurate results every time they take the assessment.

2. **Test-retest reliability:** A measurement of consistency determined by a strong positive correlation between the scores on the first and second administration of a test to the same group.

a. For example, a test for the Big Five personality trait of conscientiousness has test-retest reliability if scores for the same 100 participants on two different occasions are positively correlated.

3. **Split-half reliability:** A measurement of consistency determined by a strong positive correlation between scores on subsets of the test (e.g., odds versus evens or first versus second halves).

a. Split-half reliability involves giving the test only once.

b. For example, a test for the Big Five personality trait of neuroticism has split-half reliability if scores for participants on odd versus even questions are positively correlated.

**Test Tip**

Remember to distinguish between reliability and validity. Psychological tests, including intelligence tests, are designed to be reliable and valid. Reliability indicates the test is repeatable (consistent results), and validity indicates the test is accurate.

## F. SOCIO-CULTURALLY RESPONSIVE TESTING PRACTICES

1. Researchers strive to develop assessments of intelligence that are socio-culturally responsive. Testing practices are designed to prevent particular groups from having advantages or disadvantages on intelligence tests.

2. **Stereotype threat:** The finding that when individuals believe others will use negative stereotypes to evaluate their performance, they experience anxiety, which then leads to decreased performance.

a. For example, a female student who is reminded that women are not as successful in STEM classes will perform poorly on a science test due to the anxiety created by attempting to overcome this stereotype.

3. **Stereotype lift:** The finding that performance can be enhanced from not considering oneself to be a member of an outgroup assumed to perform poorly.

a. For example, young people who are reminded that older people have poor recall will perform better on a recall test because they know that they are not part of the outgroup that is negatively stereotyped.

## III. SYSTEMIC ISSUES OF INTELLIGENCE ASSESSMENTS

### A. FLYNN EFFECT

1. **Flynn effect:** A finding that the average IQ has risen dramatically over successive generations.

2. Most researchers believe that it is due to societal factors (e.g., higher socioeconomic status, access to better health care, better nutrition) because the changes have happened too quickly for evolution to have occurred.

**The Flynn Effect: Gains in Mean IQ for World Regions**
Gain in Mean Full Scale IQ (Intelligence Quotient)

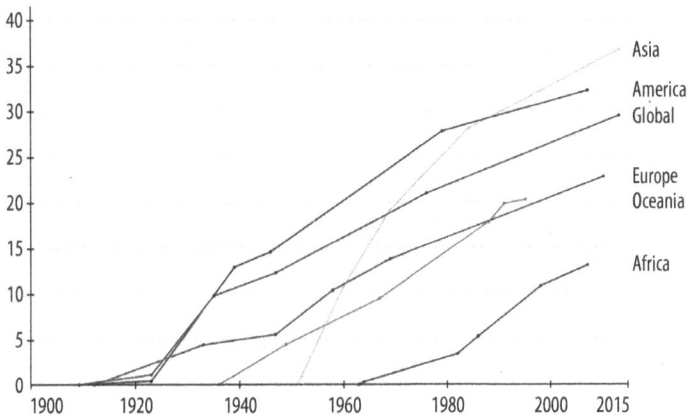

Source: Wikimedia Commons

### B. INFLUENCES ON IQ SCORES

1. IQ tends to vary more within a group than between groups.

   a. It is true that, in the United States, the IQ of certain groups are, on average, lower than other groups.

   b. However, the range of IQ for European Americans and other groups is actually the same; every race contains individuals with high intelligence.

2. Environmental factors, such as poverty, discrimination, and educational disparities, can lower intelligence scores for individuals and societal groups.

3. Misconceptions about the relationship between heredity and intelligence have caused pain for millions of people.

    a. Historically, intelligence tests have been misused to discriminate against various groups in the context of immigration and military rank.

    b. Individuals have also been denied jobs, education, and legal rights in part because of these claims.

## C. CULTURAL BIAS

1. Some cultures may have very different interpretations of what constitutes intelligence.

    a. Standardized intelligence tests that require language skills, such as the verbal section, are the most likely to be culturally biased.

    b. Tests that require subjects to be familiar with objects absent in their culture, or that have different uses or values, are also culturally biased.

2. **Culture-fair tests:** Assessments that are designed to enable all individuals, regardless of culture, the opportunity to perform equally well. They use nonacademic and nonverbal material to remove culture and are relatively unbiased.

3. **Culture-relevant tests:** Assessments designed to focus on skills and knowledge that are specific and important to a particular culture and would only be administered to members of the culture it was designed for.

**Science Tip**

Cultural factors influence the definition of intelligence. Remember, one of the science practices requires that you explain how cultural norms, expectations, and circumstances, as well as cognitive biases, apply to behavior and mental processes.

## IV. ACADEMIC ACHIEVEMENT

### A. ACADEMIC TESTS

1. Academic achievement is not considered intelligence, but rather being successful at school or having a specific skill.

2. **Achievement tests:** Assessments designed to determine the level of knowledge an individual has regarding a particular subject or skill that has resulted from experience.

   a. For example, the AP® Psychology exam determines how much material has been learned in that subject.

3. **Aptitude tests:** Assessments designed to predict the success of individuals by evaluating their general abilities, such as mathematical calculation, language ability, and reasoning. They may or may not involve the measurement of intelligence.

   a. The Stanford-Binet or Wechsler Scales determine whether an individual has the potential to learn based on the possession of basic skills.

   b. The line between achievement and aptitude tests is unclear. In reality, college entrance exams measure both aptitude (likelihood of college success) and achievement (accumulated knowledge based on high school coursework).

## B. IMPACTS TO ACADEMIC ACHIEVEMENT

1. **Fixed mindset:** The belief that abilities, intelligence, and talents cannot be significantly changed or developed.

   a. Individuals with a fixed mindset tend to avoid challenges, fear failure, and do not value effort because they believe their abilities are predetermined.

2. **Growth mindset:** The belief that abilities, intelligence, and talents can be developed and improved through dedication, effort, and learning.

   a. Individuals with a growth mindset embrace challenges, persist in the face of setbacks, and see effort as a path to mastery and success.

# Development

## I. HUMAN DEVELOPMENT

### A. THEMATIC ISSUES AND CHRONOLOGICAL ORDER

1. **Developmental psychology:** The study of physical, cognitive, and social-emotional development of humans that occurs across the lifespan from conception to death.

2. Developmental psychologists are concerned with chronological order and thematic issues.

### B. NATURE AND NURTURE THEME

1. **Nature:** The specific influences on development that are genetic or biological.

2. **Nurture:** The specific influences on development that are environmental (e.g., family, nutrition, culture, interactions with others, education, wealth).

### C. CONTINUITY AND DISCONTINUITY (STAGES) THEME

1. **Continuity:** The gradual, cumulative process of development that is similar to an escalator (e.g., Vygotsky's sociocultural theory).

2. **Discontinuity:** The sudden discrete stages that are similar to a staircase (e.g., Piaget's cognitive development theory).

### D. STABILITY AND CHANGE

1. **Stability:** The degree to which our personalities or intelligence stay the same as we age.

2. **Change:** The degree to which our personalities and intelligence transform as we age, resulting in new traits, behavior, and mental processes.

## II. RESEARCH DESIGNS

### A. CROSS-SECTIONAL DESIGNS

1. **Cross-sectional design:** A research method that compares individuals of different ages who are evaluated at a single point in time.

2. For example, several age groups (e.g., 20-, 30-, and 40-year-olds) were compared for executive functioning simultaneously.

3. For example, a 40-year-old group had significantly lower video game scores than individuals in the 20-year-old age group. However, be careful drawing conclusions from such evidence; lower scores could be due to an inability to learn new video games declining with age, a lack of experience or motivation, or some other factor.

### B. LONGITUDINAL DESIGNS

1. **Longitudinal design:** A research method that studies the same group of individuals over a lengthy period to examine stability and change in development.

2. For example, following the same group of 20-year-olds through their 30s and 40s to examine changes in executive functioning over time.

3. For example, the Minnesota Twin Study found that monozygotic twins raised apart had similarities in certain traits, including intelligence and personality.

**Science Tip**

Remember, because age cannot be manipulated (individuals cannot be randomly assigned to a particular age group), developmental research is often correlational or descriptive.

## III. PHYSICAL DEVELOPMENT

### A. PRENATAL

1. Maternal illness (e.g., infectious disease), genetic mutations, and hormonal and environmental factors (e.g., maternal health, stress,

malnutrition) can influence the major physical and psychological milestones that occur during prenatal development.

2. **Teratogens:** Any chemical, virus, or other agent that reaches the fetus and results in developmental abnormalities.

    a. Examples are certain drugs and medications, infectious diseases, and pollutants.

    b. **Fetal alcohol syndrome (FAS):** A condition that involves a group of negative health effects that are the result of heavy drinking, which is known to cause developmental problems. Typical complications of FAS include physical and cognitive abnormalities.

3. Proper health care, nutrition, and a supportive environment can positively influence prenatal development.

**Exclusion Statement:** The stages of prenatal development (zygote, embryo, and fetus) are outside the scope of the AP® Psychology exam.

## B. INFANCY AND CHILDHOOD

1. **Maturation:** The biological growth process that enables change in behavior and is connected to an individual's genetic blueprint, meaning it is relatively uninfluenced by experience.

2. **Developmental milestones:** The average age when children typically achieve particular skills. The exact age may not be the same for every infant, but the steps in the process follow the same basic pattern.

    a. Motor development milestones include learning to lift the head, roll over, sit up unassisted, crawl, and walk.

    b. Cross-cultural research indicates that motor development is also related to environmental (nurture) causes. Variation across cultures may be due to parenting styles.

3. During childhood, physical development progresses rapidly as motor skills improve and expand.

    a. **Gross motor skill:** A motor skill that involves large muscles to move the trunk or limbs and maintain balance by controlling posture.

        i. For example, walking, kicking a ball, and swimming.

    b. **Fine motor skill:** A motor skill that involves the coordination of small muscles to make precise movements, particularly in the hands and fingers.

       i. For example, handwriting, tying shoes, using a keyboard, and manipulating small objects.

4. Infants have reflexes for survival from birth. Many reflexes are lost relatively quickly after three or four months as the infant develops muscle control, but others last throughout life. The presence of the major reflexes at birth indicates normal neurological development.

    a. **Rooting reflex:** An automatic response when an infant's cheek is touched that involves turning toward the source of the touch and opening the mouth in preparation for feeding.

5. Physically, infants are already very developed and capable of receiving information from their surroundings using all their senses. However, vision in newborns is not fully developed at birth.

6. Researchers need innovative methods to study how infants perceive depth (e.g., visual cliff and more recent research) because they cannot talk.

    a. **Visual cliff:** An apparatus designed to examine if depth perception exists in infants who have just learned to crawl; it consists of a glass-topped table that creates the illusion of a drop-off on one side.

    b. The infant is placed on the table at the shallow end and encouraged to cross the perceived cliff, but most infants refuse to do this, indicating that they can perceive depth.

    c. This finding suggests that the perception of depth in humans might be innate. However, it is impossible to determine whether infants have learned to judge depth before they can crawl, so the visual cliff cannot conclusively prove that depth perception is innate in humans and not learned.

    d. Newborn animals were also tested on the visual cliff, including kittens, chickens, and a goat, all of which can move independently very soon after birth. The findings showed that these animals would also not cross the visual cliff, providing further evidence that depth perception may be innate.

7. **Critical period:** A fixed time early in life when individuals are best able to acquire specific skills that are part of normal development and cannot be learned later in life.

8. **Sensitive period:** A developmental stage when acquiring a skill or characteristic is particularly quick and easy.

9. There is evidence of a sensitive or potentially critical period for language.

   a. Very young children can easily acquire any language or even more than one language, but as individuals become older learning a second language becomes increasingly challenging.

   b. Children who are not exposed to speech early in their lives have a difficult time learning language later.

10. Time periods for attachment in animals and humans have also been explored.

    a. **Imprinting:** A phenomenon among some species in which the animal is biologically programmed to form an attachment to and follow the first moving object that it sees.

       i. For example, baby chicks form an attachment with the first moving object they see.

       ii. This inborn tendency to form a bond during a critical period is necessary for small vulnerable animals to survive. A critical period is a fixed time frame very early in life when particular events result in long-lasting effects on behavior.

    b. Human infants lack a specific time frame for building an attachment, but establishing a strong bond with caregivers is crucial for healthy development.

       i. For example, the first year of life in humans is crucial for forming secure attachments.

       ii. Unlike a critical period, missing this window doesn't permanently impair development, but it can make acquiring skills more challenging.

## C. ADOLESCENCE

1. **Adolescence:** The period beginning with the onset of puberty and spanning the teen years, typically starting at around the age of 14 for boys and the age of 12 for girls.

2. One of the earliest signs of physical changes associated with adolescence is the growth spurt.

3. **Puberty:** The period when individuals reach sexual maturity and can reproduce. The precise beginning of puberty is difficult to determine, but many agree it is marked by the first menstrual period or the first ejaculation.

     a. **Menarche:** The first menstrual period, which indicates the onset, or start, of puberty in women.

     b. **Spermarche:** The first ejaculation of semen in men.

     c. **Primary sex characteristics:** A trait directly related to reproduction, including the reproductive organs and external genitalia.

     d. **Secondary sex characteristics:** A trait that has no effect on physical reproduction.

         i. Men experience a lowering of their voice and the appearance of facial, chest, and pubic hair.

         ii. Women experience the enlargement of the breasts and the appearance of armpit and pubic hair.

4. The timing of puberty is related to both biological maturation (nature) and environmental influences (nurture). Environmental influences on puberty include nutrition and access to health care. The timing of puberty can have important social and emotional effects. Early maturation is often associated with more positive consequences for males than females.

5. The prefrontal cortex is also a focus of neural development during adolescence. The frontal lobes, critical for reasoning, planning, judgment, and impulse control, do not fully develop until individuals are in their mid-20s. Because the frontal lobe is not fully mature, adolescents are more likely to engage in risky behavior.

## D. ADULTHOOD

1. The developmental period of adulthood can be divided into three stages: early, middle, and late adulthood.

2. **Early adulthood:** The period of adulthood that is the peak of physical development, such as reaction time, speed, and strength.

3. **Middle adulthood:** The period of adulthood characterized by gradual physical decline. Hearing, visual acuity, and sense of smell become less sensitive, and reaction time decreases.

     a. **Menopause:** The end of the menstrual cycle, in which a woman's reproductive capacity decreases and eventually ends.

     b. Men do not have a comparable experience; however, sperm count declines with age.

4. **Late adulthood:** The period of adulthood characterized by a more rapid physical decline, which can be seen in lengthened reaction times, decreased mobility, and reduced sensory acuity.

## IV. GENDER DEVELOPMENT

### A. SEX AND GENDER

1. **Sex:** The biological definition of being male, female, or intersex, which is determined by anatomical differences.

2. **Gender:** The cultural, psychological, and behavioral characteristics associated with biological sex. Gender is acquired as children develop and are socialized.

3. **Gender identity:** The internal recognition that an individual is male, female, neither, or both and the assimilation of this belief into the person's self-concept. For most individuals, gender identity is consistent with one's biological sex.

4. **Sexual orientation:** The attraction to another person (e.g., heterosexual, same-sex, bisexual, asexual).

### B. GENDER ROLES

1. **Gender roles:** The expected appearance, personality traits, and behaviors connected to being male or female mainly relate to environmental factors, such as family and cultural interactions. Gender roles help individuals develop a sense of identity and understand others.

2. **Social learning theory:** The theory that gender roles may be acquired through the observation of models and operant conditioning. Children imitate individuals in their family or culture of the same sex, especially in regard to behaviors that are reinforced or punished.

   a. For example, if a boy cries and the parent frowns, this punishment will likely lead him to suppress emotions in the future, whereas if a girl cries and the parent consoles her, she learns that expressing emotions is acceptable.

3. **Cognitive-developmental theory:** The theory that explains how gender roles are acquired. According to this theory, children develop gender schemas and organize information about behavior and activities into specific gender categories.

a. For example, a girl watches a boy get punished for crying and processes that behavior to create a gender rule that will be used to build her gender schema that boys don't cry.

4. **Androgyny:** A type of gender expression that combines masculinity and femininity or does not fit traditional gender categories.

## V. COGNITIVE DEVELOPMENT

### A. THEORIES OF COGNITIVE DEVELOPMENT

1. Jean Piaget believed that children advance cognitively through an active exploration of their world resulting in the development and expansion of schemas.

   a. Schemas can be developed discontinuously (distinct changes between the four stages of cognitive development) and continuously (a more gradual change across stages).

2. **Schema:** A mental framework that organizes past experiences and aids in perception (speed and accuracy), memory, cognition, and problem-solving.

   a. For example, there are schemas for identifying various types of animals, including cats.

3. **Assimilation:** The process of trying to fit new information into existing schemas.

   a. For example, a child sees a black cat and incorporates it into the child's schema for animals (correct).

   b. For example, a child sees a skunk for the first time and thinks it is a cat because all small, four-legged furry animals are cats (incorrect).

4. **Accommodation:** If the information does not fit into an existing schema, a new one is created, or the original schema is changed to incorporate this new information.

   a. For example, after being told the animal is a skunk, the child changes the child's schema for animals to include both skunks and cats.

5. Jean Piaget described cognitive development in terms of four distinct stages that follow a fixed order from birth to adolescence.

   a. Furthermore, he hypothesized that movement from one stage to another is dependent on both biological maturation and exposure to experiences with the environment.

| Stage | Definition | Characteristics |
|---|---|---|
| **Sensorimotor** (Infancy through toddlerhood) | Piaget's first stage of cognitive development in which cognition develops through sensory and motor experiences. | **Object permanence:** The awareness that items (objects) continue to exist even when they cannot be seen. It develops at 9 months or about halfway through the stage. |
| **Preoperational** (Toddlerhood through early childhood) | Piaget's second stage of cognitive development in which cognition develops through symbolic and pre-logical thought, language, and pretend play. | **Egocentrism:** The difficulty of seeing how the world looks from the perspective of others. It is not about being selfish. Children cannot understand why others cannot tell that their drawings are of themselves and their dogs. They think that because they know what the pictures represent others do as well. |
| | | **Animism:** The preoperational error that all objects are living and capable of actions and emotions. A child thinks a teddy bear is alive and has feelings. |
| | | **Centration:** The preoperational error caused by focusing on one aspect of a problem. This is why preoperational children lack conservation. A child pours juice into a tall, narrow glass and believes it has more juice than when it was in a short, wide glass. The child is focused on the height and not the width. |

*(continued)*

| Stage | Definition | Characteristics |
|---|---|---|
| **Concrete operational** (Early through late childhood) | Piaget's third stage of cognitive development in which cognition develops through the use of logical thought about concrete concepts, which are tangible or physically present. | **Conservation:** The understanding that the mass, volume, weight, and quantity of an object(s) do not change even though the appearance has been altered in some way. |
| | | **Reversibility:** The ability to perform actions and mentally undo or reverse them. |
| **Formal operational** (Late childhood through adulthood) | Piaget's fourth stage of cognitive development in which cognition develops through the use of logical reasoning to examine abstract theoretical concepts. Piaget proposed that not all people achieve formal operational thinking. | **Abstract thought:** A type of cognition that involves considering intangible concepts, such as morality and equality. |
| | | **Hypothetical thought:** A type of problem-solving that involves exploring potential situations, drawing logical conclusions, and testing ideas beyond direct experiences. For example, an individual could imagine humans regenerating limbs or explore the problems associated with a perfect memory. |

6. **Theory of mind:** The growing awareness in children of their own mental processes and those of others that begins to develop in Piaget's preoperational stage.

   a. It is measured through a false-belief test, such as the Sally-Anne test.

7. **Sociocultural theory of cognitive development:** The theory that learning is mostly a social process influenced by language, culture, and interactions with others, such as parents, teachers, and older peers.

   a. Proposed by psychologist Lev Vygotsky.

   b. **Zone of proximal development (ZPD):** The difference between what children are capable of learning independently and what they can accomplish with assistance from a more knowledgeable other (MKO).

c. **Scaffolding:** The process of providing just enough assistance to the learner to ensure understanding. It is related to the zone of proximal development because the teacher continually adjusts how much support is needed as learning progresses.

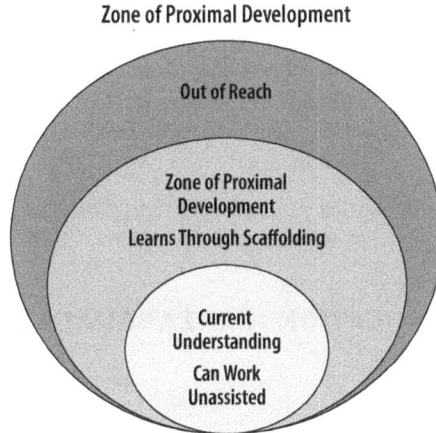

**Zone of Proximal Development**

Out of Reach

Zone of Proximal Development
Learns Through Scaffolding

Current Understanding
Can Work Unassisted

*Source: https://tracyharringtonatkinson.com*

## B. ADULTHOOD

1. Cognitive changes continue during adulthood, but specific differences exist between the abilities of individuals in early, middle, and late adulthood.

   a. Early adulthood is the peak of cognitive development, such as vocabulary expansion, planning, reasoning, and memory.

   b. Middle adulthood is the period during which mental abilities remain stable. Recall may decline, but recognition does not.

   c. Late adulthood is the period during which processing speed, working memory, and recall of episodic memories decline.

2. During adulthood, changes occur in specific intellectual abilities in relation to types of intelligence.

   a. **Crystallized Intelligence:** The acquired knowledge of vocabulary, verbal skills, cultural knowledge, and factual information remains stable throughout adulthood.

   b. **Fluid intelligence:** The rapid processing of information and memory span needed to solve new types of problems begins decreasing during middle adulthood.

c. **Dementia (neurocognitive disorder):** The significant impairment of daily functioning and independence is often caused by vascular issues or conditions such as Alzheimer's disease.

   i. Diagnosis often involves physical exams, blood tests, cognitive assessments, brain scans, and genetic tests.

   ii. Different from normal aging because it involves severe challenges with memory, thinking, language, and physical abilities, making daily tasks difficult compared to the milder changes associated with aging.

   iii. Individuals who remain physically and mentally active and eat a healthy diet can slow the signs of aging.

## VI. COMMUNICATION AND LANGUAGE DEVELOPMENT

### A. LANGUAGE

1. **Language:** A shared form of communication consisting of symbols that can be arranged to derive meaning.

   a. In spoken language, sounds represent objects and ideas, whereas sign language uses hand motions for communication.

2. **Phonemes:** The smallest units of sound in language needed to pronounce a word.

   a. For example, in the word "sun," there are three phonemes: /s/, /u/, and /n/. Each phoneme represents a unique sound that is needed to pronounce the word "sun" correctly.

3. **Morphemes:** The smallest unit of meaning in language, such as a root word, prefix, or suffix. Combinations of morphemes create words.

   a. For example, in the word "sunflowers," there are three morphemes, the root words "sun" and "flower," which describe a flowering plant that typically follows the sun's movement during the day, and the suffix -s, which indicates there is more than one sunflower.

4. **Grammar:** The rules for combining and ordering words in a language to create meaningful sentences.

   a. **Syntax:** The aspect of grammar that determines how words are ordered to form sentences in a language.

    b. **Semantics:** The aspect of grammar involving how words convey meaning individually and when combined in sentences or phrases, including both literal and implied interpretations.

## B. LANGUAGE ACQUISITION

1. Babies learn languages effortlessly and communicate through nonverbal gestures (e.g., pointing). Language development is a complex process influenced by the interaction of biology, cognition, and culture.

2. Cross-cultural studies show that babies acquire formal language through specific stages. Similar to other types of development, language acquisition varies among individuals and the ages presented are only approximate.

| Stage or Term | Description | Example |
|---|---|---|
| **Nonverbal manual gestures** | Babies use gestures to communicate with caregivers. | Facial expression for pleasure, pointing, or pushing away objects. |
| **Cooing** | Babies repeat soft vowel-like sounds often indicating contentment. They may progress by varying pitch to gain the attention of their caregivers. | "Ohhhhh" <br><br> "Ahhhhhh" |
| **Babbling** 4–6 months | Infants make repetitive meaningless sounds from various languages. | Short sound combinations, such as "ba, ba, ba," or "la, la, la." |
| **One-word stage** 10–18 months | Infants communicate by using single words often accompanied by gestures for emphasis. | Single words, such as "mama" or "dada," or significant objects, such as "doggy" or "ball." |
| **Telegraphic speech** 18–30 months | Infants use only the words essential to meaning, typically nouns and verbs, and lack other parts of speech. | "Give doll" or "Give doll me," rather than the more complete "Give the doll to me." |

**Exclusion Statement:** Pragmatics of language are outside the scope of the AP® Psychology exam.

## C. LANGUAGE ERRORS

1. During language acquisition, errors such as mispronunciations and grammatical mistakes are common.

2. **Overgeneralization:** A problem in language acquisition where learners apply grammatical rules in a language beyond the appropriate contexts, resulting in errors.

   a. For example, a child might use the past tense -ed suffix for irregular verbs by saying "I goed" instead of "I went."

   b. It reflects the learner's attempt to apply language rules consistently but can indicate a lack of complete understanding of the language's intricacies.

## D. INSIGHTS INTO LANGUAGE

1. Children acquire language through operant conditioning, imitation, modeling, and association (nurture).

   a. Children are reinforced with smiles and encouragement when they use the correct word and punished by being misunderstood or corrected when they use the wrong word.

2. Children acquire language as the result of a genetically based innate ability (nature).

   a. Children learn language much too quickly for it to be the result of only imitating others or responding to rewards and punishments. Grammar is acquired even if children are not corrected for their speech errors.

3. Language may be influenced by culture because primary language influences thought processes.

   a. The vocabulary of a language affects how colors are perceived and remembered. For example, languages with specific terms for different shades of blue can lead speakers to perceive greater distinctions between those shades compared to languages without such terms.

   b. Understanding how cultural factors impact language is an important science practice in AP® Psychology.

## VII. SOCIAL-EMOTIONAL DEVELOPMENT

### A. SOCIAL DEVELOPMENT

1. **Ecological systems theory:** A theory that examines how the social environment impacts human development.

   a. **Microsystem:** The immediate environment where individuals directly interact.

      i.  For example, a child's interactions with parents within the family setting or teachers within the school setting.

   b. **Mesosystem:** The interconnections and relationships between groups in the microsystem.

      i.  For example, how a child's home experiences influence their interactions at school and vice versa.

   c. **Exosystem:** The external environment that indirectly impacts individuals.

      i.  For example, a parent's job schedule affects family dynamics and childcare arrangements.

   d. **Macrosystem:** The broad social and cultural values that affect all other systems.

      i.  For example, the societal norms, beliefs, and practices that shape development on a larger scale.

   e. **Chronosystem:** The changes and transitions that occur over the lifespan that influence individual development.

      i.  For example, changes in family structure, societal norms, or technology can significantly influence individual development.

2. There are three main types of parenting styles of caregivers: authoritarian, authoritative, and permissive. Each style differs in terms of discipline, expectations, communication levels, and emotional warmth.

   a. Effective parenting styles vary within and across cultures.

   b. Overall, the authoritative parenting style in the United States has been found to be the most strongly correlated to positive self-esteem and high levels of self-reliance.

**Macrosystem:**
Social and cultural values

**Exosystem:**
Extended networks, media,
neighbors, parents' workplaces

**Mesosystem:**
Connections and links
between microsystems

**Microsystem:**
Family, peers, school,
health care, religion

**Individual:**
Age, gender, sex, etc.

**Chronosystem:**
Changes over time and lifespan

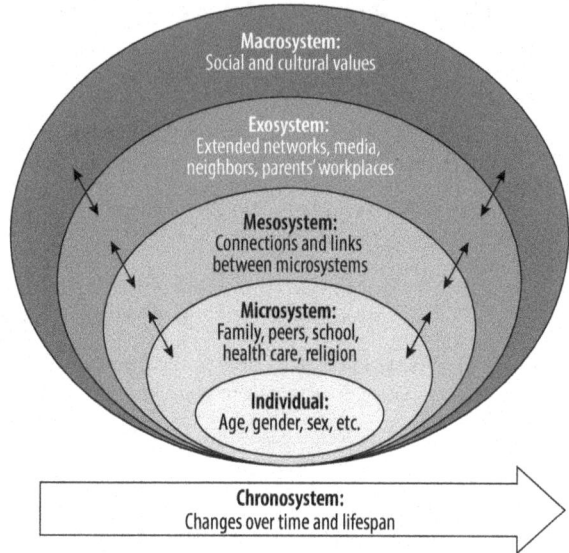

*Source: Adapted from OpenOregon,*
*"Bioecological Model of Human Development."*

**Test Tip**

To remember the layers of the ecological systems theory,
use the following mnemonic going from the outside inward.
**Ch**ange **M**akes **Ex**cellent **Me**ssy **Mi**nds.

### The Three Main Parenting Styles

| Parenting Style | Definition |
| --- | --- |
| **Authoritarian** | The parent demands obedience and controls behavior through punishment. Communication, love, and warmth are limited. |
| **Authoritative** | The parent establishes clear limits and provides explanations for consequences. Communication is open, but the parent makes the ultimate decision. This style offers the child love and warmth. |
| **Permissive** | The parent provides few expectations and allows children to make their own decisions. There are high levels of communication as well as warmth and love. |

3. **Attachment:** The long-lasting emotional bond that develops between the infant and caregiver that provides the child with a sense of security and comfort.

   a. Infants often form an attachment with their primary caregiver by the age of 6–10 months.

   b. Infant attachment is influenced by temperament (nature), parenting styles (nurture), and culture.

   c. **Separation anxiety:** The normal distress experienced by an infant when a caregiver leaves.

   d. **Strange-situation:** A test that evaluates types of attachment by examining the reactions of infants when separated and reunited with their caregivers.

The Four Attachment Styles
Caregiver-Infant Interaction

| Attachment | Caregiver Present | Caregiver Leaves | Caregiver Returns |
|---|---|---|---|
| Secure | The child explores and uses the caregiver as a secure base. | The child is distressed. | The child calms down and reestablishes contact. |
| Insecure avoidant | The child explores and seeks little contact with the caregiver. | The child shows little distress. | The child avoids or ignores the caregiver. |
| Insecure anxious | The child is unsure of whether to explore and often clings to the caregiver. | The child is distressed. | The child seems angry and resists being comforted. |
| Insecure disorganized | Less consistency across situations and involves both insecure and controlling behaviors. | Inconsistent | Inconsistent |

4. **Temperament:** An individual's biologically influenced activity level, behavioral patterns, and emotional responses.

   a. Longitudinal research has found three general types of temperament: easy, difficult, and slow-to-warm-up.

   b. Research suggests that temperament is likely to remain consistent over time, but questions remain about when temperament is stable enough to predict adult personality traits.

    c. Temperament is related to how children attach to caregivers and how caregivers may respond to the child.

## B. ATTACHMENT STUDIES

1. **Contact comfort:** The positive emotion that results when an infant has close physical touch with a caregiver, which is critical to forming healthy attachments.

    a. To test for contact comfort, baby rhesus monkeys were raised in a cage with two artificial mothers: one made of wire and holding a bottle, and the other covered in a soft cloth without a bottle.

    b. Overwhelmingly, they spent most of their day on the cloth mother. When frightened, they would run to the cloth mother to alleviate their anxiety and build their confidence. Attachment was more than a biological need and was impacted by the need for contact comfort.

    c. There were ethical concerns related to some of these non-human animal studies. Animals suffered negative long-term effects from being raised in total isolation, including aggression and withdrawal. The monkeys became disturbed and could not successfully interact with other monkeys later in life.

        i. Similar negative long-term effects have been seen when human infants are deprived of attachment and contact comfort in cases of severe abuse.

**Science Tip**

Remember, you will need to evaluate whether a psychological scenario followed appropriate ethical procedures. Practice applying ethics from Science Practice 2 to animal attachment research.

## C. PEER RELATIONSHIPS OVER TIME

1. **Pretend play:** A type of play that involves assuming different roles, such as mother, superhero, doctor, or animal.

2. Preschool children participate in social play, progressing from solitary play to parallel play.

    a. **Solitary play:** A type of play in which children are physically near others but absorbed in their own activities, such as building with blocks.

    b. **Parallel play:** A type of play in which children play near each other but don't interact directly. It is like being in the same room with a friend but doing different things.

  3. **Adolescent egocentrism:** The heightened self-consciousness of teenagers that consists of two types of social thinking.

    a. **Imaginary audience:** The belief that other people are focused on them, and they are on stage where everyone else is watching them.

    b. **Personal fable:** The belief that they are completely unique and invincible. The sense of invincibility puts them at risk of driving recklessly or using drugs, based on the idea that bad things would never happen to them, only to someone else.

## D. SOCIAL DEVELOPMENT OVER TIME

  1. Culture determines when adulthood begins and when major life events are supposed to occur.

  2. **Social clock:** The set of norms that dictate the expected ages for significant life events within a specific culture, including starting school, leaving home, getting married, having children, and retiring.

  3. **Emerging adulthood:** A developmental stage separate from both adolescence and young adulthood, typically spanning the late teens to mid-twenties.

    a. It is characterized by continued identity exploration, including matters of love, work, and worldviews.

    b. There is a gradual movement toward making lifelong decisions.

    c. Rates of residential change are high during this period because individuals see themselves as neither dependent adolescents nor independent adults.

  4. Developed from childhood experiences, attachment styles shape adult relationships and influence how we perceive and interact with others later in life.

    a. Secure attachments in childhood lead to confident, trusting adults who handle intimacy and conflict well.

    b. Conversely, insecure attachments, marked by inconsistent caregiving, can result in difficulties in understanding emotions and maintaining stable relationships.

    c. By recognizing patterns and actively working to make positive changes, individuals can build stronger connections and navigate romantic relationships more effectively.

### E. STAGE THEORIES OF SOCIAL DEVELOPMENT

1. One psychosocial stage theory created from the psychoanalytic perspective explains how personality develops through social interaction with others across the lifespan.

2. Each stage involves a psychosocial crisis or turning point that can result in either a positive or negative outcome.

| Crisis/Stage | Age | Resolution of Crisis |
|---|---|---|
| **Trust and mistrust** | Infant 0–1 years | Trust: If needs are met, infants develop basic trust. |
| **Autonomy and shame and doubt** | Toddler 1–3 years | Autonomy: If provided with opportunities to demonstrate control, toddlers develop independence. |
| **Initiative and guilt** | Preschool 3–6 years | Initiative: If exposed to a larger social world and engaged in social planning and fantasy play, preschoolers will feel capable. |
| **Industry and inferiority** | Elementary School 6–12 years | Industry: If school-age children master the knowledge and social skills required for success, they will develop competency and high self-esteem. |
| **Identity and role confusion** | Adolescence 12–20 years | Identity: If adolescents determine who they are and their individual strengths, they will develop a strong sense of self. |
| **Intimacy and isolation** | Young Adulthood 20–40 years | Intimacy: If young adults share with others without losing themselves, they will develop relationships that are open and warm. |
| **Generativity and stagnation** | Middle Adulthood 40–60 years | Generativity: If middle-aged adults take an active role in society through their family or career, they will establish feelings of usefulness and accomplishment. |
| **Integrity and despair** | Late Adulthood 60+ years | Integrity: If late adult individuals reflect back upon their lives and evaluate them favorably, they will see their lives as successful and meaningful. |

**Exclusion Statement:** The psychosexual stage theory of development is outside of the scope of the AP® Psychology exam.

3. Adolescence involves social and emotional development, including expanding one's self-concept, building an identity, pursuing autonomy, and developing relationships. Adolescents refine their self-concept, making it more accurate through self-evaluation and incorporating the opinions of others.

   a. **Identity:** A collection of many components, including career, culture, race/ethnicity, gender, sexual orientation, politics, religion, family, personality, and interests that will shape adult behavior.

   b. One theory proposes that adolescents occupy one or more of four statuses (states) at least temporarily as they develop various aspects of their identities. Each status is a combination of the adolescent's degree of commitment and whether an exploration of identity is taking place (crisis).

| Status | Definition |
|---|---|
| **Identity diffusion** | The adolescent has not committed to an identity and is not exploring possible identities. |
| **Identity foreclosure** | The adolescent has committed to an identity and is no longer exploring possible identities. Often an identity is blindly accepted. |
| **Identity moratorium** | The adolescent has not committed to an identity but is actively exploring possible identities. |
| **Identity achievement** | The adolescent has committed to an identity and continues to explore to refine it. Identity achievement is correlated with high self-esteem, achievement motivation, and emotional stability. |

F. **LIFELONG IMPACT OF CHILDHOOD EXPERIENCES**

   1. **Adverse childhood experiences (ACEs):** The negative events that happen to children before the age of 18 that can have lasting effects on their health and well-being.

      a. ACEs include different types of abuse, as well as household dysfunction, such as substance abuse, mental illness, and parental separation or divorce.

   2. In the mid-1990s, the ACE study had several thousand participants complete confidential surveys about their current health and their childhood memories.

a. Results found a positive correlation between ACEs and various physical and mental health problems that can emerge in adolescence and persist into adulthood, such as depression, substance abuse, autoimmune disease, and cardiovascular disease.

b. However, the sample was not representative of the American population and is unlikely connected to poverty-stricken or high-crime neighborhoods.

c. Follow-up studies have still linked childhood trauma and adult health problems.

3. Positive childhood experiences, such as safe and nurturing relationships, can help protect children from the negative impacts of ACEs.

**Science Tip**

Remember that Science Practice 2 asks you to determine whether the wording of the survey could lead respondents to demonstrate self-report bias or social desirability bias. Think about how this may relate to research on ACEs.

## G. ADULTHOOD AND AGING

1. The period of adulthood is dominated by concerns regarding marriage, relationships, children, family, and work.

a. Early adulthood is when the focus is on developing meaningful relationships and building careers.

b. Middle adulthood is when the focus is on establishing an active role in society through increased involvement in family and career goals to establish feelings of accomplishment or generativity.

c. Late adulthood is when the focus is on reflecting upon life experiences, which can result in feelings of fulfillment or disappointment.

# Learning

## I. LEARNING

### A. LEARNING

1. **Learning:** An enduring or relatively permanent change in an organism caused by experience or influences in the environment.

2. **Behavioral perspective:** An approach which proposes that psychology should be an objective science that studies behavior that traditionally has not referenced mental processes.

3. **Associative learning:** The acquisition of new information through pairing.

### B. ASSOCIATIVE LEARNING

1. **Classical conditioning:** A type of associative learning that involves pairing two stimuli—a neutral stimulus (NS) + an unconditioned stimulus (UCS)—to generate a learned response—a conditioned response (CR).

2. **Operant conditioning:** A type of associative learning that involves pairing a voluntary behavior with a consequence (reinforcement or punishment) that influences future behavior.

**Test Tip**

Distinguish between operant and classical conditioning by using the acronym VOICE.

V = Voluntary behavior
O = Operant conditioning
I = Involuntary behavior
C = Classical conditioning
E = *Easy!*

## II. CLASSICAL CONDITIONING

### A. FOUNDATIONAL RESEARCH

1. Ivan Pavlov began the investigation of how organisms learn by association through exploring the conditioned reflex in dogs.

2. Classical conditioning is based on involuntary responses.

### Key Elements of Classical Conditioning

| Term | Definition | Pavlov's Study | Example |
|------|-----------|----------------|---------|
| Unconditioned stimulus (UCS) | Unlearned cause | Meat powder | Chemotherapy drug |
| Unconditioned response (CR) | Unlearned effect | Salivation (to the meat powder) | Nausea (to the chemotherapy drug) |
| Neutral stimulus (NS) | No cause prior to learning | Bell (prior to acquisition) | The waiting room of the hospital (prior to acquisition) |
| Conditioned stimulus (CS) | Learned cause | Bell (after being paired with the meat powder) | The waiting room of the hospital (after being paired with the chemotherapy drug) |
| Conditioned response (CR) | Learned effect | Salivation (to the bell) | Nausea (to the waiting room) |

### B. KEY PRINCIPLES OF CLASSICAL CONDITIONING

1. **Acquisition:** The initial process of pairing two stimuli (NS + UCS) to cause a CR.

   a. For example, the bell (NS) is repeatedly paired with the meat powder (UCS) so that the bell (CS) causes the dog to salivate (CR).

2. Acquisition during classical conditioning is most effective when two stimuli are being presented close together in time.

   a. Presenting the CS before the UCS (order) increases the strength of the CR.

   b. After presenting the CS, the UCS should be presented quickly (timing) to increase the strength of the CR.

c. Repeated pairings (frequency) of the CS and UCS increase the strength of the CR.

**Exclusion Statement:** Delayed conditioning, trace conditioning, simultaneous conditioning, and backward conditioning are outside the scope of the AP® Psychology exam.

3. **Higher-order conditioning:** Turning a new NS into a new CS by pairing it with the original CS. Eventually, the new CS will produce the CR even though the new CS was never paired with the UCS.

a. For example, a light (new NS) becomes a new CS by being paired with the bell (original CS). Eventually, the light will produce salivation (CR) even though the light was never paired with the meat powder (UCS).

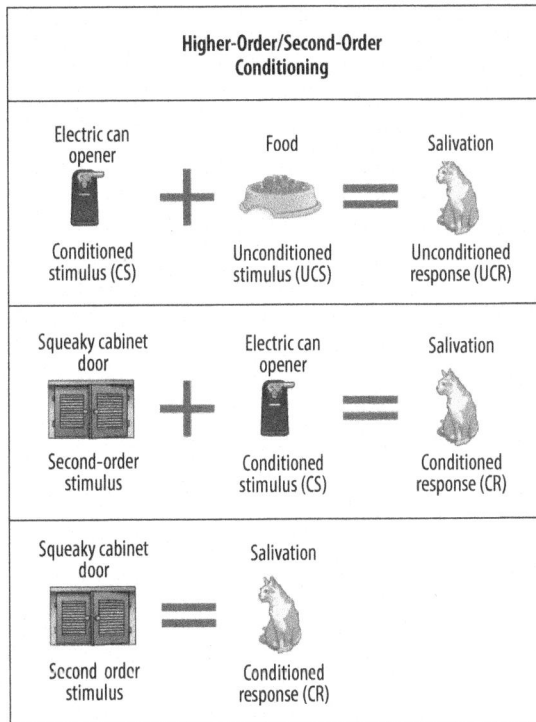

Source: Rose M. Spielman, PhD, via Wikimedia Commons

| Term | Definition | Example |
|------|-----------|---------|
| Stimulus discrimination | Learning to respond (CR) to only the CS. | A dog learns to salivate (CR) to only the bell (CS) and not a metronome or other similar stimuli. |
| Stimulus generalization | Learning to respond (CR) to stimuli that are similar to the CS. | A dog learns to salivate (CR) to a metronome or tuning fork because they sound similar to a bell (CS). |
| Extinction | The CR is weakened because the CS was presented alone. | The bell (CS) no longer causes the dog to salivate (CR) because the bell (CS) was presented several times without being paired with the meat powder (UCS). |
| Spontaneous recovery | The sudden reappearance of an extinguished CR to the CS after a delay. | The dog suddenly salivates (CR) to the presentation of a bell (CS) after the CR had been extinguished for several days. |

**Acquisition, Extinction, and Spontaneous Recovery**

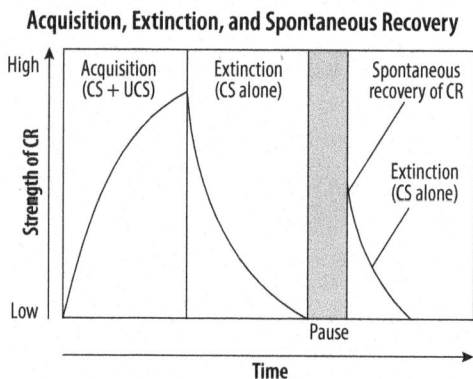

*Source: Pressbooks via BCcampus.ca*

The above figure shows the curve of acquisition, extinction, and spontaneous recovery. **Acquisition:** The CS and the US are repeatedly paired and the behavior increases (rising curve). **Extinction:** The CS is repeatedly presented alone, and the behavior gradually diminishes until it disappears (declining curve). **Spontaneous recovery:** Following a pause, the CS is again presented alone, and the previously extinguished CR reappears.

**Science Tip**

Science Practice 3 states you must identify psychological concepts in descriptions or representations of data. Be able to identify the stages of classical conditioning in a graph.

## C. CLASSICALLY CONDITIONED EMOTIONAL RESPONSES

1. John B. Watson demonstrated that complex emotions could be classically conditioned in humans by teaching Little Albert to fear a white rat.

2. Little Albert generalized his fear of the white rat to include the fear of other similar stimuli.

3. These findings form the basis of therapeutic interventions for many mental disorders, such as counterconditioning.

   a. **Counterconditioning:** A learning technique that replaces an unwanted response with a desired one by pairing the stimulus that triggers the unwanted response with a positive or neutral stimulus.

   b. For example, a dog has a fear of storms and barks when it thunders. By pairing a treat (food) when it thunders (storm), eventually, the dog will have a positive reaction to the storm and not bark when it thunders.

**Key Elements of Counterconditioning**

| Term | Definition | Watson's Study | Counterconditioning Example |
|---|---|---|---|
| Unconditioned stimulus (UCS) | Unlearned cause | Loud noise | Food |
| Unconditioned response (CR) | Unlearned effect | Fear (to loud noise) | Happiness (to food) |
| Conditioned stimulus (CS) | Learned cause | White rat | Rabbit |
| Conditioned emotional response (CER) | Learned effect | Fear (to white rat) | Happiness (to rabbit) |

**Exclusion Statement:** The expectancy theory is outside the scope of the AP® Psychology exam.

## D. CONDITIONED TASTE AVERSIONS

1. **Taste aversion:** A classically conditioned response that involves an organism learning to dislike or avoid a particular food item or liquid often after as little as one pairing with nausea.

   a. **One-trial learning:** A type of learning that occurs when the association is acquired through one pairing and is not strengthened by further pairings.

   b. Often, only one pairing is required, and the CS does not need to be presented immediately before the UCS.

   c. For example, you eat pizza (the potential CS) before becoming infected with the flu (UCS), which makes you sick (UCR). You may become nauseous (CR) when offered pizza in the future or avoid eating it altogether.

2. Taste aversions were first studied when it was noticed that rats receiving radiation treatment in their cage were avoiding their water bottles. The radiation (UCS) originally caused nausea (UCR), but then the water (CS) caused nausea (CR). The rats had learned to avoid the water because the water had been associated with the radiation.

3. **Biological preparedness:** An innate biological predisposition for animals to learn certain pairings more quickly than others.

## E. HABITUATION

1. **Habituation:** A type of learning that results when organisms get used to a stimulus and therefore have a decreased response to the repeated or enduring stimulus.

2. For example, if you live near an airport, you learn to pay less attention (decreased response) to the sound of planes.

**Test Tip**

Remember, habituation relates to behavioral changes due to repeated exposure, while sensory adaptation refers to physiological adjustments of sensory receptors to constant stimuli.

## III. OPERANT CONDITIONING

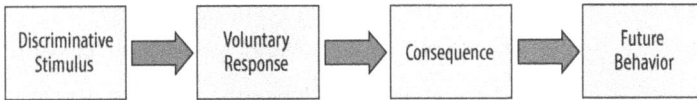

| Discriminative Stimulus | → | Voluntary Response | → | Consequence | → | Future Behavior |
|---|---|---|---|---|---|---|

### A. FOUNDATIONAL RESEARCH

1. Operant conditioning is based on voluntary responses.

2. Acquisition in operant conditioning consists of the initial process of pairing a voluntary behavior and consequence (reinforcement or punishment).

   a. For example, a pigeon pairs pecking (voluntary behavior) with getting a treat (consequence).

3. **The Law of Effect:** A voluntary behavior followed by a positive outcome is more likely to be repeated, and a voluntary behavior followed by failure is less likely to be repeated.

### B. KEY PRINCIPLES OF OPERANT CONDITIONING

1. **Reinforcement discrimination:** Learning to voluntarily respond to only the discriminative stimulus that was reinforced.

   a. For example, a pigeon pecks only when it sees a yellow light (specific discriminative stimulus) to receive food (consequence).

2. **Reinforcement generalization:** Learning to voluntarily respond to stimuli similar to the original discriminative stimulus.

   a. For example, a pigeon pecks when it sees a green light (similar stimuli to the original yellow light) to receive food (consequence).

3. **Shaping:** A behavior is taught by reinforcing successive approximations.

   a. For example, to teach a pigeon to turn in a circle, food was provided as a reinforcement as the pigeon got closer and closer to the desired behavior.

   b. For example, gradually reinforcing workouts with increasing duration and intensity to shape an exercise habit.

4. **Instinctive drift:** The tendency to abandon learned behavior for more innate behavior.

    a. For example, a raccoon taught to pick up coins may fall back to an innate behavior and start washing the coins.

    b. This provides further evidence that what organisms are capable of learning is strongly influenced by biology.

## C. APPLICATIONS

1. **Superstitious behavior:** A behavior learned when unrelated actions are reinforced by coincidental outcomes, leading individuals to mistakenly attribute cause and effect.

    a. Often seen in habits without a logical connection to desired outcomes.

2. Extinction in operant conditioning is a weakening of a voluntary response when reinforcement is not provided.

    a. For example, a pigeon no longer pecks (voluntary response) because no food is provided (consequence).

3. **Learned helplessness:** The loss of motivation and failure to attempt to escape from aversive consequences if the individual perceives an inability to exert control over a situation.

    a. This has also been applied as a cognitive theory of depression.

## D. REINFORCEMENT

1. **Reinforcement:** A process involving the addition or removal of stimuli to increase a voluntary behavior.

2. **Positive reinforcement:** An operant consequence that involves adding a desirable stimulus after a voluntary behavior to increase the likelihood of the behavior occurring in the future.

    a. For example, children make their beds and receive praise (add good), and they will continue to make their beds in the future.

3. **Negative reinforcement:** An operant consequence that involves removing an undesirable stimulus after a voluntary behavior to increase the likelihood of the behavior occurring in the future.

    a. For example, teenagers buckle their seat belts, the buzzing noise is removed (remove bad), and they continue to buckle their seat belts in the future.

    b. Aversive stimuli are unpleasant factors that often result in avoidance or escape behaviors. This type of learning can be studied in animals using a shuttle box—a device divided into two halves within which the animal is encouraged to move between compartments to gain a reward or avoid a negative stimulus.

4. **Primary reinforcer:** A consequence following a voluntary behavior that is innately (e.g., natural, unlearned) reinforcing and satisfies a biological need.

   a. For example, positive primary reinforcers include adding food, water, and sleep after a voluntary behavior.

   b. For example, negative primary reinforcers include removing pain and extreme noise after a voluntary behavior.

5. **Secondary reinforcer:** A consequence following a voluntary behavior that is reinforcing because it was learned by association.

   a. For example, positive secondary reinforcers include adding money, praise, and grades after a voluntary behavior.

   b. For example, negative secondary reinforcers include removing chores after a voluntary behavior.

## E. REINFORCEMENT SCHEDULES

1. The schedule with which reinforcement is delivered can determine the strength of the association between the consequence and the response.

2. **Continuous reinforcement schedule:** A pattern in which each and every correct behavior is reinforced.

   a. For example, a student receives points (reinforcement) for every correct homework assignment.

   b. This schedule leads to the fastest learning, but the learned response becomes extinct if reinforcements end.

3. **Partial reinforcement schedule:** A pattern in which only some correct behaviors are reinforced.

   a. For example, superstitious behavior and a child whining for a treat in a store are likely to be partially reinforced.

   b. This schedule leads to slower learning, but the learned behavior is more resistant to extinction.

   c. Ratio schedules are delivered after a number of behaviors are performed.

   d. Interval schedules are delivered after a period of time (e.g., months, minutes) has passed.

**Types of Reinforcement Schedules**

| Schedule | Definition | Example | Result | Graph |
|---|---|---|---|---|
| Fixed-ratio (FR) | Reinforcement for a predictable number of correct behaviors. | Receiving a free coffee (reinforcement) after buying 10 coffees. | Creates a rapid response rate with short pauses after the reinforcement is presented. | **Fixed-Ratio Schedule**<br><br>Cumulative number of responses → Time |
| Variable ratio (VR) | Reinforcement for an unpredictable number of correct behaviors. | Receiving a payout (reinforcement) after buying an unpredictable number of lottery tickets. | Creates a steady, rapid rate of responding. | **Variable-Ratio Schedule**<br><br>Cumulative number of responses → Time |
| Fixed-interval (FI) | Reinforcement for the first correct response after a predictable amount of time. | Receiving food (reinforcement) for entering the kitchen at a predictable time (5 pm). | Creates a moderate response rate until just prior to the delivery of the reinforcement. | **Fixed-Interval Schedule**<br><br>Cumulative number of responses → Time |

(continued)

| Schedule | Definition | Example | Result | Graph |
|----------|-----------|---------|--------|-------|
| Variable-interval (VI) | Reinforcement for the first correct response after an unpredictable amount of time. | Receiving a text message (reinforcement) for checking your phone after an unpredictable amount of time has passed. | Creates a slow, steady rate of responding that is resistant to extinction. | **Variable-Interval Schedule** |

Comparison of Reinforcement Schedule Response Patterns

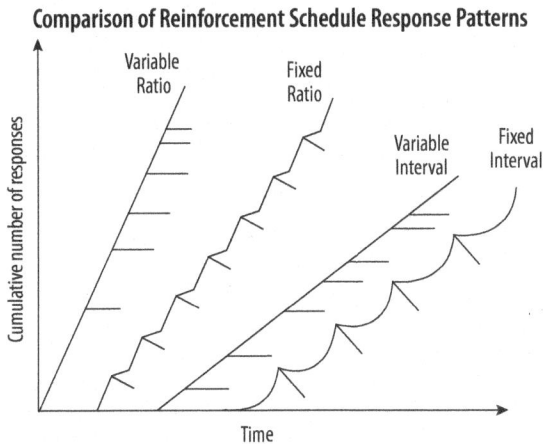

*Source: Wikimedia Commons*

**Science Tip**

Science Practice 3 states you must identify psychological concepts in descriptions or representations of data. Be able to identify each schedule of reinforcement on the graph and whether it produces a steady or scalloped response.

### F. PUNISHMENT

1. **Punishment:** A process involving the addition or removal of a stimulus to decrease a voluntary behavior.

2. **Positive punishment:** An operant consequence that involves adding an undesirable (aversive) stimulus, also known as a punisher, after a voluntary behavior to decrease the likelihood of the behavior occurring in the future.

   a. For example, a teenager arrives at work late and gets yelled at (add bad), and is less likely to arrive late again (decrease behavior).

3. **Negative punishment:** An operant consequence that involves the process of removing a desirable stimulus after a voluntary behavior to decrease the likelihood of the behavior occurring in the future.

   a. For example, a teenager uses a cellphone, and the teacher takes it away (remove good), which will make the teenager less likely to use the phone again in the future (decrease behavior).

4. Punishment can be quick and effective but must be used with caution because of its many potential drawbacks.

   a. It fails to teach an alternative response to the frustrating stimulus.

   b. It may create anger, fear, or hostility toward the punisher.

   c. It may lead to learned helplessness, lying, or avoidance behaviors.

### G. COMPARISON OF REINFORCEMENT AND PUNISHMENT

|  | Desirable Stimulus | Undesirable Stimulus |
|---|---|---|
| **Positive** (Add) | **Positive reinforcement**<br><br>After a voluntary response, a desirable stimulus is added to increase the likelihood of the behavior occurring again. | **Positive punishment**<br><br>After a voluntary response, an undesirable (aversive) stimulus is added to decrease the likelihood of the behavior occurring again. |
| **Negative** (Remove) | **Negative punishment**<br><br>After a voluntary response, a desirable stimulus is removed to decrease the likelihood of the behavior occurring again. | **Negative reinforcement**<br><br>After a voluntary response, an undesirable (aversive) stimulus is removed to increase the likelihood of the behavior occurring again. |

Keep in mind that in regard to conditioning, the terms "positive" and "negative" are not related to emotions but indicate the addition or subtraction of stimuli that will ultimately increase or decrease the chance that an organism will repeat a particular behavior.

## IV. COMPARISON OF CLASSICAL AND OPERANT CONDITIONING

### A. SIMILARITIES

1. They are both types of association learning.

2. They both involve acquisition, generalization, and discrimination.

### B. DIFFERENCES

1. Classical conditioning involves involuntary responses that occur from the pairing of stimuli.

2. Operant conditioning involves voluntary behaviors that are guided by consequences.

## V. SOCIAL, COGNITIVE, AND NEUROBIOLOGICAL LEARNING

### A. SOCIAL LEARNING

1. **Social learning theory (observational learning):** The theory that learning is the result of observation and imitation.

   a. For example, little children often surprise their parents by displaying behavior (e.g., applying makeup, using swear words) that they gain from watching and imitating parents, older siblings, or others.

   b. There are four processes involved in observational learning: attention, retention (memory), reproduction, and motivation.

2. **Vicarious conditioning:** A type of learning that occurs as a result of watching others or hearing of others receiving consequences (reinforcements or punishments) without direct experience.

   a. For example, a student sees a friend praised for turning in assignments on time, prompting the student to do the same for recognition.

**143**

b. For example, observing a classmate being corrected by the teacher for disruption leads a student to avoid similar behavior to prevent the consequences.

3. **Model:** A person demonstrating a behavior that will be repeated as a result of social learning.

   a. The more similar a model is to the observer, the more likely the behavior is to be learned.

   b. Albert Bandura conducted the Bobo doll study to investigate the social learning of aggression by observing children's behavior after watching an adult act aggressively toward a Bobo doll.

## B. COGNITIVE FACTORS IN LEARNING

1. **Cognitive learning:** A type of learning that occurs as a result of thoughts, perceptions, and expectations.

2. **Insight learning:** A type of learning that involves arriving at a sudden solution to a problem without association, consequence, or model.

   a. For example, leaving the classroom and suddenly a test answer comes to mind.

3. **Latent learning:** A type of learning that is hidden and not demonstrated until there are reinforcements.

   a. Edward Tolman believed the rapid increase in learning displayed in the third group in the table below indicated that the animals could create a mental picture of the maze.

4. **Cognitive map:** A mental representation or picture of a physical space.

### Tolman's Latent Learning and Cognitive Maps Study

| Group | Condition | Results |
|-------|-----------|---------|
| Group 1 | Rats were not given reinforcement at the end of the maze. | Lowest rate of learning because the rats made the most errors. |
| Group 2 | Rats were given reinforcement (food) every time they reached the end of the maze. | Decrease in the number of errors demonstrating learning. |
| Group 3 | Rats were not given reinforcement at the end of the maze for the first 10 days but were then reinforced for the final 7 days of the trials. | Similar number of errors as group 1 during the first 10 days of the trial, but made significantly fewer errors on day 11 demonstrating latent learning. |

**Tolman's Study Results**

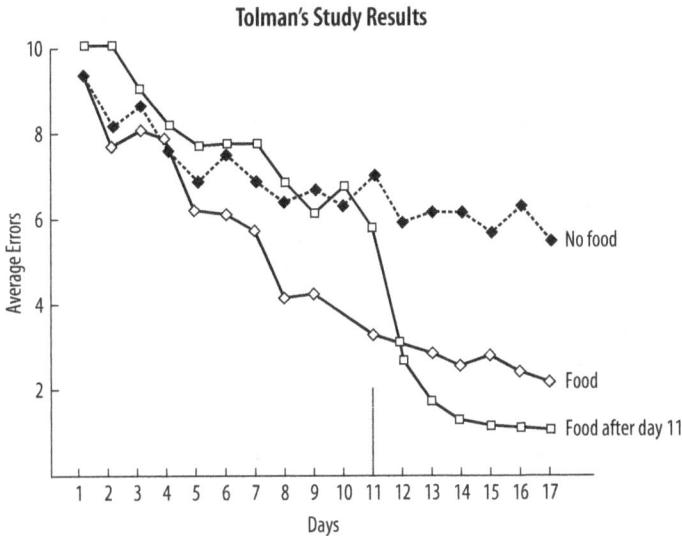

Science Practice 3 states you must identify psychological concepts in descriptions or representations of data. Be able to identify where latent learning becomes apparent on a graph.

## VI. BIOLOGICAL INFLUENCES OF LEARNING

### A. EVOLUTIONARY

1. The evolutionary approach suggests that each species has evolved biological predispositions enabling them to learn behaviors that elevate the likelihood of their survival.

2. For example, humans easily learn certain phobias (e.g., heights, spiders) because they would have posed danger in the past to our ancestors, but do not learn phobias to nonthreatening objects or events (e.g., flowers, daylight, music).

### B. PREPAREDNESS VERSUS CONSTRAINT

1. **Biological preparedness:** A biological predisposition for organisms to more readily learn certain behaviors by pairing particular stimuli over others.

    a.  Rats easily learn to associate taste stimuli and nauseous responses.

    b.  Pigeons easily learn to flap their wings to avoid shock.

2.  **Biological constraint:** A biological limitation regarding what organisms are capable of learning. '

    a.  Rats do not learn to associate taste stimuli and pain responses.

    b.  Pigeons do not learn to peck in order to avoid shock.

## C. NEUROBIOLOGICAL LEARNING

1.  **Long-term potentiation (LTP):** A biological theory that explains that the repeated stimulation of neural networks strengthens the synaptic connections between neurons and results in learning and memory creation.

    a.  Learning as the result of synaptic changes was studied with rats in enriched environments.

    b.  Rats with early enriched experiences had increased brain weight, had more synapses, and demonstrated improved performance on learning and memory tests.

2.  **Brain plasticity:** The ability of the brain to modify itself in response to injury or as a result of learning.

# Social Psychology

## I. ATTRIBUTION THEORY

### A. TYPES OF ATTRIBUTIONS

1. **Attribution:** The explanation for your own or others' behavior. It is influenced and potentially biased by culture, personality, prior experience, and perceptual errors.

2. **Dispositional attribution:** The explanation of behavior in terms of consistent factors inside the person (e.g., personality, intelligence).

   a. For example, I did well on the test because I am smart.

3. **Situational attribution:** The explanation of behavior in terms of factors outside the person (e.g., luck, outside circumstances).

   a. For example, my friend did well on the test because of luck.

### B. EXPLANATORY STYLES

1. **Explanatory style:** An individual's distinctive manner of describing and understanding a phenomenon, event, or personal history.

2. **Optimistic explanatory style:** The tendency for individuals to describe...

   a. negative events in terms that are external, specific, and unstable (temporary).

   b. positive events in terms that are internal, global (everything), and stable (permanent).

3. **Pessimistic explanatory style:** The tendency for individuals to describe...

   a. negative events in terms that are internal, global (everything), and stable (permanent).

   b. positive events in terms of external, specific, and unstable (temporary).

### C. ATTRIBUTIONAL BIASES

| Bias | Definition | Tip | Example |
|------|-----------|-----|---------|
| **Actor/ observer bias** | Tendency to explain the behavior of others with dispositional factors, but one's own behavior with situational factors. | Involves two individuals in comparison; "you" the person who is making the attribution and "them" to whom you assigned an attribution. | When my classmate stumbles during a speech, it is due to carelessness (disposition), but when I stumble it is because I have a headache (situation). |
| **Fundamental attribution error (FAE)** *More common in individualistic cultures.* | Tendency to explain others' behavior with dispositional factors and overlook the situation. | FAE occurs only when explaining someone else's behavior—it is about "them." | I think a student (other) who cut me off is rude (disposition), and I overlook that the student may have been in a hurry (situation). |
| **Self-serving bias** *More common in individualistic cultures.* | Tendency to see oneself in a positive way by explaining one's successes to dispositional factors and one's failures to situational factors. | Involves only your behavior "you" and choosing attributions that make "you" look good. | A soccer player attributes winning to their own athleticism (dispositional), but blames a loss on the referee (situation). |

## II. LOCUS OF CONTROL

### A. TYPES

1. **Locus of control:** The amount of confidence people have regarding the level of influence (control) they believe they have over events in their lives.

2. **External locus of control:** The idea that motivation is determined by a belief that one's life is the product of circumstances outside of one's control (e.g., fate/destiny, luck, circumstances, or the actions of others).

3. **Internal locus of control:** The idea that motivation is determined by a belief that people are capable of influencing what happens to them through their hard work or effort.

a. Correlational studies show that individuals with an internal locus of control are more successful, are less likely to become depressed, are more likable, and have higher levels of self-esteem.

**Test Tip** Be prepared to distinguish the types of locus of control (internal, external) versus motivation (intrinsic, extrinsic).

B. APPLICATIONS

1. An external locus of control has been associated with learned helplessness.

a. **Learned helplessness:** A phenomenon where individuals, after facing repeated exposure to uncontrollable situations, stop trying to change or influence their circumstances due to diminished motivation.

2. An external locus of control often leads to anxiety and frustration because individuals feel they have no control. They view events as threats (distress) as opposed to challenges (eustress).

## III. PERSON PERCEPTION

A. PERSON PERCEPTION

1. **Person perception:** How people understand themselves and others.

2. People's perception of how much they like something can be influenced by the mere exposure effect.

a. **Mere exposure effect:** The tendency to like something more after having been repeatedly exposed to It.

b. For example, hearing a song multiple times increases liking for the song.

3. **Self-fulfilling prophecy:** The tendency for our beliefs about ourselves or another person to lead us to act in a way that

brings about the behaviors we expect and confirms our original impression.

   a. For example, a student expects that he will do poorly on his paper, so he does not try and earns a low grade, confirming his belief.

   b. For example, a teacher expects a student to do well on a paper and gives the student extra attention. The student earns a high grade, thereby confirming this belief.

4. **Social comparison theory:** Person perception that involves evaluating your own abilities and attitudes in relation to other members of a society or social circles.

   a. **Upward comparison:** Comparing yourself to those better than you in a particular skill. These comparisons can damage your self-esteem or inspire positive change.

   b. **Downward comparison:** Comparing yourself to those worse than you in a particular skill. These comparisons often help enhance your self-esteem.

5. **Relative deprivation:** The perception that occurs when you compare yourself with your reference group and find that regardless of how much wealth, status, and appreciation you are receiving, it is less than what others similar to you have.

   a. For example, a recent college graduate making $60,000 may feel he is not getting what he deserves if others in his reference group are making over $100,000.

## IV. ATTITUDE FORMATION AND ATTITUDE CHANGE

### A. PREJUDICIAL ATTITUDE COMPONENTS

| Prejudicial Attitude | Attitude Components | Explanation |
|---|---|---|
| Discrimination | Behavioral | Actions that involve treating individuals differently due to their membership in a particular group. |
| Emotion | Affective | The emotional aspect of an attitude (e.g., prejudice: hostility, envy, fear). |
| Stereotype | Cognitive | A schema or generalized concept for an entire group that assumes that all or most of the members share the same negative traits. |

1. Stereotypes can simplify thinking (reduce cognitive load), which leads to faster decisions.

2. They can also be the cause or result of biased perceptions and experiences.

3. They often lead to prejudicial attitudes with negative emotions and discriminatory actions.

B. **IMPLICIT ATTITUDES AND NEGATIVE EVALUATIONS OF OTHERS**

1. **Implicit attitude:** A hidden and automatic evaluation that can lead to discrimination.

   a. For example, when evaluators unknowingly give higher ratings to the same résumé when it has a male- rather than female-sounding name.

2. **Just-world phenomenon:** The tendency to view the world as fair and believe that individuals get what they deserve.

   a. The belief in a just world may lead individuals to blame the victim.

3. **Outgroup:** Any group of individuals you do not belong to and thus view as different from yourself.

   a. **Out-group homogeneity bias:** An assumption that outgroup members are similar, while ingroup members have differences. This often leads to stereotyping and discrimination.

   b. For example, individuals may think all rival fans are disrespectful, but only some of their own fans show poor sportsmanship.

4. **Ingroup:** Any group of individuals that you belong to and view as similar to yourself and different from others.

   a. **In-group bias:** The preference for "us" or people in our group.

   b. It can be used to elevate your self-esteem by associating yourself with successful groups and putting down members of outgroups.

5. **Ethnocentrism:** The tendency to favor one's own cultural, racial, or ethnic group and hold negative stereotypes about other cultures.

   a. This prejudice is directed toward cultural, racial, or ethnic membership.

   b. For example, believing your country's education system is superior to other countries, leading to biases against students or professionals educated elsewhere.

## C. FACTORS THAT INFLUENCE ATTITUDE FORMATION AND CHANGE

1. **Belief perseverance:** A cognitive bias that involves holding onto an assumption after it has been disproven.

   a. Belief perseverance and confirmation bias are both related to attitude formation and change. Belief perseverance is often reinforced by confirmation bias—selectively seeking out information that supports one's own beliefs while disregarding opposing viewpoints.

   b. For example, even after losing a lot of money in risky investments, investors may continue to believe they can beat the market (belief perseverance), which is reinforced by their selective focus on past successes while ignoring failures (confirmation bias).

2. **Cognitive dissonance:** The unpleasant state (tension) experienced when holding two conflicting beliefs or when actions do not match beliefs.

   a. The tension must be internal and not between you and another person.

   b. For example, An individual thinks smoking can kill (belief) but continues to smoke (behavior), and this inconsistency causes discomfort.

   c. This tension motivates us to reduce cognitive dissonance by either changing our behavior or altering our beliefs.

   d. For example, because it is easier to alter beliefs, individuals are likely to rationalize that they will not get cancer because they only smoke a little and can quit anytime.

## V. PSYCHOLOGY OF SOCIAL SITUATIONS

### A. SOCIAL SITUATION

1. **Social norms:** The learned general guidelines for expected behaviors related to a specific social context.

   a. For example, the norm when driving is to stop at a red light.

2. **Social roles:** The expected patterns of behavior required by specific situations or social positions.

   a. Certain behaviors are associated with particular social roles, such as mother, employer, student, and teacher.

b. Philip Zimbardo conducted the famous Stanford Prison Study, which investigated the power of social roles and the impact of the situation on behavior. The power of the situation led both the guards and the prisoners to alter their thoughts and behaviors to align with the social roles they were assigned.

c. The study was terminated after six days due to the negative consequences of participants assuming their social roles.

3. **Social influence theory:** A theory that examines how thoughts, feelings, and behaviors are shaped by others, offering insights into conformity, obedience, persuasion, group dynamics, and social norms in various social settings.

a. **Normative social influence:** The process of conforming because you want to be accepted or liked.

   i. This leads to public acceptance but not necessarily an internal change.

   ii. For example, students say they like a band their friends like (conformity) even if they do not like the band, because they want to fit in.

b. **Informational social influence:** The process of conforming because you want to be correct.

   i. This often leads to private acceptance, in which one believes the attitude or behavior change is correct. When unsure, people often look to others as information sources.

   ii. For example, a student unsure of which concert door to enter joins a line (conformity) based on the assumption that others have chosen the correct line.

## B. PERSUASION

1. **Persuasion:** The various methods designed to change the behavior or beliefs of yourself or others.

a. The effectiveness of a persuasive message is influenced by the source (who says it), the nature of the communication (how it is said), and the audience. All of these persuasion factors can be applied to print and broadcast media, as well as social media and face-to-face interactions.

2. **Elaboration-likelihood model:** A theory of persuasion that offers two general methods that individuals use to process the claims being presented to them in a persuasive message.

a. **Central route to persuasion:** A method of persuasion that focuses on the facts and uses evidence and logic.

    i. For example, an advertisement for a car that includes data, such as safety rating or miles per gallon.

    ii. It involves high levels of elaboration, creating stronger attitudes more resistant to change.

b. **Peripheral route to persuasion:** A method of persuasion that focuses on emotional appeals and attention-grabbing components.

    i. For example, an advertisement for a car that includes an emotional appeal, such as a celebrity endorsement.

    ii. It involves low elaboration and minimal information processing, leading to attitudes that are less predictive of behavior and more likely to change.

c. The halo effect connects to a peripheral route to persuasion.

    i. **Halo effect:** The tendency to assume that people with a positive general impression or one positive trait (e.g., attractiveness) also have other positive traits (e.g., intelligence, happiness, friendliness).

    ii. For example, when viewing a model in a commercial, you may assume that people who are physically attractive (one positive trait) are also intelligent (another positive trait), and you buy the product they are endorsing.

3. Persuasion can depend on how information is presented.

a. **Foot-in-the-door technique:** A two-step procedure that makes you more likely to comply with a larger request after having initially complied with a smaller request.

    i. For example, a teacher is more likely to answer several questions (large request) after complying by answering one question (small request).

b. **Door-in-the-face technique:** A two-step procedure that makes you more likely to comply with a smaller request after having initially refused a larger request.

    i. For example, a teacher is more likely to extend the due date for a class assignment by one day (small request) after denying a request for a one-week extension (large request).

## C. CONFORMITY

1. **Conformity:** The process of changing one's behavior or beliefs to match the unspoken rules, norms, or expectations of the group.

   a. Solomon Asch conducted the famous Line Study, which investigated whether participants would conform to the incorrect judgment of line length given by a group of confederates.

   b. Approximately 70% of the participants conformed to the group's wrong answer at least once.

2. Research has identified specific conditions that increase conformity including group size, unanimity, attraction to the group, having no strong pre-existing opinion, and being presented with a situation in which the answer is unclear or ambiguous.

3. The two main factors that cause individuals to conform are normative and informational social influence.

## D. OBEDIENCE

1. **Obedience:** The process of changing one's behavior in response to a demand from an authority figure.

   a. Stanley Milgram conducted the famous Shock Study, which investigated whether participants would obey an authority figure.

   b. Approximately 65% of the participants obeyed and administered what they believed was the maximum shock level to the learner. It demonstrated that people will obey orders from an authority figure even to the point of committing cruel and harmful actions.

2. Research has identified specific conditions that increase obedience, including the prestige of the institution, the proximity of the authority figure, the presence of others who disobeyed, and the depersonalization of the victim.

## VI. GROUP DYNAMICS

### A. CULTURAL PHENOMENA

1. **Individualism:** A group of values that emphasize the self and personal goals, as well as values of independence and self-reliance.

   a. Found in individualistic cultures, such as the United States, Western Europe, and Australia.

**155**

2. **Collectivism:** A belief system that emphasizes group membership and harmony above individual achievement.

   a. Found in collectivistic cultures, such as many in Asia, Africa, and South America.

3. **Multiculturalism:** A belief system that emphasizes advocacy and celebration of cultural variety within a community.

## B. GROUP PROCESSES

1. **Group polarization:** A group of like-minded individuals interacts, resulting in an amplification of their existing attitudes and tendency to make more extreme decisions.

   a. For example, a group of like-minded parents discusses the need for curfews, and their overall opinion becomes even stronger.

2. **Groupthink:** The practice of making decisions collectively in a way that promotes harmony while discouraging participants from sharing different viewpoints or evaluating possible alternatives.

   a. For example, the student council is working on a prom theme. Although many members disagree with the leader's idea, nobody says anything in order to maintain group harmony, which keeps the problem from being evaluated completely.

   b. The likelihood of groupthink increases when contradictory evidence is ignored, disagreement is discouraged, and group members feel pressured to make a quick decision.

**Test Tip**

Be prepared to look at ways to minimize both group polarization and groupthink. To reduce group polarization, encourage open-minded discussion and diverse perspectives. To reduce the likelihood of groupthink, promote sharing of dissenting views and allow time for thoughtful decision-making.

3. **Social loafing:** The tendency to exert less individual effort in a group than when doing the same task alone due to less accountability.

   a. For example, individuals contribute less in a group project than when working alone because any individual's lack of effort is less likely to be noticed in the group.

4. **Deindividuation:** A state of lessened personal responsibility and self-restraint due to feelings of anonymity created by being part of a crowd or in situations in which individuals feel anonymous (e.g., interacting online, wearing a mask, or taking other action that obscures their identity).

   a. For example, an individual feels less responsible and more anonymous online and is thus more willing to post a harsh comment or review.

5. **Diffusion of responsibility:** The belief in which individuals feel no need to take action in a group because they assume someone else will.

   a. It can contribute to various group phenomena including the bystander effect, deindividuation, social loafing, and social dilemmas.

6. **Social facilitation:** The tendency to perform an easy or well-rehearsed task better in the presence of an audience.

   a. For example, in front of an audience, an experienced actor delivers an award-winning performance.

7. **False consensus effect:** The tendency to overestimate how many others share one's belief and/or behavior.

   a. For example, a student does well on his test and thus assumes everyone else was successful.

**Science Tip**

Science Practice 3 states that you must identify psychological concepts in descriptions or representations of data. Be able to identify the group processes in images, graphs, and figures.

## C. COMPETITION

1. **Superordinate goals:** An objective that can be achieved only when members of groups collaborate, combining their skills, efforts, and resources.

a. Sherif's Robber's Cave Study involved a group of boys attending a summer camp who were divided into two opposing teams. The researchers created in-group bias and prejudice and then utilized contact theory and superordinate goals to create harmony between the two groups.

2. **Social traps:** Situations in which individuals face a conflict requiring them to choose whether to cooperate or compete with others. In social traps, choosing to compete will provide one individual with an advantage, but if all parties compete it will result in harmful consequences for everyone.

a. For example, an arms race is a social trap. Countries compete to build their military capabilities out of self-interest. This leads to increased tensions, economic strain, and a security dilemma in which all the countries feel less secure despite their efforts to secure their own safety.

3. Some social traps involve shared resources.

a. **Commons dilemma:** A social trap or resource dilemma in which individuals need to determine how much to take from a shared supply.

   i. For example, your class agrees to share a bowl of candy. Taking only one piece of candy is in everyone's best interest, but if everyone wants to take more and does so the candy will run out before the supply is scheduled to be replenished.

b. **Public goods dilemma:** A social trap or resource dilemma in which individuals must decide how much to contribute to a shared resource.

   i. For example, money is needed to fund government services. It is in the best interest of each citizen not to pay taxes, but if everyone chose to behave this way, government services would shut down.

## D. INDUSTRIAL-ORGANIZATIONAL PSYCHOLOGY

1. **Industrial-organizational (I/O) psychology:** A subfield concerned with the work environment that investigates how research can be applied to employee motivation or workplace improvement.

a. Research may involve examining ways to decrease burnout.

   i. **Burnout:** The result of work-related stress that involves physical and psychological exhaustion.

      ii. It is more likely to occur in professions that involve caring for others (e.g., health care professionals, air traffic controllers, and police officers and other first responders). It is not inevitable, however, and like other stressors can be mediated.

2. There are several branches within industrial-organizational psychology.

    a. **Human factors psychology:** A branch of I/O psychology concerned with creating, designing, and producing machines and systems that are functional and easy to use by people.

      i. Effective product design requires understanding sensation, perception, psychomotor behavior, and cognitive processes.

      ii. For example, designing an instrument panel for an airplane that is easy to read and enables pilots to immediately notice potential problems.

    b. **Personnel psychology:** A branch of I/O psychology that assists companies with the process of hiring and evaluating worker performance based on data from empirical research.

      i. Administers tests and provides employee training.

    c. **Organizational psychology:** A branch of I/O psychology that supports companies by creating more productive work climates to increase employee morale and productivity.

      i. Examines effective management methods and how to foster leadership and motivation among the employees.

      ii. Identifies two leadership styles.

| Leadership Style | Definition |
|---|---|
| Relationship-motivated leadership | Leadership style that emphasizes developing and maintaining strong supportive bonds among coworkers, minimizing conflict, and offering encouragement. Communication and feedback are designed to develop positive, team-centered environments. |
| Task-motivated leadership | Leadership style that emphasizes specific goals (tasks) that groups or teams are required to complete. Communication and feedback are specifically related to goal attainment. |

## VII. PROSOCIAL BEHAVIOR

### A. PROSOCIAL BEHAVIOR

1. **Prosocial behavior:** Any behavior that benefits another person.

   a. Conditions that increase helping behavior include when the individual is similar, attractive, or female, or appears to deserve help.

   b. People are also more likely to help after observing others who help, when not in a hurry, when in a small town, or when feeling guilty, not distracted, or in a good mood.

2. **Altruism:** The act of helping another with unselfish regard and at a potential personal cost to oneself.

   a. **Social reciprocity norm:** The expectation that individuals will receive help in return for helping others OR will help those who have helped them in return.

   b. **Social responsibility norm:** The expectation that individuals help those in need, such as individuals who are dependent and deserving.

      i. For example, helping children, the elderly, or those physically unable to complete a task.

**Science Tip**

Cultural factors influence altruism. Keep in mind that Science Practice 1 requires that you explain how cultural norms, expectations, and circumstances, as well as cognitive biases, apply to behavior and mental processes.

3. In order to offer assistance, individuals would need to notice the event, interpret it as an emergency, and assume responsibility.

   a. Situational and attentional variables predict whether someone is likely to help another person.

4. **Bystander effect:** The tendency for individuals to be less likely to assist in an emergency situation when other people are present.

   a. Diffusion of responsibility, when connected to bystander effect, occurs when people in a crowd fail to take action assuming someone else has taken, or will take, appropriate action.

# Personality

## I. PERSONALITY THEORY

### A. INTRODUCTION TO PERSONALITY

1. **Personality:** The pattern of behaviors, thoughts, and characteristics an individual possesses and displays consistently that differentiates one person from another.

2. Each personality theory approaches personality development with somewhat different assumptions, strategies, and objectives.

### B. PSYCHODYNAMIC THEORY OF PERSONALITY

1. Sigmund Freud explained that personality is the result of unresolved unconscious conflicts from childhood or unconscious sexual and aggressive instincts.

2. Freud described the mind as structured in three levels, and it is often described symbolically as an iceberg.

   a. **Unconscious:** In psychodynamic theory, the part of the mind that contains hidden thoughts, wishes, memories, and feelings.

      i. Freud believed it included unacceptable sexual or aggressive thoughts and wishes and unresolved conflicts from childhood which could result in personality difficulties.

   b. **Preconscious:** In psychodynamic theory, the part of the mind that contains information an individual is aware of but not thinking about currently.

      i. For example, individuals may not be thinking of what they had for dinner the night before, but if asked they could easily pull that information from their preconscious.

   c. **Conscious:** In psychodynamic theory, the part of the mind that is currently active and responsive to events and stimuli in the environment.

**Exclusion Statement:** The stage theory of psychosexual development is outside the scope of the AP® Psychology exam.

3. According to Freud, personality is divided into three components.

   a. **Id**: The completely unconscious aspect of personality that consists of innate sexual and aggressive drives. It operates on the pleasure principle, seeking immediate gratification and the avoidance of discomfort.

   b. **Ego**: The problem-solving and rational aspect of personality that operates on the reality principle, seeking to balance the conflicting demands of the id and superego.

   c. **Superego**: The aspect of the personality that reminds individuals of ideal behavior and operates on the morality principle, seeking to enforce ethical conduct.

4. **Ego defense mechanisms:** The unconscious methods to protect the ego from threats and reduce anxiety.

| Ego Defense Mechanism | Definition | Example |
| --- | --- | --- |
| Denial | Unconsciously reducing anxiety by refusing to accept reality even when presented with large amounts of evidence. | Refusing to admit a substance abuse problem. |
| Displacement | Unconsciously reducing anxiety by taking out aggression on someone or something that is less powerful or threatening than the true source of anxiety. | Athletes taking out their aggression on teammates (less powerful) rather than the referee (the true source of anxiety). |
| Projection | Unconsciously reducing anxiety by attributing one's own fears, feelings, faults, or unacceptable thoughts and behaviors to another person or group. | Accusing a friend of wanting to cheat on a test, when you are wanting to cheat. |
| Rationalization | Unconsciously reducing anxiety by creating logical excuses for unacceptable thoughts and behaviors. | Creating the excuse of not really wanting to go to a certain college after having been denied admission to it. |

(continued)

| Ego Defense Mechanism | Definition | Example |
|---|---|---|
| **Reaction formation** | Unconsciously reducing anxiety by acting or saying the exact opposite of the morally or socially unacceptable beliefs held by an individual. | Being overly nice to a supervisor you really dislike. |
| **Regression** | Unconsciously reducing anxiety by reverting to thoughts and behaviors that would be more appropriate during an earlier period of development. Individuals may behave in a childlike manner. | Reverting to an earlier developmental stage and sucking one's thumb upon receiving a negative evaluation. |
| **Repression** | Unconsciously reducing anxiety by blocking a painful event from awareness and preventing retrieval. | Blocking a tragic accident from awareness. |
| **Sublimation** | Unconsciously reducing anxiety by directing aggression toward a more socially acceptable outlet, such as exercise, hard work, sports, or hobbies.<br><br>Note: Sublimation is a healthy version of displacement. | Dealing with relationship conflict by going for a run. |

**Test Tip**

Remember to distinguish between similar defense mechanisms. Displacement involves taking out anxiety on someone innocent, while projection is accusing someone else of how you really feel.

  a. Defense mechanisms may be healthy if used in moderation.

  b. Excessive use can result in stress due to the large amount of cognitive energy being wasted on maintaining them.

5. This psychoanalytic perspective has been criticized for various reasons.

  a. The theory is unscientific because it cannot be tested empirically and is not falsifiable.

b. It is based on an unrepresentative sample, involving case studies from one cultural group, which cannot be generalized to the larger population.

c. It is gender biased.

## C. HUMANISTIC THEORY OF PERSONALITY

1. Emphasizes the human capacity for goodness, creativity, and freedom in the development of personality.

2. This perspective identifies two primary motivating factors in personality.

   a. **Self-actualizing tendency:** The drive to fulfill one's full potential.

   b. **Unconditional positive regard:** The acceptance and appreciation of an individual (faults and all). This unwavering acceptance allows individuals to develop a sense of innate goodness and reach their full potential.

3. This perspective has been criticized for various reasons.

   a. It is difficult to test scientifically because ideas, such as self-actualizing tendency, are hard to measure and operationally define.

   b. The idea that individuals are innately good and striving for perfection may be too optimistic because the aggressive and selfish aspects of human nature are not being recognized.

   c. Despite the criticisms, the perspective focuses more on healthy individuals, which in part leads to positive psychology.

---

**Exclusion Statement:** Maslow's hierarchy of needs is outside the scope of the AP® Psychology exam.

---

## D. SOCIAL-COGNITIVE THEORY OF PERSONALITY

1. **Social-cognitive personality theory:** The theory of personality that combines behavioral and cognitive approaches.

   a. Behavioral theories assume that personality is learned through experience and often is the result of reinforcements and punishments.

b. Cognitive theories assume that people construct their personality based on beliefs, thoughts, and how they perceive the world around them.

2. **Reciprocal determinism:** The theory that the individual's personal/cognitive, behavioral, and environmental variables all interact with one another to influence personality.

   a. For example, if you are interested in tennis (personal trait), you will consistently choose to play or watch tennis (behavior) and you will be rewarded by being around people who share your enthusiasm for tennis (environment), further strengthening your interest in it.

3. **Self-concept:** The description and evaluation of who one is as an individual (e.g., traits, values, accomplishments, abilities).

   a. Self-concept is influenced by culture. Everyone's self-concept has elements from both independent and interdependent selves.

   b. An independent sense of self involves defining oneself as separate and unique and focuses less on group membership. It is more common in individualistic cultures.

   c. An interdependent sense of self involves defining oneself as part of a social group and focuses less on individual uniqueness. It is more common in collectivist cultures.

4. **Self-esteem:** The evaluation of the components of an individual's self-concept.

5. **Self-efficacy:** The level of confidence individuals have regarding their ability to perform a specific task or skill.

   a. The theory that the individual's personal/cognitive, behavioral, and environmental variables all interact with one another to influence personality.

   b. For example, people with high personal self-efficacy in baking are confident in their ability to make a cake and will be more likely to persist at that task and be successful.

   c. This perspective has been criticized for overemphasizing the situation's importance without considering an individual's personality traits.

**Test Tip**

Be prepared to distinguish between words using the prefix self-. *Self-concept* is our overall description and evaluation of ourselves including our traits and skills. *Self-esteem* reflects our self-worth. *Self-efficacy* involves the level of confidence (high or low) we have in our ability to achieve a specific task.

## E. TRAIT THEORY OF PERSONALITY

1. **Trait:** An enduring and stable characteristic that influences a person to act in a consistent way.

   a. Through factor analysis, five main traits have been identified.

   b. **Factor analysis:** A statistical procedure that identifies clusters of variables that are highly correlated with one another.

2. **Big Five theory of personality:** A theory that describes an individual's personality traits on a continuum across five dimensions: agreeableness, conscientiousness, extraversion, neuroticism, and openness.

| Big Five Personality Traits | High | Low |
|---|---|---|
| **Agreeableness** | Cooperative, kind, likable, trusting, good-natured | Unkind, cold, grumpy, untrusting |
| **Conscientiousness** | Hardworking, organized, dependable, self-controlled, responsible, prepared | Negligent, disorganized, careless |
| **Extraversion** | Outgoing, sociable, active, assertive, draw energy from others | Reserved, quiet, drawn to private thoughts and feelings, prefers to work independently |
| **Neuroticism** (Emotional stability) | Anxious, tense, hostile, excitable | Calm, emotionally stable, low anxiety |
| **Openness to experience** | Creative, curious, imaginative, wide range of interests, inquiring, willing to explore | Conventional, traditional, low curiosity, practical, prefers routine |

3. This perspective has been criticized for various reasons.

   a. Characterizing individuals solely in terms of their personality traits fails to account for how people behave differently depending on the situation. Consequently, the predictive power of a personality inventory is limited.

b. Some counter this criticism by saying that individual behavior is consistent under most circumstances. Most research shows that traits, on average, accurately predict behavior in most situations.

## II. PERSONALITY ASSESSMENT TECHNIQUES

### A. ASSESSMENT METHODS

1. Personality psychologists have taken various approaches in their attempts to create psychometric measures that are reliable and valid for assessing personality.

    a. Psychodynamic theories investigate differences through the use of case studies and projective testing.

    b. Humanistic personality theories attempt to measure theoretical ideas, such as self-concept and self-actualization, based on data obtained via interviews or questionnaires.

    c. Social-cognitive theories utilize data from questionnaires.

    d. Trait theory is based on data created through factor analysis and specialized personality inventories.

### B. SPECIALIZED PERSONALITY INVENTORIES

1. **Personality inventory:** An assessment with a restricted format (e.g., true/false, Likert scale) that asks individuals to indicate whether specific statements about behaviors, symptoms, emotions, or thoughts are related to them personally.

    a. For example, the Minnesota Multiphasic Personality Inventory (MMPI) is a test that measures differences in personality and identifies emotional and behavioral problems. Individuals answer a large number of statements as *true, false,* or *cannot say* with respect to their own behavior.

    b. For example, the NEO Personality Inventory (NEO-PI) is a test that measures the Big Five traits. Individuals answer a large number of statements on a 5-point Likert scale.

2. Strengths of personality inventories include the following:

    a. They are easy to administer and generate a great deal of information.

    b. They are used in cross-cultural studies and have high levels of reliability and validity.

  3. Weaknesses of personality inventories include the following:

    a. They must be carefully evaluated for potential cultural biases.

    b. Individuals may not answer personal questions honestly to depict themselves in a positive way (social desirability bias).

    c. Individuals may interpret the questions to mean something other than was intended.

## C. PROJECTIVE PERSONALITY TEST

  1. **Projective personality test:** An assessment that asks individuals to respond to ambiguous stimuli to determine aspects of their personality.

    a. For example, the Rorschach Inkblot Test involves presenting individuals with a series of cards containing ambiguous blots of ink. Individuals must explain what they see, and their response is interpreted by the test administrator to reveal aspects of their personality.

    b. For example, the Thematic Apperception Test (TAT) involves presenting individuals with a series of cards that have an ambiguous picture. Individuals create a story about the picture, and what the person chooses to discuss is considered important. The TAT is frequently used to measure both achievement and affiliation motivations or as a starting point for conversations between clients and psychologists.

  2. Strengths of projective tests include the following:

    a. They provide more information about the client, which is especially helpful in psychotherapy.

    b. They make it difficult for individuals to be deceptive or know the socially desirable response.

  3. Weaknesses of projective tests include the following:

    a. They are vulnerable to experimenter bias, because test examiners may unintentionally influence how individuals respond or how they interpret responses.

    b. While problems exist with reliability and validity for most projective tests, they continue to be used in clinical settings.

# Motivation and Emotion

## I. BIOLOGICAL-BASED MOTIVATIONAL THEORIES

### A. INSTINCT

1. **Instinct theory:** The idea that an organism's behavior is influenced by innate, fixed responses to particular stimuli.

2. Instinctual motivation is more typical of nonhuman animals.

### B. DRIVE REDUCTION

1. **Drive-reduction theory:** The idea that an unmet physiological need creates tension that motivates individuals to do a behavior to bring their body back to homeostasis (balance).

2. For example, when Kurt needs water, he gets thirsty and is motivated to drink water to bring his body back to homeostasis.

### C. AROUSAL THEORY

1. **Arousal theory:** The idea that the physical environment can motivate individuals to seek an optimal level of physiological stimulation or arousal.

2. For example, to escape boredom, individuals are motivated to increase their arousal.

3. For example, to escape stress, individuals are motivated to decrease their arousal.

### D. YERKES-DODSON LAW

1. **Yerkes-Dodson Law:** The theory that describes the relationship between arousal and performance.

2. Performance is best for most tasks at a moderate level of arousal.

3. On simple tasks, performance is better if arousal levels are somewhat higher than moderate levels.

4. On difficult tasks, performance is better if arousal levels are slightly lower than moderate levels.

5. The graph below illustrates the Yerkes-Dodson law regarding the relationship between arousal and performance, which forms an upside-down U-shaped curve.

**Yerkes-Dodson Law**

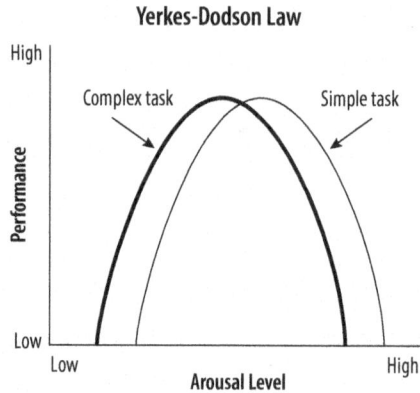

*Source: OpenStax*

## II. PSYCHOLOGICAL-BASED MOTIVATIONAL THEORIES

### A. SELF-DETERMINATION THEORY

1. **Self-determination theory:** The idea that individuals are motivated by the need for competence, autonomy, and relatedness, and behavior is regulated on a continuum from intrinsic to extrinsic motivations.

2. When these needs are fulfilled and individuals are intrinsically motivated, they tend to achieve more, have increased self-esteem, and experience better health.

3. **Intrinsic motivation:** The desire to perform a behavior out of genuine interest.

   a. For example, reading a book for pleasure.

4. **Extrinsic motivation:** The desire to perform a behavior to obtain a reward or avoid punishment.

   a. For example, reading a book to pass a class.

## B. INCENTIVE THEORY

1. **Incentive theory:** The idea that individuals are motivated by the pull of external stimuli.

2. The effect of a particular incentive varies among individuals and can change from one situation to another.

## C. LEWIN'S MOTIVATION CONFLICT THEORY

1. **Approach-approach:** A psychological conflict in which an individual must choose between two desirable options.

   a. For example, choosing between going to a baseball game and hanging out with friends, with both options enjoyable.

2. **Approach-avoidance:** A psychological conflict characterized by the simultaneous attraction and aversion to a single goal or choice.

   a. For example, choosing whether to buy a new item that is both cool (attractive) and expensive (unattractive).

3. **Avoidance-avoidance:** A psychological conflict in which an individual must choose between two undesirable options.

   a. For example, choosing between cleaning your room or studying, with both options disliked.

## D. SENSATION-SEEKING THEORY

1. **Sensation-seeking theory:** The idea that individuals with this personality type (e.g., thrill or adventure seeking, experience seeking, disinhibition, and boredom susceptibility) seek varied or novel experiences to reach optimal arousal.

2. People vary in the level of sensation seeking, with some individuals scoring very high on sensation-seeking scales and others very low while most are at a moderate level.

   a. For example, extreme-sports enthusiasts would have high levels of sensation seeking and thrive on activities such as rock climbing, bungee jumping, and whitewater rafting, constantly seeking new challenges and adrenaline rushes.

   b. For example, individuals who prefer quiet nights at home and hobbies such as gardening, cooking, or crafting and are content in familiar surroundings are likely to have low levels of sensation seeking.

### III. HUNGER MOTIVATION

#### A. BIOLOGICAL FACTORS

1. The hypothalamus, via the pituitary gland, signals hormone release and regulates hunger and satiety.

   a. **Leptin:** A hormone produced and secreted by fat cells that assists in decreasing food intake and reducing hunger (satiation).

   b. **Ghrelin:** A hormone secreted by the stomach to arouse hunger.

2. Set point theory suggests that individuals have a genetically determined range of weight maintained by biological processes without effort.

**Test Tip**

Remember "ghrelin" with the mnemonic "Ghrelin is in your growling stomach."

#### B. PSYCHOLOGICAL AND SOCIOCULTURAL FACTORS

1. Internal psychological cues, such as memories and moods, impact eating behaviors.

2. External factors, such as environmental and social influences, impact eating behaviors.

   a. For example, the appearance of food or seeing the time on the clock impacts whether an individual eats.

   b. For example, individuals may be motivated to eat during a social gathering.

3. Social learning theory proposes that watching and copying others impacts eating behaviors, including table manners and portion sizes.

4. Learned associations develop between eating and specific times of day, so we eat at lunchtime, even if we have eaten a large breakfast.

5. Cultural traditions provide information regarding when to eat, how fast to eat, how much to eat, and what types of foods are appropriate.

**Test Tip** Remember the term "satiety" by associating it with the word "satisfied." Satiety involves the general feeling of being full that decreases hunger motivation.

## IV. SOCIAL MOTIVATION

### A. AFFILIATION MOTIVATION

1. **Affiliation motivation:** The desire to belong and form attachments with others.

2. This drive to develop social bonds leads individuals to seek connections with others by establishing friendships and romantic relationships, participating in clubs, and attending events.

### B. ACHIEVEMENT MOTIVATION

1. **Achievement motivation:** The desire to attain a level of excellence or success by overcoming difficult challenges.

2. Individuals with high levels of achievement motivation select tasks that are moderately challenging.

3. Several factors are often associated with achievement motivation.

   a. **Intrinsic motivation:** The drive to perform a behavior out of genuine interest.

   b. **Growth mindset:** The belief that one's abilities can change and improve with effort.

4. The impact of culture on achievement motivation can be illustrated in terms of the differences discovered between individualist and collectivist cultures.

   a. Achievement in individualist cultures emphasizes reaching goals and overcoming difficulties for individual or personal satisfaction.

   b. Achievement in collectivist cultures emphasizes attaining excellence by being part of a larger group, such as a family or community.

## V. EMOTION THEORIES

### A. EXPLAINING EMOTION

1. **Emotion (a type of affect):** A complex psychological process that involves physiological, cognitive, and behavioral aspects.

   a. The physiological aspect involves the arousal of the autonomic nervous system, more specifically the sympathetic nervous system (e.g., changes in heart rate, blood pressure, breathing, sweating, pupil dilation), and hormone release.

      i. In general, the stronger the arousal level the more intense the emotion.

      ii. Different emotional states lead to different bodily changes.

   b. The behavioral aspect involves the observable actions and expressions accompanying emotional experiences, including facial expressions and gestures, as well as avoidance or approaching reactions.

   c. **Facial-feedback hypothesis:** A theory that proposes that activity generated by the facial muscles creates expressions that cue the brain to determine the emotion experienced. Research on this theory has had mixed results.

2. Current theories describe emotions as positive or negative responses to external and internal factors.

   a. For example, fear can be triggered by an external factor, such as a car alarm going off.

   b. For example, fear can be triggered by an internal factor, such as an embarrassing event (episodic memory).

3. Neural systems are involved in emotion processing.

   a. External factors of emotion can trigger the sensory system.

   b. Internal factors of emotion can trigger the memory system.

   c. Physiological components of emotion can trigger the autonomic nervous system.

   d. The limbic system is involved with the processing of emotions.

4. Some theories propose that arousal precedes (comes before) emotion.

   a. Order of events for an emotion: stimulus, then physiological arousal, and then emotional reaction.

      i. For example, you see a snake, then tremble, and then experience fear.

   b. The James-Lange theory proposes that physiological responses precede and automatically create the experience of an emotion.

   c. The facial-feedback hypothesis proposes that activity generated by the facial muscles creates expressions that cue the brain to determine the emotion experienced. Research on this theory has had mixed results.

5. Some theories propose that arousal and emotion are simultaneous.

   a. Order of events for an emotion: stimulus, followed by simultaneous physiological arousal and emotional reaction.

      i. For example, you see a snake, and then your heart rate increases and you experience fear simultaneously.

   b. The Cannon-Bard theory proposes that the physiological response and the experience of emotion occur simultaneously.

6. Some theories propose that a cognitive label/appraisal is needed for an emotion.

   a. Order of events for an emotion: stimulus, then physiological response, then cognitive label, and then emotional reaction.

      i. For example, you see a snake, then your heart rate increases, then you cognitively label it as dangerous, and then you experience fear.

      ii. Two-factor theory proposes that emotions are the result of a physiological response and the individual's cognitive labeling of the response. The cognitive label requires noticing and interpreting aspects of the environment to identify emotions.

   b. Alternative order: stimulus, then cognitive appraisal, then physiological arousal, and then emotional reaction.

      i. For example, you see a snake, then appraise it as a threat, then recognize you lack the resources to cope, then have an increased heart rate, and then experience fear.

      ii. Cognitive appraisal theory proposes an initial evaluation (primary appraisal) of whether an event is irrelevant, challenging, or threatening; followed by another evaluation (secondary appraisal) of the available coping resources.

7. Some theories propose that emotion precedes (comes before) cognition.

    a. Order of events for an emotion: stimulus, then emotional reaction, and then cognition.

      i. For example, you see a snake and then experience fear (emotion) before knowing what is going on (cognition).

    b. Alternative order: stimulus, then activation of the amygdala and cortex simultaneously.

      i. For example, you see a long, dark shadow; then the information travels to the amygdala (via the fast low road) for a quick emotion of fear; and then the information travels to the cortex (via the slow high road) for you to interpret it as a stick, which reduces fear.

      ii. Dual road theory proposes that information travels to the thalamus from where it can be routed along two pathways to separate brain structures.

8. Researchers continue to debate the order and/or if all components are involved in emotion.

**Exclusion Statement:** Specific names of theories of emotion are outside the scope of the AP® Psychology exam.

## B. EXPERIENCING POSITIVE EMOTIONS

1. **Broaden-and-build theory:** The idea that positive emotional experiences tend to expand your thoughts and actions (broaden), enabling you to develop personal resources (build), which drives personal growth.

    a. Experiencing positive emotions enables individuals to think about novel solutions and ideas (broaden thinking).

    b. The expanded thinking results in the development (building) of skills, resilience, and relationships that enhance health, making people better prepared to handle stressors and setbacks.

    c. Enhanced health produces more positive emotions.

2. Positive emotions create expanded (broadened) mindsets, while negative emotions create narrow mindsets.

**Broaden-and-Build Theory of Positive Emotions**

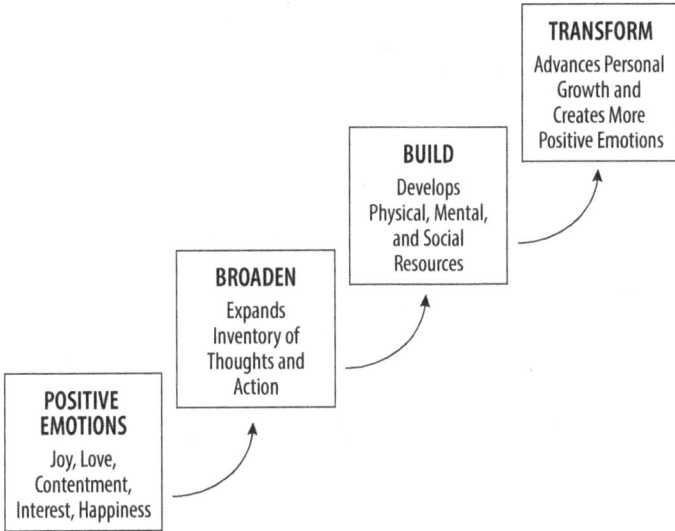

**TRANSFORM**
Advances Personal Growth and Creates More Positive Emotions

**BUILD**
Develops Physical, Mental, and Social Resources

**BROADEN**
Expands Inventory of Thoughts and Action

**POSITIVE EMOTIONS**
Joy, Love, Contentment, Interest, Happiness

## VI. THE IMPACT OF SOCIAL AND CULTURAL FACTORS ON EMOTION

### A. CROSS-CULTURAL RESEARCH

1. Some primary emotions that may be universally recognized across cultures include anger, disgust, sadness, happiness, surprise, and fear.

2. Research on the universality of emotions shows mixed results.

### B. EMOTIONAL EXPRESSION

1. **Facial expressions:** A specific type of nonverbal communication involving the activation of different combinations of facial muscles.

   a. For example, happiness is expressed with a smile and lifted cheeks that create crinkles around the eyes.

   b. Cross-cultural research supports the universality of smiling to express happiness, but other facial expressions vary in meaning across cultures.

2. Emotional expression is evident in differences in voice, posture, gestures, and facial expressions.

   a. Anger is usually expressed in a sharp, loud, high-pitched voice.

   b. Anger gestures may include fist clenching.

3. Emotional expression is impacted by experience (nurture) through operant conditioning, social learning, and cultural values.

   a. **Display rules:** The culturally acceptable learned guidelines for when and how emotions can be expressed in particular social situations.

      i. For example, public displays of affection, such as kissing a cheek as a greeting, are acceptable in some cultures but not in others.

**Test Tip**

Remember that rules are learned; therefore, display rules are culturally learned.

# Health and Positive Psychology

## I. WELLNESS

### A. HEALTH PSYCHOLOGY

1. **Health psychology:** A subfield of psychology that applies research to understanding the biological, psychological, and sociocultural factors that impact physical and mental health with the goals of identifying causes of health issues, preventing illness, improving health, and positively influencing public policy.

2. Health is often measured in two ways.

   a. Objective measures are the observable factors (e.g., infection rates, life expectancy) used to measure health.

   b. Subjective measures are the personal explanations (e.g., personal ratings or self-appraisals of health status) used to measure health.

### B. BIOPSYCHOSOCIAL APPROACH

1. Biological influences (e.g., genetic vulnerability, epigenetic influences, nervous system, and endocrine system differences) impact health and wellness.

2. Psychological influences (e.g., beliefs and attitudes, personality, emotions, stress, coping strategies, level of control) impact health and wellness.

3. Social or cultural influences (e.g., environments, family, social support, socioeconomic status [SES], ethnicity, gender) impact health and wellness.

## II. STRESS

### A. PSYCHOPHYSIOLOGICAL ILLNESSES

1. Genetics, health behaviors (e.g., unhealthy diet, smoking, inactivity), and psychophysiological and personality traits (e.g., hostility, aggression) relate to how people respond to stress and impact illness.

2. Psychophysiological illnesses result from, or are worsened by, stress and other emotional factors. The physical symptoms are real and can be produced or exaggerated by psychological factors.

   a. Physiological factors include genetics (e.g., family history of cancer) and lifestyle choices (e.g., unhealthy diet, smoking, inactivity).

   b. Psychological factors are personality traits (e.g., hostility, aggression) that influence how people respond to stress and that impact health.

3. Types of psychophysiological illnesses include hypertension, headaches, and immune suppression.

   a. **Hypertension:** A medical condition involving high blood pressure that is a major risk factor for heart disease (a type of cardiovascular disease). If not regulated, serious consequences, including death, can result.

   b. Stress can produce headaches, including tension headaches, and increase sensitivity to pain.

   c. Acute stress can increase immunity, while chronic stress can cause immune suppression (decreased immunity).

      i. Immune system: The body's defense mechanism to protect against infection and disease.

      ii. Stress is linked to slowed wound healing and increased chances of getting infections.

### B. STRESS AND STRESSORS

1. Stress can be adaptive, such as when it motivates us in constructive ways, or maladaptive when it causes health risks.

   a. **Eustress:** The positive stress response from accepting challenges and pursuing worthwhile or enjoyable goals.

        i.  Individuals need some level of eustress to be productive, happy, and inspired.

    b.  **Distress:** The negative stress response from being overwhelmed by threats.

        i.  Distress involves high levels of tension, resulting in impaired decision-making, negative physical consequences, and appetite or sleep disturbances.

2.  **Stressor:** A stimulus or event in the environment resulting in psychological tension and threats to internal homeostasis.

    a.  Individuals can encounter potential stressors early in life.

        i.  **Adverse childhood experiences (ACEs):** The negative events that happen to children before the age of 18 that can have lasting effects on their health and well-being.

        ii.  The counterpart is positive childhood experiences (PCEs), which can lead to good emotional health and well-being in adults because they feel protected and cared for during their childhood. Providing emotional care for pregnant women and families with young children can be beneficial.

    b.  Daily hassles or common everyday stressors are often a significant source of stress.

        i.  The frequency (how often), duration (how long), and intensity of these daily hassles impact the stress reaction.

        ii.  The counterpart is daily uplifts, such as receiving praise for a job well done, which can help protect against the negative effects of stress.

    c.  Additional examples of stressors include significant life events, catastrophes, poverty, discrimination, or a lack of social support.

## C. STRESS REACTIONS

1.  **General adaptation syndrome (GAS):** A three-stage physical stress response to prolonged stress—Alarm, Resistance, Exhaustion (ARE).

    a.  **Alarm:** The first stage of GAS in which the body's emergency response activates the sympathetic nervous system, resulting in physiological changes such as increased heart rate.

b. **Resistance:** The second stage of GAS in which the body's defense response involves continued increased physiological arousal, such as ongoing elevated levels of adrenaline.

c. **Exhaustion:** The third stage of GAS in which the body's immune system is depleted, causing vulnerability to illness.

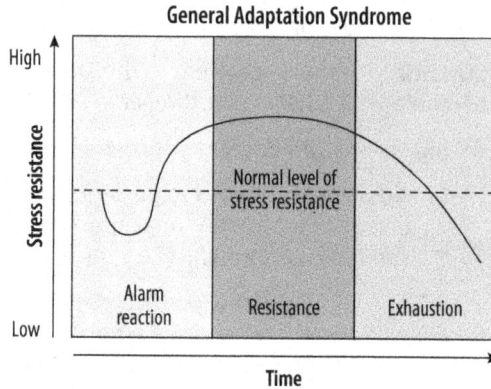

**General Adaptation Syndrome**

*Source: Pressbooks via BCcampus.ca*

2. The body follows a typical stress response.

a. **Fight-flight-freeze response:** The physiological response to a stressor that prepares an individual for a behavioral response for fighting, fleeing, or freezing (immobilized).

b. First, the hypothalamus activates the sympathetic nervous system to release epinephrine and norepinephrine into the bloodstream.

c. Second, the hypothalamus and pituitary glands send messages that release stress hormones, including cortisol.

3. Another response to stress is a social reaction.

a. **Tend-and-befriend theory:** The idea that individuals, especially females, respond to stress by engaging in caregiving behaviors and seeking social support.

i. For example, when stressed at school, you may help a classmate and seek support from friends.

**Test Tip**

Remember to make connections between neurotransmitters and behavior and mental processes. The tend-and-befriend theory has been linked to the neurotransmitter oxytocin, which promotes social bonding.

4. The cognitive appraisal theory is an attempt to explain how individuals evaluate stressors.

   a. Individuals evaluate stressors as either a challenge (eustress) or a threat (distress), impacting the experience of stress.

   b. Two types of appraisal lead to an emotion.

      i. Primary appraisal: The initial assessment of a situation, which involves deciding whether an event will affect an individual personally by determining whether the stressor is neutral, positive, or negative.

      ii. Secondary appraisal: The second assessment, which involves deciding whether the stressor can be dealt with and how to cope.

5. **Coping:** The cognitive, behavioral, and emotional ways of dealing with stress.

   a. **Problem-focused coping:** The process of dealing with a stressor directly.

      i. For example, when anxious about a test, study more or break up the material into smaller sessions.

      ii. Strategies to solve the problem (stressor) involve time management, asking for assistance, working harder,[1] reducing or removing the stressor, etc.

   b. **Emotion-focused coping:** The process of dealing with a stressor by managing one's feelings.

      i. For example, when anxious about a test, venting to a friend and seeking social support.

      ii. Strategies to reduce discomfort involve meditating, deep breathing, using medications, expressing emotions, seeking support, denial, avoidance, self-blame, rumination, etc.

   c. Coping strategies vary with the situation but also in relation to individual differences in gender, personality, genetics, and socioeconomic status (SES).

   d. Culture plays a role in coping strategies and the degree of stress an individual experiences.

**Test Tip** Keep in mind that problem-focused coping is often effective when you feel that you have the control to solve the problem. Emotion-focused coping may be better in situations in which you have less control and more of a desire for comfort.

## III. FACTORS THAT CONTRIBUTE TO POSITIVE SUBJECTIVE EXPERIENCES

### A. POSITIVE PSYCHOLOGY

1. **Positive psychology:** The subfield of psychology that explores positive experiences and emotions, positive traits (strengths and virtues), and positive institutions (e.g., groups, communities, cultures) that help people thrive. It seeks to find factors that lead to well-being, resilience, positive emotions, and psychological health.

2. Research in this field has focused on what makes people happy and increases subjective well-being.

### B. POSITIVITY AND RESILIENCE

1. **Positive emotions:** The pleasant feelings associated with happiness and well-being that lead to better physical and psychological health outcomes and to increased resilience.

2. **Well-being:** A state associated with perceived control, environmental mastery, personal growth, positive relationships, living a meaningful life, self-acceptance, relaxation, spirituality, curiosity, and self-efficacy.

3. **Resilience:** The ability to bounce back from stressful experiences and successfully adapt to changing situations. Resiliency comes from individual traits, autonomy, positive self-image, positive life experiences, healthy habits, and social support.

### C. CULTIVATING GRATITUDE

1. **Gratitude:** A sense of appreciation and thankfulness that serves as an effective method for coping with stress and increases subjective well-being.

2. Practicing gratitude leads to increased well-being, happiness, strengthened relationships, positive emotions, life satisfaction, optimism, less anxiety, and lowered blood pressure.

3. Cross-cultural research supports the benefits of expressing gratitude for health and well-being.

### D. 24 CHARACTER STRENGTHS

1. **Character strength:** A positive quality of one's personality.

2. Positive psychologists have developed a list of 24 character strengths organized around six virtue categories that cross cultures.

3. Everyone has each character strength as part of their personality to different degrees. As a result, each person has a unique profile.

| Category | Character Strengths |
|---|---|
| Courage | Bravery, honesty, perseverance, zest (enthusiastic and energetic) |
| Humanity | Kindness, love, social intelligence |
| Justice | Fairness, leadership, teamwork |
| Temperance | Forgiveness, humility, prudence (cautious), self-regulation |
| Transcendence | Appreciation of beauty and excellence, gratitude, hope, humor, spirituality |
| Wisdom | Creativity, curiosity, judgment, love of learning, perspective |

### E. ADDRESSING ADVERSITY

1. **Mindfulness:** A state of thoughtful awareness or being present with one's thoughts, emotions, feelings, and sensations.

   a. Mindfulness increases happiness and creates greater life engagement.

   b. Various mindfulness-based treatments using meditation have been used in treating anxiety, depression, and stress.

2. **Social support:** The care, comfort, and help provided by others (e.g., family, friends, doctors, community groups).

   a. Social support counteracts the effects of stressful events.

   b. Those who have close relationships have better immune functioning, lower blood pressure, lower levels of stress hormones, and better coping than those who feel alone.

3. **Posttraumatic growth:** The positive changes resulting from facing a challenging life event.

   a. For example, when someone goes through a major life event like a serious illness that challenges their view of the world, it can lead to a shift in their thinking. This cognitive restructuring can result in several positive outcomes, including a deeper appreciation for life, increased personal strength, stronger relationships, a recognition of new possibilities, and enhanced spiritual understanding.

   b. Psychologists assess positive changes using self-report measures.

# Psychological Disorders

## I. DEFINING PSYCHOLOGICAL DISORDERS

### A. CRITERIA OF PSYCHOLOGICAL DISORDERS

1. **Dysfunction:** Any impairment or disturbance in thoughts or behaviors that prevents individuals from caring for themselves, meeting obligations, or being productive at work or in social situations.

   a. For example, the behavior of a person struggling with addiction who continues to use drugs despite severe consequences, such as losing their job and going bankrupt.

2. **Distress:** Physical or mental pain, suffering, or discomfort.

   a. Although stress and worry are typical emotions that everyone experiences, they become abnormal if they are excessive, constant, and long-lasting.

3. **Deviance:** Thoughts and behaviors that differ from culturally or socially accepted standards.

   a. Cultural norms can change over time.

   b. For example, in the United States it would have been considered deviant, until recently, for the father to stay home and raise the children while the mother worked to support the family.

## II. DIAGNOSING MENTAL ILLNESS

### A. DIAGNOSING AND CLASSIFYING

1. A formal diagnosis is a precise determination made by a trained mental health professional based on information gathered and

evaluated during the assessment process, including interviews and tests.

2. Positive consequences are associated with diagnosing and classifying disorders.

   a. Labels help individuals better understand and predict their behaviors and enable clear communication among mental health professionals.

3. Negative consequences are associated with diagnosing and classifying disorders.

   a. The use of the *DSM* and the need for a diagnosis required by insurance companies creates a label that can be stigmatizing.

   b. Prejudices, such as racism, sexism, and ageism, can affect diagnosis and treatment, stressing the need for cultural sensitivity.

4. Before a person's behavior and/or thoughts are classified as a psychological disorder, a thorough consideration of all relevant factors (e.g., nature of the disorder, individual being diagnosed, cultural norms) must be considered.

## B. Evidence-Based Diagnostic Tools

1. *Diagnostic and Statistical Manual of Mental Disorders (DSM)*: The classification system created by the American Psychiatric Association for psychological disorders most often used in the United States.

   a. The *DSM-5-TR* (2022) provides information for each disorder, including diagnostic criteria, prevalence rate, risk factors, sex- and gender- and culture-related diagnostic issues, suicide risk, differential diagnosis, and comorbidity.

2. *International Classification of Mental Disorders (ICD)*: The classification system for psychological disorders created by the World Health Organization.

   a. The *DSM-5-TR* (2022) includes ICD-11 (2022) codes for enhanced global research and communication.

3. These classification systems are updated regularly to be responsive to new research and advances in the field.

## III. MODELS OF PSYCHOLOGICAL DISORDERS

### A. CONTEMPORARY MODELS

1. Currently, modern psychologists use various theories based on psychological perspectives to explain psychological disorders.

   a. **Behavioral perspective:** Causes for psychological disorders focus on maladaptive learned associations acquired through classical conditioning, operant conditioning, and social learning.

   b. **Biological perspective:** Causes for psychological disorders focus on physical differences in brain structure and function, including problems with specific neurotransmitters and hormones, as well as genetic factors.

   c. **Cognitive perspective:** Causes for psychological disorders focus on irrational and maladaptive thoughts, beliefs, attitudes, and emotions.

   d. **Evolutionary perspective:** Causes for psychological disorders focus on exaggerated versions of behaviors that were naturally selected for survival. For example, anxiety disorders may be exaggerated versions of thoughts or actions that aided the survival of the species along the evolutionary timeline.

   e. **Humanistic perspective:** Causes for psychological disorders focus on a lack of social support, such as a lack of unconditional positive regard, or the inability to reach one's full potential.

   f. **Psychodynamic perspective:** Causes for psychological disorders focus on unconscious thoughts often originating in childhood.

   g. **Sociocultural perspective:** Causes for psychological disorders focus on maladaptive social and cultural relationships and dynamics. Family relationships, social interactions, culture, race, ethnicity, gender, and similar factors affect behavior and thought. Although this perspective cannot predict abnormality in specific individuals, it helps explain abnormality due to specific external pressures, such as poverty or discrimination, experienced by members of a group.

2. **Eclectic approach:** Using more than one theoretical perspective to diagnose and treat the client's needs.

### B. INTERACTIONIST MODELS

1. **Biopsychosocial:** Psychological disorders are due to a combination of biological, psychological (e.g., thoughts and actions, emotions), and social (e.g., culture, family, social support) influences.

2. **Diathesis-stress:** Psychological disorders are due to the interaction of both a vulnerability (genetic or environmental) and a stressful life event. Exposure to stressful life events triggers the disorder.

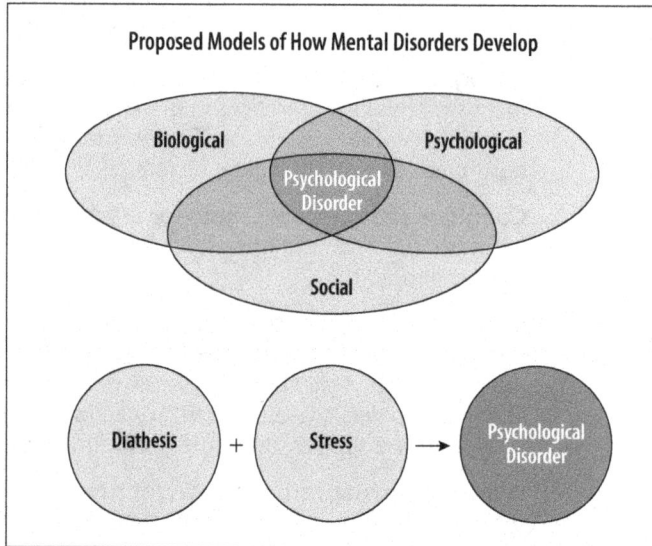

Proposed Models of How Mental Disorders Develop

**Test Tip**

Be sure to carefully differentiate the two major interactionist models. The biopsychosocial model considers biological, psychological, and social factors as overlapping influences that explain disorders. The diathesis-stress model emphasizes a linear relationship in which an inherited vulnerability interacts with stressors later in life to trigger the onset of a disorder.

## IV. DIAGNOSTIC CATEGORIES

**Exclusion Statement:** While there are many disorders listed in diagnostic manuals used by professionals in the field, the AP® Psychology exam focuses on the disorders listed in Topic 5.4 as representative of an introductory understanding of psychological disorders.

## A. NEURODEVELOPMENTAL DISORDERS

1. **Neurodevelopmental disorders:** A category of psychological disorders that start in childhood and are marked by a difference in brain processing that produces impairments in functioning.

   a. **Attention-deficit hyperactivity disorder (ADHD):** A persistent pattern of inattention (e.g., difficulty focusing, off-task, lack of follow-through, disorganized) and/or hyperactivity and impulsivity (e.g., fidgets, leaves their seat, is on the go, excessive talking, blurts out, interrupts) that impairs functioning.

   b. **Autism spectrum disorder:** Difficulties in social communication and interactions in multiple contexts, along with the presence of restrictive interests, repetitive behaviors, and/or the insistence on sameness. The severity level determines the amount of support needed.

2. Symptoms are evaluated in terms of whether the individual is displaying behaviors suitable for their age or level of maturity.

3. Possible causes of neurodevelopmental disorders involve genetic, biological, and/or environmental factors.

## B. SCHIZOPHRENIA SPECTRUM AND OTHER PSYCHOTIC DISORDERS

1. **Schizophrenia:** A disorder involving significant disturbances in cognition, emotion, perception, behavior, and/or speech that dramatically impair functioning in work, relationships, or self-care.

2. Schizophrenia can be experienced as an acute or chronic condition.

   a. **Acute schizophrenic episode:** A short-term episode of schizophrenic symptoms characterized by sudden onset. The symptoms may emerge suddenly and intensely, often requiring immediate intervention and treatment.

   b. **Chronic schizophrenia:** A long-term and persistent form of the disorder characterized by symptoms that may be less severe but endure and recur over an extended period. Despite periods of relative stability, individuals typically experience ongoing challenges in various aspects of their lives, including social interactions, work, and self-care.

3. Symptoms are often described as being either positive or negative.

   a. **Positive symptoms:** A symptom of schizophrenia that is an excess or distortion of normal thoughts and functioning.

    i. For example, delusions, hallucinations, disorganized thinking or speech, and catatonic excitement.

  b. **Negative symptoms:** A symptom of schizophrenia involving the absence or dramatically decreased levels of normal thoughts, emotions, and functioning.

    i. For example, social withdrawal, flat affect, and catatonic stupor.

**Test Tip**

Remember in regard to symptoms, the terms "positive" and "negative" do not suggest good or bad qualities; instead, they indicate the addition of inappropriate cognitions/behaviors or the subtraction of appropriate cognitions/emotions/behaviors.

4. Diagnosis of schizophrenia requires the presence of symptoms from two or more of the following five diagnostic domains—delusions, hallucinations, disorganized thinking or speech, disorganized motor behavior, and negative symptoms.

  a. **Delusions:** The false beliefs contrary to reality in one's culture and firmly held despite conflicting evidence.

    i. **Delusion of persecution:** The false belief that someone is plotting against you or the fear of being followed or watched.

      ➤ Individuals are overly vigilant, experience extreme levels of agitation, and are extremely mistrustful.

      ➤ The most common type of delusion.

    ii. **Delusion of grandeur:** The false belief that an individual holds special powers or is especially important, famous, or influential when they are not. This may lead them to demand special treatment.

  b. **Hallucinations:** False perceptual experiences characterized by hearing, seeing, smelling, tasting, or feeling something that is not present.

    i. Auditory hallucinations involve hearing voices or sounds that are not present and are the most common type.

  c. **Disorganized thinking:** Irrational, disjointed, or incoherent thoughts or speech.

        i.  **Word salad:** A type of disorganized speech that involves using loose associations and may be incomprehensible.

    d.  **Disorganized motor behavior:** A variety of obvious and bizarre behaviors that include arbitrary movements, agitation, or extreme silliness.

        i.  Disorganized motor behavior includes a wide range of catatonic behaviors, such as muscle rigidity, adoption of unusual postures, and extreme agitation without an observable cause.

      ii.  **Catatonia:** Disordered movement.

         1. Catatonia as excitement is a positive symptom.

         2. Catatonia as stupor is a negative symptom.

    e.  **Negative symptoms:** Deficiencies in cognition, movement, social activity, or other abilities.

        i.  **Flat affect:** Reduced levels of emotional expression (e.g., facial expression, eye contact, speech intonation).

      ii.  **Catatonic stupor:** A lack of movement.

     iii.  Social withdrawal or problems initiating or completing activities.

5. Biological factors may contribute to causing schizophrenia.

    a.  Genetic—Twin and family studies indicate that genetics play a part in these disorders.

    b.  Neurotransmitters—High levels of the neurotransmitter dopamine (dopamine hypothesis) may be involved in schizophrenia. Others, such as serotonin and glutamate, may also be involved.

    c.  Brain structures and activity—Enlarged ventricles and decreased frontal lobe activity may be involved in schizophrenia.

6. Several environmental and interacting factors may contribute to causing schizophrenia.

    a.  Prenatal exposure—Viruses or infections and complications during birth may play a role.

    b.  Diathesis-stress model—The idea that a psychological disorder develops when a genetic susceptibility to the disorder is triggered by a stressor, such as a family dysfunction or a traumatic event.

## C. DEPRESSIVE DISORDERS

1. **Depressive disorders:** A category of psychological disorders marked by symptoms of extreme sadness, emptiness, irritability, and difficulty functioning.

   a. **Major depressive disorder:** Key symptoms (e.g., depressed mood, loss of interest, appetite issues, sleep issues, fatigue, worthlessness or guilt, lack of concentration) are present for at least two weeks. Suicidal risk is a significant concern.

   b. **Persistent depressive disorder:** Key symptoms are milder and persist for more than two years. Everyday functioning is less impaired than with major depressive disorder. Thoughts of death or suicide are not included in the criteria for a diagnosis.

**Test Tip** The difference between these depressive disorders is related to severity and the duration of symptoms.

2. Biological factors may contribute to causing depressive disorders.

   a. Genetic—Twin and family studies indicate genetics play a part in these disorders.

   b. Neurotransmitters—Low serotonin and/or norepinephrine levels may be involved in depressive disorders. Mania, however, is often related to elevated levels of norepinephrine.

   c. Other—Problems with the endocrine system, biological rhythms, differences in brain structure, or brain activity may play a role.

3. Cognitive factors may play a role in causing depressive disorders.

   a. Exaggerated negative thoughts and maladaptive beliefs contribute to mood disturbances.

   b. Three key factors, collectively referred to as the negative cognitive triad—negative views about oneself, the world, and the future—may play a role.

4. Social-cognitive factors may contribute to causing depressive disorders.

   a. **Learned helplessness:** A phenomenon in which individuals, after facing repeated exposure to uncontrollable situations, stop trying to change or influence their circumstances due to diminished motivation.

b. **Pessimistic explanatory style:** The tendency to explain negative events in terms that are internal, stable (things will not improve), and global (affects all areas of one's life). It is associated with a higher risk for depression.

c. **Optimistic explanatory style:** The tendency to explain negative events in terms that are external, unstable (things will get better), and specific (impacting only part of one's life). It is associated with resistance to depression.

## D. BIPOLAR DISORDERS

1. **Bipolar disorders:** A category of psychological disorders marked by mood episodes such as manic episodes, hypomanic episodes, and/or depressive episodes.

   a. **Mania:** A mood state that involves an elevated or irritable mood and increased activity.

      i. It is characterized by a decreased need for sleep, extreme talkativeness, inflated self-esteem, and foolish or risky choices.

      ii. **Flight of ideas:** A symptom of mania that involves rapid shifts in conversation from one subject to another.

   b. **Hypomania:** A less severe (milder) form of mania characterized by elevated mood and increased energy and activity.

   c. **Bipolar I disorder:** A mood disorder involving mania or alternating periods of mania and major depression. Suicidal risk is a significant concern associated with a major depressive episode in this diagnosis.

   d. **Bipolar II disorder:** A mood disorder involving at least one hypomanic episode and major depressive episodes. Suicidal risk is a significant concern associated with a major depressive episode in this diagnosis.

2. Bipolar cycling entails alternating periods of depression and mania, with durations varying widely.

3. Possible causes of bipolar disorders involve genetic, biological, and/or environmental factors.

**Test Tip**
To receive a diagnosis of Bipolar I, someone must experience at least one manic episode. Having a hypomanic episode is not sufficient for a diagnosis of Bipolar I.

### E. ANXIETY DISORDERS

1. **Anxiety disorders:** A category of disorders marked by symptoms of fear and/or anxiety that are extreme and chronic (lasting at least six months).

   a. **Agoraphobia:** An intense fear of public transportation, wide-open areas, enclosed locations, standing in line or being in a crowd, or being outside of the home due to the worry of being unable to escape or receive help if needed. Individuals can be completely homebound or unable to work.

   b. **Generalized anxiety disorder (GAD):** A widespread and persistent worry related to various areas or activities occurring most days. The anxiety is free-floating, not specific to one event, and is difficult to control. Physical symptoms must also be present.

   c. **Panic disorder:** Following a panic attack, at least one month of fearing future panic attacks or major dysfunctional change in behavior.

   d. **Social anxiety disorder:** An intense fear of being scrutinized while interacting with others that is severe enough to prevent social interactions, being observed, or performing due to the potential threat of embarrassment or judgment.

   e. **Specific phobia:** An irrational fear or anxiety of a particular object or situation that is unreasonable concerning the real danger and often leads to avoidance behaviors.

      i. For example, acrophobia (fear of heights) or arachnophobia (fear of spiders).

2. Specific symptoms include physical symptoms (e.g., accelerated heart rate, rapid breathing, sweating, dizziness, muscle tension, trembling, nausea), cognitive symptoms (e.g., worry, fear, irritability), and behavioral symptoms (e.g., avoidance, escape, aggression).

3. Biological factors may play a role in causing anxiety disorders.

   a. Genetic—Twin and family studies indicate that genetics plays a part in these disorders.

   b. Neurotransmitters—Low levels of the neurotransmitters GABA and serotonin may be involved in anxiety disorders.

   c. Brain structures—Most anxiety and trauma- and stressor-related conditions appear to be related to overactivity in the amygdala and fear circuits in the brain.

4. Cognitive and behavioral factors may play a role in anxiety disorders.

   a. Learned associations—Phobias are often developed through classical conditioning and maintained with operant conditioning.

   b. Irrational thoughts—Distorted or exaggerated thinking patterns can trigger feelings of anxiety.

5. Some anxiety disorders can manifest as culture-bound disorders.

   a. **Culture-bound disorder:** A psychological condition involving a set of symptoms that seem strongly shaped by cultural influences, thus occurring much less frequently or exhibiting highly varied expressions in different cultural contexts.

   b. *Ataque de nervios*: A culture-bound anxiety disorder characterized by a range of symptoms, such as convulsions, partial loss of consciousness, heart palpitations, numbness, sudden emotional outbursts, and sensations of heat ascending to the head.

      i. It often occurs quickly after a stressful event, especially violence.

      ii. It is mainly diagnosed in people of Caribbean or Iberian descent.

      iii. It is influenced by cultural norms dictating acceptable emotional responses to challenges, especially within family relations.

      iv. Although symptoms overlap, most individuals do not meet the criteria for a diagnosis of panic disorder.

   c. *Taijin kyofusho (TKS)*: A culture-bound anxiety disorder characterized by anxiety and avoidance of social interactions due to the perception that personal appearance and behavior might not meet societal standards or could potentially offend others.

      i. This condition has two cultural forms.

         ➤ The sensitive type involves heightened social sensitivity and anxiety in interpersonal interactions.

         ➤ The offensive type is characterized by the fear that others will find their bodies undesirable or offensive.

      ii. Mainly diagnosed in Japanese cultural contexts. It is known as "interpersonal fear disorder" in Japanese.

iii. It involves a broader range of symptoms than social anxiety disorder.

> ➤ While individuals with social anxiety disorder typically worry about embarrassing themselves in social settings, TKS involves physical symptoms, such as blushing, heightened body odor, and sweating.

## F. OBSESSIVE-COMPULSIVE AND RELATED DISORDERS

1. **Obsessive-compulsive and related disorders:** A category of psychological disorders marked by repeated unwanted thoughts or urges, and/or ritualized behavior.

    a. **Hoarding disorder:** Difficulty getting rid of one's possessions regardless of their actual value because of a perceived need to save items or distress with discarding them. The inability to discard items leads to an accumulation of items that creates clutter, making living spaces dysfunctional.

    b. **Obsessive-compulsive disorder (OCD):** Usually unwanted persistent thoughts or urges (obsessions) and/or specific behaviors or rituals an individual feels compelled to perform (compulsions) that reduce or prevent anxiety. The symptoms must consume more than one hour per day or cause distress or dysfunction.

2. **Obsessions:** Intrusive persistent thoughts or urges, usually unwanted, that result in anxiety.

    a. Common obsessions include fear of contamination, an overwhelming desire for symmetry, forbidden thoughts (e.g., sexual, aggressive), fear that something terrible will happen to the person or someone else, or fear of hurting someone else.

3. **Compulsions:** The usually unwanted repetitive behaviors or mental acts (e.g., counting) that individuals use to reduce anxiety.

    a. Common compulsions include hand washing, checking doors or light switches, or ordering (e.g., lining up objects by size or color).

4. Possible causes of obsessive-compulsive disorders include genetic, biological, behavioral, and/or cognitive factors.

## G. DISSOCIATIVE DISORDERS

1. **Dissociative disorders:** A category of psychological disorders marked by a disruption in the individual's conscious awareness,

perception, memory, emotion, identity, body representation, motor control, or behavior.

   a. **Dissociative amnesia (without fugue):** An inability to recall personal information, which cannot be attributed to a medical cause, such as a tumor or brain disease; can be reversed and is often caused by a traumatic event or stressful occurrence.

   b. **Dissociative amnesia (with fugue):** An inability to recall personal information, accompanied by travel from one's usual location/environment.

   c. **Dissociative identity disorder (DID):** The presence of two or more separate and distinct personalities in one person with recurring gaps in memory. The individual personalities are quite distinctive from one another and may be of different ages and genders. Transitions in identity are self-reported or observed by others.

2. Possible causes for dissociative disorders involve the experiences of trauma or stress.

**Test Tip**

Remember to distinguish between dissociative identity disorder and schizophrenia. Schizophrenia means a split from reality, not a split in personality.

## H. TRAUMA AND STRESSOR-RELATED DISORDERS

1. **Trauma and stressor-related disorders:** A category of psychological disorders marked by exposure to a traumatic or stressful event with subsequent psychological distress.

   a. **Posttraumatic stress disorder (PTSD):** A disorder resulting from exposure to an event that threatened death, serious injury, or sexual violence; causes persistent symptoms such as hypervigilance, flashbacks, severe anxiety, insomnia, emotional detachment, and hostility that are severe enough to interfere with work and social situations and relationships.

2. Exposure to a traumatic event can include direct experience, witnessing, learning about the event that happened to a close family member/friend, or experiencing repeated or extreme exposure to the event's details, as can happen with first responders, such as police, firefighters, and EMTs.

3. Symptoms may include intrusion (e.g., distressing memories, flashbacks, nightmares), avoidance (e.g., hiding from memories or reminders of the event), negative changes in thoughts and mood (e.g., numbness, detachment from others), and arousal and reactivity (e.g., exaggerated startle response, irritability, problems concentrating, sleep difficulties).

4. Possible causes of trauma and stressor-related disorders involve the experience of trauma or stress.

I.  **FEEDING AND EATING DISORDERS**

1. **Feeding and eating disorders:** A category of psychological disorders marked by a persistent disturbance in an individual's relationship with food that impairs functioning or physical health.

a. **Anorexia nervosa:** A disorder involving extreme food restriction that leads to excessive weight loss. Criteria also include fear of weight gain and a severely distorted body image.

b. **Bulimia nervosa:** A disorder involving repeated episodes of binging (extreme overeating in a certain period and a lack of control over eating) and behaviors to prevent weight gain (e.g., vomiting, laxatives, excessive exercise). Self-image is influenced by body shape and weight.

2. Symptoms include extreme food restriction or the intake of large amounts of calories in short periods and stress and worry regarding weight and appearance.

3. Possible causes of feeding and eating disorders involve genetic, biological, behavioral, cognitive, and/or social factors.

J.  **PERSONALITY DISORDERS**

1. **Personality disorders:** A category of disorders marked by enduring patterns of thought, behavior, perception, or emotion that deviate from one's culture.

2. This pattern of behavior begins in adolescence or early adulthood and may lead to personal distress or impairment.

3. Personality disorders are divided into three clusters.

a. **Cluster A personality disorders:** Odd or eccentric traits.

i. **Paranoid:** The essential feature is a pattern of extreme suspiciousness and distrust.

      ii.  **Schizoid:** The essential feature is a pattern of social detachment and a narrow range of emotional responses in social situations.

     iii.  **Schizotypal:** The essential feature is a pattern of social isolation and odd beliefs, speech, and behaviors. It is also listed under schizophrenia spectrum disorders in the *DSM-5-TR*.

  b.  **Cluster B personality disorders:** Dramatic, emotional, or erratic traits.

      i.  **Antisocial:** The essential feature is a pattern of disregard and violation of the rights of others and a lack of remorse. Most closely associated with criminal behavior.

      ii.  **Borderline:** The essential feature is a pattern of instability in relationships, self-image, and emotions. It is marked by impulsiveness that is self-damaging.

     iii.  **Histrionic:** The essential feature is a pattern of highly emotional and attention-seeking behaviors.

     iv.  **Narcissistic:** The essential feature is a pattern of entitlement, a need for undeserved admiration and praise, and a lack of empathy.

  c.  **Cluster C personality disorders:** Anxious or fearful traits.

      i.  **Avoidant:** The essential feature is a pattern of excessive shyness in social situations, feeling inadequate, and hypersensitivity to negative evaluations.

      ii.  **Dependent:** The essential feature is a pattern of excessive need to be taken care of, leading to clingy and submissive behaviors and fears of separation.

     iii.  **Obsessive-Compulsive:** The essential feature is a pattern of preoccupation with orderliness, perfectionism, and rigid control.

4.  Possible causes of personality disorders include genetic, biological, behavioral, cognitive, and/or social factors.

# Treatment of Psychological Disorders

## I. RESEARCH ON PSYCHOTHERAPY

### A. EVALUATIONS OF THE EFFECTIVENESS OF PSYCHOTHERAPY

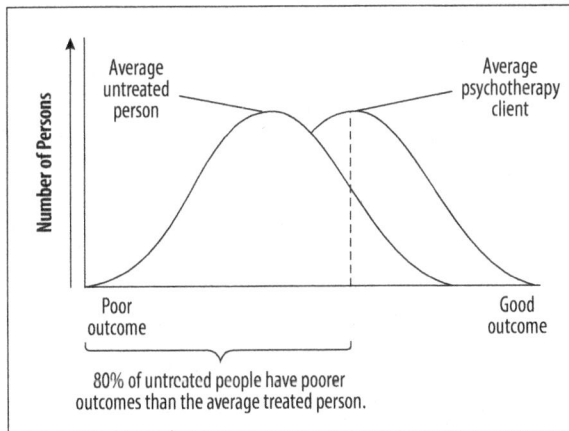

1.  Experimental research compares people receiving therapy with similar people who do not receive treatment to determine its effectiveness.

    a.  **Meta-analysis:** The statistical technique for combining effect size estimates (results) from numerous studies on the same topic into a single effect size.

    b.  Meta-analyses indicate that individuals improve more when they receive treatment.

The Effectiveness of Psychotherapy

Number of Persons

Average untreated person

Average psychotherapy client

Poor outcome

Good outcome

80% of untreated people have poorer outcomes than the average treated person.

**Science Tip**

Keep in mind that meta-analysis is a non-experimental methodology.

2. **Evidence-based practice:** A treatment supported by scientific evidence, along with clinician knowledge and the patient's values and expectations.

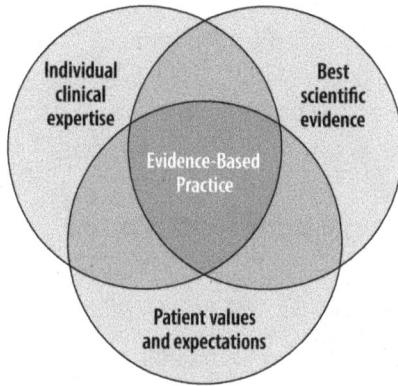

3. **Regression toward the mean:** The tendency for unusual or extreme events to move toward the average when remeasured over time.

   a. For example, in studies evaluating treatment for a specific psychological disorder, participants with initially severe symptoms may show improvement after treatment. However, improvement in symptoms may be due to regression toward the mean.

**Science Tip**

Remember Science Practice 3 requires you to explain how regression toward the mean occurs as more data are collected. This concept needs to be considered when studying the effectiveness of psychotherapy. Someone's mood could improve due to regression toward the mean rather than due to psychotherapy.

## B. INFLUENCES ON THE EFFECTIVENESS OF PSYCHOTHERAPY

1. **Therapeutic alliance:** The cooperative relationship between the therapist and client needed for successful therapy.

   a. Trusting and open relationships increase success and decrease the chances of individuals dropping out.

   b. Entering and continuing therapy can be impacted by gender and/or culture. Therapists should be sensitive and adapt to their client's needs.

2. **Cultural humility:** A mindset in psychotherapy and health care that emphasizes embracing diverse cultures with openness and respect through self-reflection and learning, fostering curiosity, and active listening to improve relationships and promote societal understanding.

3. Research indicates that education and coaching improve relationships between clients and therapists and prevent individuals from discontinuing treatment early.

## II. TRENDS OF PSYCHOTHERAPY

### A. HISTORICAL TRENDS

1. Psychological disorders were once treated with harsh methods based on an etiology (cause) of possession.

2. Reformers pushed for more humane methods in the moral treatment movement.

3. **Deinstitutionalization:** The closing of asylums and government-run hospitals and instead providing care to individuals with psychological disorders through outpatient facilities or group homes in the community.

   a. It was made possible partly by the increased use and effectiveness of psychotropic medication therapy in the 1950s.

   b. Although many patients thrived outside of institutions, many had insufficient support and became homeless after they stopped taking their medications.

### B. MODERN TRENDS

1. Therapists now prefer decentralized treatments that combine medication and psychological therapies.

2. The community mental health movement was designed to offer care for individuals formerly treated in mental hospitals by providing therapy and support through outpatient facilities that would be used by individuals with psychological disorders living with family members or in group homes.

3. **Community psychology:** A subfield of psychology that focuses on methods to prevent or reduce the prevalence of psychological disorders by understanding how social interactions in neighborhoods, families, and the larger culture impact functioning.

## III. ETHICAL PRINCIPLES IN PSYCHOTHERAPY

### A. ETHICAL CODE OF CONDUCT

1. Psychotherapists are required to follow the ethical code of conduct established by the American Psychological Association (APA).

2. The ethical code applies across various contexts, such as in-person and technology-based treatment.

### B. GENERAL PRINCIPLES

1. **Nonmaleficence:** The ethical principle to avoid harming clients.

2. **Fidelity:** The ethical principle of establishing trust and upholding professional standards.

3. **Integrity:** The ethical principle to be honest and keep promises.

4. **Respect for client's rights and dignity:** The ethical principle to value the dignity and worth of all individuals.

   a. **Confidentiality:** The ethical duty of a therapist to maintain client privacy is upheld by state and federal laws.

   b. Therapists are aware and respectful of individual differences including those based on gender, age, race, ethnicity, language, disability, and socioeconomic status (SES).

   c. Therapists are aware of how personal biases could impact the therapeutic relationship.

**Test Tip**

The general APA ethical principles outlined here refer to guidelines for psychotherapy as opposed to the ethical guidelines for research.

## IV. PSYCHOLOGICAL THERAPY TECHNIQUES

### A. PSYCHODYNAMIC THERAPIES

1. **Psychoanalysis:** A specific therapy method developed by Sigmund Freud to discover unresolved unconscious conflicts that cause difficulties for individuals.

2. **Psychodynamic therapy:** The modern group of therapies that focus on a client's current social issues and conscious processes.

3. **Dream interpretation:** A technique in which the therapist interprets the underlying unconscious meaning of the dreams of the client.

4. **Free association:** A process in which the client is asked to speak without self-censorship about whatever comes to mind during therapy to reveal unconscious conflicts that the therapist interprets.

5. The therapist's role is to interpret and resolve a client's unconscious conflicts.

## B. COGNITIVE THERAPIES

1. **Cognitive therapy:** A group of therapies that focus on helping individuals identify faulty thought processes and replace them with healthy ways to think about and perceive the world.

2. The therapist's role is to directly challenge clients to identify their current faulty thought processes and replace them with alternative thoughts that are more logical and rational.

3. **Cognitive restructuring:** A technique in which the client identifies, disputes, and replaces irrational thoughts with more realistic and adaptive ones.

    a. Replacing negative thoughts with positive ones can lead to better physical or psychological health.

    b. For example, identifying a stressful situation as a challenge, as opposed to a threat, can be beneficial to one's health.

4. **Negative cognitive triad:** Negative beliefs about the self, world, and future held by depressed individuals. Cognitive therapy focuses on replacing these irrational thoughts.

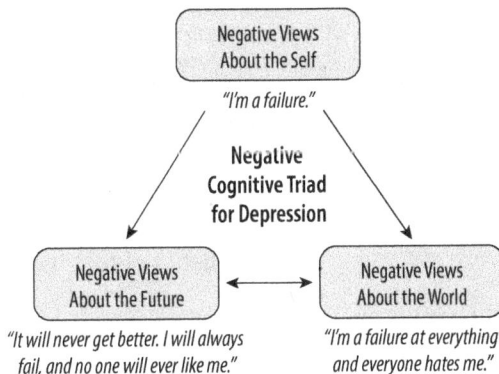

Negative Views About the Self

*"I'm a failure."*

Negative Cognitive Triad for Depression

Negative Views About the Future

Negative Views About the World

*"It will never get better. I will always fail, and no one will ever like me."*

*"I'm a failure at everything and everyone hates me."*

## C. BEHAVIORAL THERAPIES

1. **Applied behavioral analysis:** A group of therapies based on using techniques of classical, operant, or social learning to change dysfunctional behaviors.

2. The therapist's role is to act as a mentor to demonstrate and instruct how to change unwanted behaviors.

3. **Exposure therapy:** A group of therapies, often used to treat anxiety disorders, that involve individuals confronting the fear-inducing stimuli safely until they no longer respond negatively.

4. **Systematic desensitization:** A technique in which clients create a hierarchy related to their fear that they work through gradually while practicing relaxation methods. The goal is to replace the anxiety response with one of relaxation based on the theory that simultaneously experiencing these two opposite responses is impossible.

### The Three Steps of Systematic Desensitization

| Step | Systematic Desensitization Technique | Example for a Specific Phobia (Acrophobia—Fear of Heights) |
|---|---|---|
| Step one | The therapist teaches the client specific relaxation techniques. | The client is taught deep breathing and muscle relaxation. |
| Step two | The client and therapist create an anxiety hierarchy or series of scenarios related to the fear, ranging from mild to extremely threatening in incremental steps. | The anxiety hierarchy consists of first looking at a picture of a ladder, next standing on a short step stool, and finally standing on the top of a 12-foot ladder. |
| Step three | The therapist helps the client work through the hierarchy while simultaneously practicing relaxation methods. | The client begins by talking about heights while relaxing before progressing to the next level on the anxiety hierarchy. |

5. **Aversion therapy:** A classical conditioning technique in which a client pairs a negative stimulus with an undesired behavior, leading to a reduction in the frequency of that behavior.

6. **Token economy:** An operant conditioning technique in which a client is reinforced for demonstrating a desirable behavior with a token that can be traded in for a reinforcer.

7. **Biofeedback:** A technique in which a client uses a device to monitor physiological responses (sympathetic and parasympathetic systems) to achieve some degree of control. It is often used for the treatment of anxiety and depression.

## D. COGNITIVE-BEHAVIORAL THERAPIES

1. **Cognitive-behavioral therapy (CBT):** A group of therapies that combine cognitive and behavioral techniques to identify and alter faulty thoughts, emotions, and behaviors that are causing distress.

2. **Rational-emotive behavior therapy (REBT):** A technique in which clients alter their irrational thoughts, which in turn changes their negative emotions and behaviors. The framework underlying REBT is the ABCDE technique.

   a. **A**ctivating event: I fail a test.

   b. **B**elief: I irrationally believe I will never be successful at anything.

   c. **C**onsequence: Experiencing negative feelings and not trying to learn from my mistake.

   d. **D**isputing irrational belief: Challenging the catastrophizing thought and replacing it with a rational thought, such as that I merely experienced a setback.

   e. **E**ffects: Rationally accepting the one low test score and using it as motivation for improvement.

3. **Dialectical behavior therapy (DBT):** A technique that combines cognitive and behavioral ideas with mindfulness practices to lead to greater self-acceptance. It was initially developed for difficult-to-treat individuals, such as those with borderline personality disorder who often have black-and-white thinking (viewing things in extremes or absolutes).

   a. Phase I addresses the most extreme and dysfunctional behaviors (e.g., self-harm and suicidal threats/attempts) by taking a dialectical approach to discuss opposing ideas using logic and reasoning to reconcile them. Clients are trained to build problem-solving skills and use mindfulness to cope with negative emotions and prevent self-destructive behaviors.

      b. Phase II involves having the client examine traumatic experiences in their past that may be the cause of their emotional problems.

      c. Phase III involves helping the client build a sense of self-respect and independence.

## E. HUMANISTIC THERAPIES

1. **Humanistic therapies:** A group of therapies that emphasize the positive capacities of individuals and stress the importance of free will and personal growth.

2. The therapist's role is to provide a supportive emotional climate of acceptance, genuineness, and empathy. Therapists are nondirective and place the client at the center of the process while encouraging and clarifying their ideas.

      a. **Person-centered therapy:** A technique that uses active listening and unconditional positive regard to help individuals reach their full potential as they gain a more accurate self-concept.

      b. **Active listening:** A technique in which the therapist listens closely, asks clarifying questions, and paraphrases the client's statements to confirm mutual understanding.

      c. **Unconditional positive regard:** A technique in which the therapist does not necessarily agree or approve of everything the client says but does provide a caring and accepting environment that supports the client's capacity for future growth.

## F. GROUP THERAPY

1. **Group therapy:** A form of psychotherapy in which a group of patients meet to discuss their conditions and relevant experiences and insights under the supervision of a therapist who uses a variety of techniques to facilitate discussion and provide therapy to group members.

      a. Advantages include that it is more affordable than individual therapy, it creates a supportive environment that allows individuals to know they are not alone, and it provides models of effective coping. Social pressures promote accountability, and therapists can gain insight into how clients interact with others.

b. Disadvantages are that individuals need to share the time, they may not feel they can speak freely in front of others, and some may be unable to tolerate a group setting.

2. **Family therapy:** A form of psychotherapy in which the family is viewed as a client, and the family members are treated together to improve how the family functions and strengthen relationships among family members.

3. **Couples therapy:** A form of psychotherapy in which the therapist works with both individuals and focuses on improving the relationship by increasing intimacy and facilitating effective communication.

## G. HYPNOTHERAPY

1. Hypnosis has been successfully used in therapy to treat pain and anxiety.

2. The use of hypnosis for age regression or memory retrieval has not been supported by research.

## V. TREATMENTS FROM THE BIOLOGICAL PERSPECTIVE

### A. PSYCHOACTIVE MEDICATION THERAPY

1. Psychoactive medications impact physical, cognitive, and behavioral functioning by interacting with the nervous system.

   a. These medications increase (agonist) or decrease (antagonist) neurotransmission to reduce or eliminate symptoms.

   b. They are not a cure but a method for controlling symptoms that often return when a patient stops taking the medication.

2. Psychoactive medications almost always involve side effects and require monitoring and possible adjustment by a medical professional.

   a. Individuals may stop taking medications for various reasons, including unpleasant side effects.

   b. **Tardive dyskinesia:** A movement disorder characterized by involuntary movements of the face, tongue, or limbs. It is associated with long-term use of antipsychotics that regulate dopamine.

Psychoactive Medications

| Category | Main Disorder | Examples | Main Neurotransmitter |
|---|---|---|---|
| Antipsychotics | Schizophrenia | Typical | Dopamine |
| | | Atypical | Serotonin |
| Antianxiety | Anxiety disorders | Barbiturates | GABA |
| | | Benzodiazepines | |
| Antidepressants | Depressive disorders, Anxiety disorders, OCD, PTSD | MAOIs, TCAs | Serotonin |
| | | SSRIs, SNRIs | Norepinephrine |
| Antimanics | Bipolar disorders | Lithium | Glutamate |
| | | | Dopamine |
| | | | GABA |

## B. PSYCHOSURGERY OR INVASIVE INTERVENTIONS

1. **Psychosurgery:** The most extreme form of biomedical therapy that involves lesioning.

2. **Lesioning:** The purposeful surgical removal or destruction of particular areas in the brain.

3. **Lobotomy:** A technique in which specific areas of the prefrontal cortex of the brain are removed or connections between the prefrontal cortex and the rest of the brain are severed.

   a. It was a popular technique used in the 1930s and 1940s to control violent and psychotic behaviors.

   b. The procedure was replaced with medications and more precise surgical procedures.

4. **Electroconvulsive therapy (ECT):** A technique that administers a brief passage of electric current to produce a brain seizure while the patient is under anesthesia.

   a. It is an effective and rapid treatment for severe depression that is not responsive to medication and psychotherapy.

   b. Potential side effects can include temporary memory loss, disorientation, and confusion.

   c. Currently, no scientific explanation for why ECT is effective has been provided, and the results are often temporary.

5. **Transcranial magnetic stimulation (TMS):** A noninvasive technique in which specific brain areas are stimulated using an electromagnetic coil placed on the skull.

   a. It can be used to treat depression, obsessive-compulsive disorder, Tourette's disorder, and movement disorders.

   b. It can also be used to study the brain, such as electrical stimulation of the motor cortex.

# PART III

## TEST-TAKING STRATEGIES AND PRACTICE QUESTIONS

# Mastering the Multiple-Choice Questions

## I. TIMING AND SCORING FOR MULTIPLE-CHOICE QUESTIONS (MCQs)

A. The exam contains 75 multiple-choice questions, each of which has four possible answer choices (A–D).

B. The multiple-choice section of the exam lasts 90 minutes (1.5 hours).

C. The multiple-choice section accounts for 66.7% of your total score.

D. Your score for the multiple-choice section of the exam is based on the total number of questions you answer correctly. Points are not deducted for incorrect answers, so you should answer every question, even if you have to guess.

E. The exam is equally weighted 15%–25% for each of the five units.

## II. TOP 5 TEST TIPS FOR MCQs

The exam is delivered in a digital format through the College Board's Bluebook digital testing application. All tips listed below apply to this format.

A. Read carefully to be sure you understand what is being asked. In other words, read the full question (RTFQ).

B. Use the digital tools available with the digital exam. You can preview these resources in the AP® Classroom online platform and the Bluebook app. Your teacher may be using practice modules in AP® Classroom throughout the year, but the AP® exam will be completed in the Bluebook app.

C. Mark the questions you want to return to at the end. Questions will vary in difficulty level throughout the test. Answer the easy ones and reason through the difficult ones; but don't waste time. You will NOT be allowed to move between the multiple-choice questions (MCQs) and free-response questions (FRQs).

**D.** Occasionally, you may see something unfamiliar. Eliminate unlikely answers and then make an educated guess. No worries—you will not need to know 100% of the material on the multiple-choice section to score a 5.

**E.** Test-taking is a skill! Spend time carefully reviewing the sample questions and take the online practice test accompanying this book (*www.rea.com/studycenter*). Answer all the AP® Classroom practice questions you can. Use your results to help focus your study time on areas where you need improvement.

1. Take advantage of any practice opportunities in Bluebook before the exam. Bluebook will have a test preview and a full-length practice.

2. While doing the practice questions in Bluebook, the test preview is untimed. However, on exam day there will be a running timer at the top of the page. In the directions it will say you can go back and forth between questions in the multiple-choice section until time expires. The timer will turn red when there are 5 minutes left and the proctor will not provide any time warnings. If you have an approved extra-time accommodation, you will receive that accommodation on exam day in Bluebook.

3. You will have tools available to you in the upper right-hand corner under "Highlights and Notes" and under "More."

4. You will have a strikethrough feature available, with which you can cross off answers while reading and evaluating the question. This feature is especially important for questions you will mark for review. It will save time when you return to a question in which an option or two has already been eliminated.

5. You will be able to "Mark for Review" any multiple-choice question by flagging it near the number in the upper left corner.

6. Questions marked "For Review" and "Unanswered" will be pointed out to you before you exit the section. You can also navigate between questions from a pop-up box at the bottom of the screen.

## III. TYPES OF MCQs

**A.** The exam includes set-based and discrete questions.

**B.** Three types of multiple-choice questions are based on Science Practices 1–3. Each type of question is explained in detail below and followed with examples of the particular type of question. Remember that some questions will take longer to answer than others, especially if the question involves a longer question stem or analyzing a data set.

**Test Tip** **Navigating Questions:** You are free to move between questions within the multiple-choice section (Section I) until time expires. There will then be a short break between the multiple-choice and free-response sections. Once you start the free responses (Section II) you will *not* be able to return to the multiple-choice section. However, you will be able to navigate between the two free-response questions during the time allotted for Section II. Use this flexibility to revisit and improve your free-response answers, ensuring all parts of the questions are fully addressed.

## IV. CONCEPT APPLICATION QUESTIONS

A. This question format constitutes about 65% of the multiple-choice section.

   1. You will be required to apply psychological perspectives, theories, concepts, and research findings to a scenario.

   2. You will be required to explain how cultural norms, expectations, and circumstances, as well as cognitive biases, apply to behavior and mental processes.

B. Sample Questions and Answers

   1. Psychologists conducting research on the effects of morphine on the body discovered that even though morphine is an artificial chemical, the human body seems to have neural receptor sites that are "built" to receive morphine. This happens because the drug morphine closely mimics the chemical structure of which of the following naturally occurring hormones that inhibits pain?

      (A) GABA

      (B) Norepinephrine

      (C) Glutamate

      (D) Endorphins

2. Jasmine took part in a sleep study during which she was awakened by psychologists every time she entered REM sleep. Which of the following would happen to Jasmine when she was allowed to sleep again?

   (A) She would spend a greater amount of time in REM sleep.

   (B) She would spend a greater amount of time in stage 3 deep sleep.

   (C) She would spend more time sleepwalking.

   (D) She would have a greater amount of sleep spindles and K-complexes.

3. Bethany and Aliza are walking down the hall, and Bethany announces that they must be late to the pep rally because she can already hear the band playing the school song. Aliza cannot hear the band yet compared to Bethany because of which of the following concepts?

   (A) Absolute threshold

   (B) Just-noticeable difference

   (C) Sensory interaction

   (D) Sensory adaptation

4. Pranav is trying to decide how likely it is that he will enjoy a new class being offered at his college on positive psychology and decides to compare the characteristics of the class, such as the teacher, or other students taking the course, with other courses he has liked. Pranav is ultimately asking himself how similar one event (the positive psychology course) is to his prototype for an enjoyable class (other classes he has liked) that are familiar to him. Which problem-solving technique is Pranav using?

   (A) Representativeness heuristic

   (B) Availability heuristic

   (C) Belief perseverance

   (D) Overconfidence

5. Each person who completes an 8-item personality test is given a total score for their ratings of item numbers 1, 3, 5, and 7, as well as a total score for their ratings of item numbers 2, 4, 6, and 8. Each person ends up with two scores. The correlation across these individuals' odd-number total and even-number total are then computed. Which of the following procedures was used for this assessment?

(A) Test-retest reliability

(B) Split-half reliability

(C) Construct validity

(D) Predictive validity

6. Veronica had a stroke that damaged her hippocampus. After the stroke, she was no longer able to form new memories. However, she could still remember everything that happened in her life before the stroke. What type of amnesia is Veronica experiencing?

(A) Dissociative

(B) Anterograde

(C) Retrograde

(D) Infantile

7. Three-year-old Jimmy, who sees lots of cows on the family farm, sees a rhinoceros at the zoo and thinks it, too, is a cow. Which of the cognitive processes described by Jean Piaget does this illustrate?

(A) Assimilation

(B) Accommodation

(C) Conservation

(D) Egocentrism

8. Luke stopped hitting his brother after seeing a boy on a TV show hit someone and get punished for it. What type of learning on Luke's part does this illustrate?

   (A) Latent learning

   (B) Partial reinforcement

   (C) Generalization

   (D) Vicarious conditioning

9. Becky is strongly in favor of requiring students at public high schools to wear uniforms. During a class debate on the topic, she is assigned to generate arguments against creating a uniform policy. Which of the following will help reduce cognitive dissonance for Becky?

   (A) Becky's classmates will now be more in favor of requiring uniforms.

   (B) Becky's classmates will now be less in favor of requiring uniforms.

   (C) Becky will now be less in favor of requiring uniforms.

   (D) Becky will now be more in favor of requiring uniforms.

10. Zoey and Zach have been dating for two years, and it is almost time to start making plans for prom. Zach has told Zoey that he does not want to go to prom this year, and she is very disappointed and angry. Zoey is afraid to tell Zach how she really feels because she is afraid he might break up with her. That night at dinner, Zoey is extremely rude to her mom and dad. Which defense mechanism is Zoey most likely using?

    (A) Regression

    (B) Displacement

    (C) Reaction formation

    (D) Sublimation

11. Archie is a star athlete at his school and hopes to be drafted to play professional sports after he graduates. One day, a teammate offers to sell Archie performance-enhancing drugs that allegedly cannot be detected in drug tests. On the one hand, Archie believes that taking the drugs will give him a competitive advantage, but on the other hand, the drugs are illegal and dangerous to his long-term health. In what type of situation has Archie found himself?

    (A) Social trap

    (B) Approach-approach conflict

    (C) Approach-avoidance conflict

    (D) Avoidance-avoidance conflict

12. Cheyanna is extremely shy and anxious in social situations due to a fear of rejection or being evaluated negatively. Although she wants to have relationships, her fears of rejection and failure prevent her from being able to form friendships. Which of the following personality disorders would Cheyanna most likely be diagnosed with?

    (A) Avoidant

    (B) Schizoid

    (C) Antisocial

    (D) Borderline

13. Over the past six months, Renee has had unpredictable episodes during which she experiences a fear that something bad is about to happen. Her heart begins to race, she feels dizzy, and she has trouble catching her breath. Between episodes, Renee worries a great deal about future incidents. Which anxiety disorder does Renee most likely suffer from?

    (A) Generalized anxiety disorder

    (B) Social anxiety disorder

    (C) Panic disorder

    (D) Obsessive-compulsive disorder

14. Kenzo, who was born in Japan, experiences intense anxiety and avoids social interactions due to fear that his appearance or behavior might offend others. Which of the following conditions best describes the symptoms Kenzo is experiencing?

    (A) Tardive dyskinesia

    (B) Taijin kyofusho

    (C) Catatonic excitability

    (D) Ataque de nervios

15. Eli is sixteen and recently failed his driver's test. After the test, he concludes that he could have predicted the failure all along. He thinks he is the focus of others' attention more than his peers, demonstrating adolescent egocentrism. Which cognitive bias is being illustrated in this scenario?

    (A) Halo effect

    (B) Hindsight bias

    (C) False consensus effect

    (D) Cognitive dissonance

**Test Tip**

**Exam-Day Restrictions:** On exam day, your device will be able to run only the Bluebook digital testing app. Other apps or programs will be blocked during the actual exam, unlike when you run Bluebook for your untimed test preview and practice sessions.

## V. RESEARCH METHODS AND DESIGN QUESTIONS

A. This question format constitutes about 25% of the multiple-choice section.

1. You will be required to determine the type of research design(s) used in a given study.

2. You will be required to evaluate the appropriate use of research design elements in experimental methodology.

3. You will be required to evaluate the appropriate use of research design elements in non-experimental methodology.

4. You will be required to evaluate whether a psychological research scenario followed appropriate ethical procedures.

**B.** Sample Questions and Answers

16. Dr. Ruiz has published his research regarding Howard Gardner's theory of multiple intelligences in a scientific journal. After comparing the test scores of all the participants, the results indicate that participants who scored high in mathematical intelligence also scored fairly high in musical intelligence. Which research method did Dr. Ruiz use?

    (A) Case study

    (B) Experiment

    (C) Meta-analysis

    (D) Correlational

17. A study was conducted to determine whether looking at 3D optical illusions results in individuals leaning back and forth more than looking at 2D optical illusions. Participants were asked to view both types of images for four minutes while standing. The researchers then carefully measured how often the participants shifted their weight while viewing each type of image. What does the number of times participants shift their weight represent?

    (A) Effect size

    (B) Confounding variable

    (C) Operational definition of the independent variable

    (D) Operational definition of the dependent variable

18. In a study of general adaptation syndrome (GAS), researchers explored how mindfulness meditation strategies impacted the body's response to stress across the stages of alarm, resistance, and exhaustion. Participants had an equal chance of being placed in either a group that received meditation training or continued their usual activities without intervention. This procedure was designed to ensure that the average behavior of participants in the control group would not differ from participants in the experimental group. What procedure does this statement represent?

    (A) Random sampling

    (B) Statistical significance

    (C) Generalizability

    (D) Random assignment

19. In a study investigating posttraumatic growth, researchers aim to explore the relationship between the level of social support and the degree of positive psychological changes experienced after traumatic events. Data is collected through a survey of a representative sample. The survey measures levels of posttraumatic growth (e.g., changes in personal strength, appreciation of life) and perceived social support. The study seeks to identify whether higher levels of social support are associated with greater posttraumatic growth without manipulating the variables. Which of the following is the most significant weakness of this study?

    (A) It is difficult to obtain informed consent for research using the survey method.

    (B) The data may be inaccurate due to social desirability bias.

    (C) It is difficult to operationally define self-reported levels of social support.

    (D) The sample does not include individuals from the desired population.

20. A study examining the relationship between sleep duration and academic performance among college students revealed a correlation coefficient ($(r)=+0.63$) between the number of hours of sleep an individual receives per night and their grade point average (GPA). What does this correlation coefficient indicate about the results of the study?

    (A) A greater number of hours of sleep causes students to earn a higher GPA.

    (B) A higher GPA causes students to get more hours of sleep.

    (C) Fewer hours of sleep will predict a higher GPA.

    (D) More hours of sleep will predict a higher GPA.

21. In a study designed to understand the impact of emotions on memory, participants were told they would be tested using neutral tasks. However, some were presented with emotionally charged images to see how emotions influence memory. Participants were misled about the nature of the tasks to ensure their reactions were unaffected by their expectations. As a result of this deception, which of the following procedures must take place?

    (A) Random assignment

    (B) Double-blind procedure

    (C) Informed consent

    (D) Debriefing

22. Psychologists conducting research are required to tell all the participants that they will be involved in research, explain the procedures, and obtain written permission from each individual participant prior to the start of the study. This represents which of the following ethical requirements?

    (A) Informed consent

    (B) Debriefing

    (C) Deception

    (D) Confidentiality

## VI. DATA INTERPRETATION QUESTIONS

**A.** This question format constitutes 10% of the multiple-choice section.

1. You will be required to identify psychology-related concepts in descriptions or representations of data.

2. You will be required to calculate and interpret measures of central tendency, variation, and percentile rank for a data set.

3. You will be required to interpret quantitative and qualitative data from a table, graph, chart, figure, or diagram.

**B.** Sample Questions and Answers

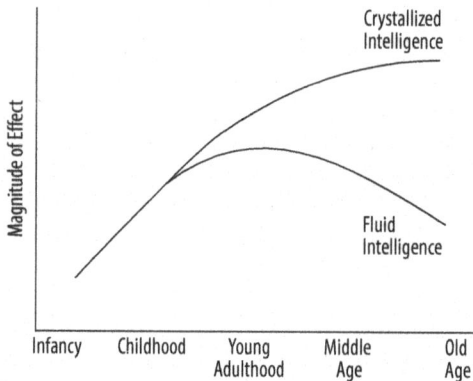

Source: ResearchGate

23. Based on the graph above, which of the following best illustrates the concepts of cognitive development and aging by examining the relationship between age and performance on tasks measuring crystallized and fluid intelligence?

   (A) Older adults tend to perform better on vocabulary tests compared to younger adults, while younger adults excel in tasks requiring abstract reasoning.

   (B) Younger adults consistently outperform older adults on vocabulary tasks.

(C) There is no significant relationship between age and performance on tasks measuring crystallized and fluid intelligence, suggesting that cognitive abilities remain stable across the lifespan.

(D) As individuals age, their performance on vocabulary tests declines significantly, while their performance on tasks requiring abstract reasoning remains relatively stable.

**Customer Arrivals by Time of Day**

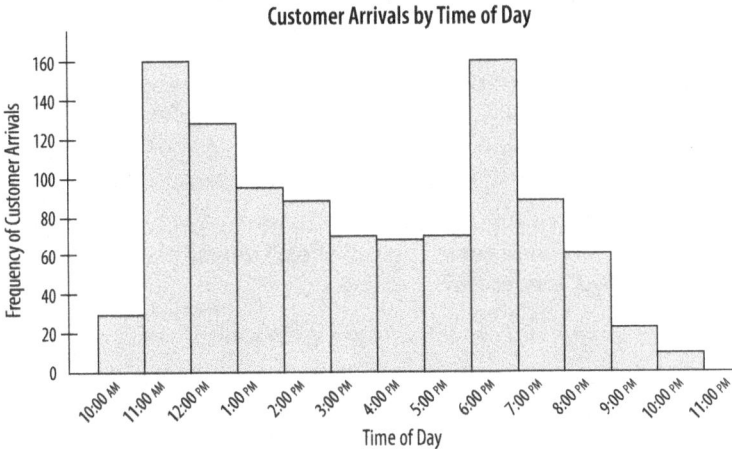

24. A restaurant owner is analyzing the distribution of customer arrivals at her new location throughout the day. She wants to identify the social norms for this neighborhood and create an appropriate staffing schedule. The graph above represents the times when customers entered the restaurant. Which of the following best describes this data?

(A) Normal

(B) Bimodal

(C) Positive skew

(D) Negative skew

25. In a study comparing the effectiveness of a new teaching method versus traditional methods on students' math performance, students were randomly assigned to one of two groups. In group A, the experimental students were exposed to a new teaching method for three months and then given an exam. The mean was 85, with a standard deviation of 10. In group B, the control group, students were exposed to a traditional teaching method for three months and then given an exam. The mean was 75, with a standard deviation of 12. Researchers calculated the effect size for group A, which was found to be large. This indicates that the new teaching method substantially improved math scores compared to the traditional method. Additionally, statistical analysis indicated that the results were likely not due to chance but were the result of the independent variable.

Given these findings, which of the following statements is accurate regarding the effect size and statistical significance of the results?

(A) large effect size, yes statistically significant

(B) small effect size, not statistically significant

(C) large effect size, not statistically significant

(D) small effect size, yes statistically significant

# ANSWERS

1. (D) is correct. The term endorphin is short for "endogenous morphine," which is the naturally occurring painkiller produced in the body. Endorphins are released in response to pain and strenuous exercise. Morphine is an effective painkiller because it is an agonist for endorphins, which means morphine binds to the same receptor sites as endorphins. GABA (A) is incorrect. It is the major inhibitory neurotransmitter and is associated with sleep and calming effects. Norepinephrine (B) is incorrect. It is associated with alertness and arousal. In the endocrine system, it is a hormone produced in the adrenal glands associated with the fight-or-flight response. Glutamate (C) is incorrect. It is the major excitatory neurotransmitter and is associated with memory and learning. *Science Practice 1.A. Apply*

*psychological perspectives, theories, concepts, and research findings to a scenario.*

2. (A) is correct. Individuals deprived of REM sleep, the stage when most dreams occur, experience REM rebound when they are allowed to return to sleep. (B) and (C) are incorrect. After being deprived of REM, an individual would not spend more time in stage 3 sleep. (D) is incorrect. After being deprived of REM, an individual would not have a greater amount of sleep spindles and K-complexes, which are associated with stage 2 sleep. *Science Practice 1.A. Apply psychological perspectives, theories, concepts, and research findings to a scenario.*

3. (A) is correct. Absolute threshold refers to the minimum level of stimulation that can be detected by an individual 50% of the time. The just-noticeable difference (B) is incorrect. It is the smallest change in or between stimuli that can be detected 50% of the time. Sensory interaction (C) is incorrect. It is when the sensory systems work together to influence how we perceive the world. Sensory adaptation (D) is incorrect. It is the reduced responsiveness in sensory receptor cells due to constant or prolonged exposure to a stimulus. *Science Practice 1.A. Apply psychological perspectives, theories, concepts, and research findings to a scenario.*

4. (A) is correct. The representativeness heuristic is being used by Pranav because he is judging the likelihood of an event (liking the new class) based on how well it matches a prototype (previous academic experiences that were positive). The availability heuristic (B) is incorrect. It is a problem-solving shortcut that involves judging the likelihood of an event in terms of how readily it comes to mind, which can result in either a correct or incorrect decision. Belief perseverance (C) is incorrect. It is a cognitive error in which individuals have a tendency to hold onto an assumption or belief even after it has been disproven. Overconfidence bias (D) is incorrect. It is a cognitive error in which individuals have a tendency to overestimate how correct their predictions and beliefs about ideas actually are. *Science Practice 1.A. Apply psychological perspectives, theories, concepts, and research findings to a scenario.*

5. (B) is correct. Split-half reliability is a measurement of consistency determined by a strong positive correlation between scores on subsets of the test (e.g., odds vs. evens or first vs. second halves). Test-retest reliability (A) is incorrect. It is a measurement of consistency determined by a strong positive correlation between the scores on the first and second administering of a test to the same group. Construct validity (C) is incorrect. It is the extent to which a test accurately measures a particular theoretical idea (construct), such as intelligence,

assertiveness, or aggression. Predictive validity (D) is incorrect. It is the extent to which a test is accurate based on how well scores correlate with scores on an established test or criterion that measures the same topic given in the future. *Science Practice 1.A. Apply psychological perspectives, theories, concepts, and research findings to a scenario.*

6.  (B) is correct. Anterograde amnesia is the inability to form new memories after the event that caused the amnesia. Dissociative amnesia (A) is incorrect. It is characterized by a partial or total inability to recall past experiences and information that does not have a biological cause. Dissociative amnesia is usually associated with a traumatic experience. Retrograde amnesia (C) is incorrect. It is an inability to recall memories that were formed prior to the event that caused the amnesia. Infantile amnesia (D) is incorrect. It is the inability to remember events before the approximate age of three due to immature brain development and cognitive abilities. *Science Practice 1.A. Apply psychological perspectives, theories, concepts, and research findings to a scenario.*

7.  (A) is correct. Assimilation, according to Piaget, is the process of taking in new information without changing the schema. Jimmy interpreted what he saw in terms of his current framework for understanding animals. Accommodation (B) is incorrect. It is the process of taking in new information and changing the schema or creating a new schema. Had Jimmy changed his understanding of animals (cows and rhinos are different), he would have been accommodating. Conservation (C) is incorrect. It is Piaget's term for the understanding that the mass, volume, weight, and quantity of an object(s) do not change even though the appearance has been altered in some way. Egocentrism (D) is incorrect. It is the difficulty of seeing how the world looks from the perspective of others. It is not about being selfish. Egocentrism is present during the stage of cognitive development that Jimmy is in currently, the preoperational stage, but is not evident in the example. *Science Practice 1.A. Apply psychological perspectives, theories, concepts, and research findings to a scenario.*

8.  (D) is correct. Vicarious conditioning is learning that occurs by observation and does not have to involve personal experience with a consequence. Luke learned that hitting would produce a punishment by seeing that someone else received a punishment for that same behavior. Latent learning (A) is incorrect. It is a type of learning that involves an organism mastering a new behavior without effort, awareness, or reinforcement; this behavior is not demonstrated unless a need or reinforcement is presented. Partial reinforcement (B) is incorrect. It is the operant conditioning technique of reinforcing the desired behavior only some of the time. Generalization (C) is incorrect.

It refers to a phenomenon that can occur during either classical or operant conditioning. In classical conditioning, it occurs when an organism learns to respond (conditioned response, CR) to stimuli that are similar to the conditioned stimulus (CS). In operant conditioning, it occurs when an organism learns to respond voluntarily to stimuli that are similar to the original stimulus. *Science Practice 1.A. Apply psychological perspectives, theories, concepts, and research findings to a scenario.*

9. (C) is correct. Becky's behavior (generating arguments against uniforms) is inconsistent with her preexisting attitude (a favorable view about uniforms). This inconsistency produces discomfort, motivating Becky to reduce the tension by changing her attitude to one that is more consistent with her behavior. Options (A) and (B) are incorrect, Cognitive dissonance theory does not apply to situations involving the behaviors of others. Option (D) is incorrect. Becky's thoughts and behaviors continue to be in conflict; therefore, cognitive dissonance is not being reduced. *Science Practice 1.A. Apply psychological perspectives, theories, concepts, and research findings to a scenario.*

10. (B) is correct. Zoey is using the defense mechanism of displacement that involves unconsciously reducing anxiety by taking out aggression on someone or something that is less powerful or threatening than the true source of anxiety. Zoey is really angry at her boyfriend Zach but unconsciously takes her aggression out on her parents because she knows they will still love her, making them a safer target. Regression (A) is incorrect. It involves unconsciously reducing anxiety by reverting to thoughts and behaviors that would be more appropriate during an earlier period of development. Reaction formation (C) is incorrect. It involves unconsciously reducing anxiety by acting or saying the exact opposite of the morally or socially unacceptable beliefs held by an individual. Sublimation (D) is incorrect. It involves unconsciously reducing anxiety by directing aggression toward a more socially acceptable outlet, such as exercise, hard work, sports, or hobbies. Sublimation is viewed as a healthier version of displacement. *Science Practice 1.A. Apply psychological perspectives, theories, concepts, and research findings to a scenario.*

11. (C) is correct. Archie is involved in an approach-avoidance conflict because he must make a decision about a situation in which he is both attracted to and repelled by the same option. It is a situation that offers advantages and disadvantages. A social trap (A) is incorrect. A social trap is a situation in which individuals must choose whether to cooperate or compete with others. An approach-approach conflict (B) is incorrect. It is a situation in which an individual is forced to make a choice between two equally desirable goals. Both

options are appealing, which makes the choice difficult. If Archie is offered a position on two professional sports teams and he likes both of them, that would be an approach-approach conflict. An avoidance-avoidance conflict (D) is incorrect. It is a situation in which an individual is forced to make a choice between two equally undesirable or threatening options. Neither choice is good, so the individual is essentially choosing the lesser of two evils. By the way, in case you are wondering, Archie made the right decision and did not take the drugs. *Science Practice 1.A. Apply psychological perspectives, theories, concepts, and research findings to a scenario.*

12. (A) is correct. The essential feature of avoidant personality disorder is a pattern of excessive shyness in social situations, feeling inadequate, and hypersensitivity to negative evaluations. A schizoid personality disorder (B) is incorrect. Its essential feature is a pattern of social detachment and a narrow range of emotional responses in social situations. An antisocial personality disorder (C) is incorrect. Its essential feature is a pattern of disregard and violation of the rights of others and a lack of remorse. It is most closely associated with criminal behavior. A borderline personality disorder (D) is incorrect. Its essential feature is a pattern of instability in relationships, self-image, and emotions. It is marked by impulsiveness that is self-damaging. *Science Practice 1.A. Apply psychological perspectives, theories, concepts, and research findings to a scenario.*

13. (C) is correct. Panic disorder is an anxiety disorder that lasts a minimum of one month following a panic attack and involves fear about future panic attacks or a major dysfunctional change in behavior. Generalized anxiety disorder (A) is incorrect. It is an anxiety disorder that involves a widespread and persistent worry (anxiety) related to various areas or activities and is present most days. The anxiety is free-floating, not specific to one event, and difficult to control. Social anxiety disorder (B) is incorrect. It is an anxiety disorder that involves an intense fear of being scrutinized while interacting with others that prevents social interactions because of the potential threat of embarrassment or judgment. Obsessive-compulsive disorder (D) is incorrect. It is a disorder involving unreasonable thoughts that result in anxiety (obsessions) and/or specific behaviors or rituals an individual feels compelled to perform (compulsions) that reduce or prevent anxiety. The symptoms must consume more than one hour per day or cause distress or dysfunction. *Science Practice 1.A. Apply psychological perspectives, theories, concepts, and research findings to a scenario.*

14. (B) is correct. Taijin kyofusho is a culture-bound anxiety disorder experienced mainly by Japanese people characterized by an intense fear that others are judging their bodies as offensive or unpleasant.

Tardive dyskinesia (A) is incorrect. It is a movement disorder characterized by involuntary movements of the face, tongue, or limbs. It is associated with long-term use of antipsychotics that regulate dopamine. Catatonic excitability (C) is incorrect. It is a type of disorganized motor behavior that is considered a positive symptom of schizophrenia. Ataque de nervios (D) is incorrect. It is a culture-bound anxiety disorder experienced mainly by individuals of Caribbean or Iberian descent characterized by a range of symptoms, such as convulsions, partial loss of consciousness, heart palpitations, numbness, sudden emotional outbursts, and sensations of heat ascending to the head. *Science Practice 1.B. Explain how cultural norms, expectations, and circumstances, as well as cognitive biases, apply to behavior and mental processes.*

15. (B) Hindsight bias is correct. It is the tendency to think the outcome is obvious after it is known. Halo effect (A) is incorrect. It is the tendency to assume that people with a positive general impression or one positive trait (e.g., attractiveness) also have other positive traits (e.g., intelligence, happiness, friendliness). False consensus effect (C) is incorrect. This occurs when an individual overestimates how many others agree with them or share their beliefs. Cognitive dissonance (D) is incorrect. It involves the unpleasant state (tension) experienced when holding two conflicting beliefs or when behaviors and beliefs do not match. *Science Practice 1.B. Explain how cultural norms, expectations, and circumstances, as well as cognitive biases, apply to behavior and mental processes.*

16. (D) is correct. Correlational research was used because Dr. Ruiz determined a relationship between scores on two different portions of the test. Correlational studies can show the strength and direction of the relationship between variables. This study reveals a positive correlation between mathematical and musical intelligence. Case study (A) is incorrect. A case study involves investigating an individual or group in great depth. Experiment (B) is incorrect. There is no indication that participants were randomly assigned to different conditions, a key component of experimental research. Meta-analysis (C) is incorrect. A meta-analysis involves statistically combining data from multiple studies to draw broader conclusions. Dr. Ruiz's study, however, analyzed data from a single group of participants to identify correlations, not multiple studies. *Science Practice 2.A. Determine the type of research design(s) used in a given study.*

17. (D) is correct. The number of times participants shifted their weight is the dependent variable, which is operationally defined because it is specific and measurable. Effect size (A) is incorrect. It is the meaningfulness of a relationship between variables. It often indicates

the practical significance of the findings. Confounding variable (B) is incorrect. They are factors other than the independent variable (IV) that impacted the dependent variable (DV) but are not intentionally studied. Operational definition of the independent variable (C) is incorrect. The IV is the type of image (three-dimensional vs. two-dimensional optical illusions). *Science Practice 2.B. Evaluate the appropriate use of research design elements in experimental methodology.*

18. (D) is correct. Random assignment is correct because it ensures that each participant has an equal chance of being assigned to either the control or experimental group. Random sampling (A) is incorrect. It refers to choosing participants from a population so that each has an equal chance of being included in the sample. Statistical significance (B) is incorrect. It relates to the probability that a study's observed results are likely not due to chance and are instead the result of the experimental manipulations. Generalizability (C) is incorrect. It refers to the extent to which a study's results can be applied to the population. *Science Practice 2.B. Evaluate the appropriate use of research design elements in experimental methodology.*

19. (B) is correct. The data's self-report nature may lead to the social desirability bias, affecting the accuracy of the results. Participants may respond in ways they perceive as favorable rather than providing authentic answers when asked about subjective experiences like social support and personal growth. Option (A) is incorrect. Obtaining informed consent for survey research is generally straightforward when the study design and purpose are clearly communicated. Option (C) is incorrect. Self-reported levels of social support can be operationally defined by using well-constructed survey items validated in previous research. Option (D) is incorrect. A representative sample was used, which means they match the population being studied. *Science Practice 2.C. Evaluate the appropriate use of research design elements in non-experimental methodologies.*

20. (D) is correct. This is correct because the correlation coefficient of +0.63 indicates that an increase in sleep hours is associated with an increase in GPA. Correlations provide a prediction, not a causal statement. Option (A) is incorrect. Correlation does not prove causation. The correlation coefficient indicates a positive association between the two variables. An experiment that uses random assignment would be necessary to determine causation. Option (B) is incorrect. Correlation does not prove causation. The correlation coefficient indicates a positive association between the two variables. An experiment that uses random assignment would be necessary to determine causation. Option (C) is incorrect. This option describes a negative correlation, in which one variable decreases while the other

increases. The correlation coefficient from the study was positive. *Science Practice 2.C. Evaluate the appropriate use of research design elements in non-experimental methodologies.*

21. (D) is correct. Debriefing is required when deception is used. It is intended to explain the true purpose of the research and make the participants feel comfortable with their participation before leaving. Random assignment (A) is incorrect. It is a process used in experiments to control for confounding variables and establish cause-and-effect relationships. Double-blind procedure (B) is incorrect. It is a research procedure in which both the experimenter and the participants are unaware of who is in the control or experimental group. Informed consent (C) is incorrect. Before the study, researchers must explain the details, and participants must agree to participate. *Science Practice 2.D. Evaluate whether a psychological research scenario followed appropriate ethical procedures.*

22. (A) is correct. Informed consent involves researchers telling (informing) participants about the features of the experiment prior to the study and obtaining their signed agreements to participate based on a full understanding of their rights. Debriefing (B) is incorrect. It requires psychologists to fully explain the research and inform participants if any deception was involved immediately after the study ends. Deception (C) is incorrect. It is the purposeful misleading of participants to obtain more genuine results. If deception is used in research, it must be revealed in the debriefing process. Confidentiality (D) is incorrect. It requires researchers to protect the identity of all participants. Researchers are permitted to break confidentiality if the individual provides written permission or is in danger of causing harm to themselves or others. *Science Practice 2.D. Evaluate whether a psychological research scenario followed appropriate ethical procedures.*

23. (A) is correct. Crystallized intelligence is the acquired knowledge of vocabulary, verbal skills, cultural knowledge, and factual information that would be measured on a vocabulary test. Fluid intelligence is the rapid processing of information and memory span used to solve novel problems and make new associations with existing knowledge that would be measured with tasks requiring abstract reasoning. The two intelligences become more distinct with age. Crystallized intelligence remains stable with age, but fluid intelligence peaks in young adulthood and then declines. Option (B) is incorrect. Older adults typically perform better on tasks that depend on accumulated knowledge and experience, such as vocabulary. Crystallized intelligence (like vocabulary skills) generally improves or remains stable with age. Option (C) is incorrect. The graph indicates distinct age-related trends in different cognitive abilities. While some aspects

of cognitive abilities, such as crystallized intelligence, may remain stable or decrease slightly, others, such as fluid intelligence, typically decline with old age. Option (D) is incorrect. Generally, performance on tasks requiring crystallized intelligence, like vocabulary tests, does not decline significantly with age but remains stable or decreases slightly. Performance on tasks requiring fluid intelligence, such as abstract reasoning, typically declines with age. *Science Practice 3.A. Identify psychology-related concepts in descriptions or representations of data.*

24. **(B) is correct.** The data is bimodal because it has two distinct peaks around midday and evening. This pattern is characteristic of a bimodal distribution, in which two separate modes are prominent. Normal (A) is incorrect. A normal distribution is characterized by a single, central peak, with data symmetrically distributed around the mean. Positive skew (C) is incorrect. A positively skewed distribution has a tail that extends to the right, meaning most of the data are concentrated on the left. Negative skew (D) is incorrect. A negatively skewed distribution has a tail that extends to the left, indicating that most of the data are concentrated on the right. *Science Practice 3.B. Calculate and interpret measures of central tendency, variation, and percentile rank in a given data set.*

25. **(A) is correct.** The study had a large effect size and was statistically significant, meaning the results are unlikely to have occurred by chance. (B) is incorrect. The correct answer is opposite of both of these options. The results have both a large effect size and are statistically significant. (C) is incorrect. While this option correctly identifies a large effect size, it incorrectly suggests the results are not statistically significant. (D) is incorrect. This option incorrectly reports a small effect size, but correctly indicates the results are statistically significant. *Science Practice 3.C. Interpret quantitative or qualitative inferential data from a given table, graph, chart, figure, or diagram.*

# Mastering the Free-Response Questions

## I. TIMING AND SCORING OF FREE-RESPONSE QUESTIONS (FRQs)

A. Your score for the free-response questions (FRQs) on the exam is based on your answers to two questions and comprises 33.3% of your total AP® exam score. Each of the two free-response questions is equally weighted. You will have 70 minutes (one hour and 10 minutes) to complete your responses to both the questions.

B. The free-response questions assess all four science practices and involve summarized peer-reviewed research.

C. Following is a chart showing the breakdown of the FRQ section of the exam.

FRQ Overview

| Question Type | Number of Sources | Suggested Time Limit | Science Practices Assessed | Percentage of Exam Score |
|---|---|---|---|---|
| Article Analysis Question (AAQ) | 1 | 25 minutes total<br><br>10-minute reading period<br><br>15 minutes writing | 2: Research methods and design<br><br>3: Data interpretation<br><br>4: Argumentation | 16.65% |
| Evidence-Based Question (EBQ) | 3 | 45 minutes total<br><br>15-minute reading period<br><br>30 minutes writing | 1: Concept application<br><br>4: Argumentation | 16.65% |

## II.   TOP 5 TIPS FOR ANSWERING A FREE-RESPONSE QUESTION

A. Read the question and be sure you understand what the question is asking you. In other words, read the full question (RTFQ).

B. Use the digital tools available to help you evaluate questions. Take a few minutes to create a plan for how you will answer the question.

   1. You can preview these resources in the AP® Classroom online platform and the Bluebook app. Your teacher may be using practice in AP® Classroom throughout the year, but the AP® exam will be completed in the Bluebook application.

   2. While doing the practice questions in Bluebook, the test preview is untimed. However, on exam day there will be a running timer at the top of the page. In the directions it will say you can go back and forth between questions in the free-response section until time expires. You will NOT be able to return to the multiple-choice section. The timer will turn red when there are 5 minutes left and the proctor will NOT give you any time warnings. If you have an extra time accommodation, you will receive that accommodation on exam day in Bluebook.

   3. You will be able to annotate the articles with a variety of tools, such as highlighting in multiple colors, underlining, and making notes. These tools are located in the upper-right corner of the screen.

   4. You will have access to keyboard shortcuts listed under the "More" option in the upper-right corner of the screen.

   5. You will be allowed to copy and paste in your boxes, but not from the actual documents.

   6. You will have access to a line reader to help you focus as you read the article. This is a tool you will want to practice with so you can be completely comfortable with it on exam day, and use it to its full advantage.

C. Send in a "reserve player" (an extra answer that may be able to score the point).

   1. On the EBQ, you will be asked to support your claim with a piece of evidence and support your claim using a psychological concept, perspective, theory, or research finding.

   2. Sending in a "reserve player" by giving an additional example helps you earn the point in case one of your required responses is wrong. This approach offers you protection because if one of your

examples is incomplete or inaccurate, you might be able to score a point with your extra example.

3. Even if you are confident in your original answer, take a moment to call in a "reserve player" if you have additional time available!

D. Time management is essential, so take into account the suggested pacing for each question.

1. You have 25 minutes for the AAQ, including a suggested 10-minute reading period and a 15-minute writing period.

2. You have 45 minutes for the EBQ, including a suggested 15-minute reading period and a 30-minute writing period.

3. You can move between the two FRQs at any time. If you finish the AAQ early, you may move ahead to the EBQ, and if you have any time left at the end, you should go back and review your answers and add in "reserve players"for the EBQ.

E. Be aware of what is being asked of you based on the verb used in each part of the question. Mark the verb in each part of the question to remind yourself of the directions. Some of the most commonly used verbs on the FRQs and what they mean in terms of your response are provided in the chart that follows.

**Test Tip**

**Line Reader Tool:** Use this feature on exam day to help stay focused while reading questions, prompts, and articles. It will help keep you from missing key details.

## III. AAQ FREE-RESPONSE VERBS

| FRQ Verb | Question Stem |
|---|---|
| Identify/ State | Express the psychological concept briefly and clearly. This verb will appear in parts A, B, and D of the AAQ. <br><br> • Part A Question Stem: **Identify** the research method used in the study. <br><br> • Part B Question Stem: **State** the operational definition of a variable indicated in the study. <br><br> • Part D Question Stem: **Identify** at least one ethical guideline applied by the researchers. |

*(continued)*

| FRQ Verb | Question Stem |
|---|---|
| **Describe** | Provide specific and relevant qualities of the psychological concept.<br><br>This verb will appear in part C of the AAQ.<br><br>• Part C Question Stem: **Describe** the identified statistic in the study. |
| **Explain** | Give enough of a description or information to make something easy to understand.<br><br>This verb will appear in part E and part F of the AAQ.<br><br>• Part E Question Stem: **Explain** the extent to which the research findings may or may not be generalizable using specific and relevant evidence from the study.<br><br>• Part F Question Stem: **Explain** how at least one of the research findings supports or refutes a psychological concept or the researcher's hypothesis. |
| **Use Evidence** | Use specific information from the documents to provide reasoning to explain whether a claim should be upheld. Specific details may include data, rationales, or conclusions.<br><br>This verb will appear in part E of the AAQ.<br><br>• Part E Question Stem: Explain the extent to which the research findings may or may not be generalizable **using specific and relevant evidence** from the study. |
| **Support or Refute** | Provide reasoning that explains whether a statement should be upheld or rejected.<br><br>This verb will appear in part F of the AAQ.<br><br>• Part F Question Stem: Explain how at least one of the research findings **supports or refutes** a psychological concept or the researcher's hypothesis. |

## IV. EBQ FREE-RESPONSE VERBS

| FRQ Verb | Question Stem |
|---|---|
| **Propose** | Suggest a claim.<br><br>This verb will appear in part A of the EBQ.<br><br>• Part A Question Stem: **Propose** a specific and defensible claim based in psychological science that responds to the question. |
| **Support/ Use Evidence** | Use specific information from the documents to provide reasoning to explain whether a claim should be upheld. Specific details may include data, rationales, hypotheses, or conclusions.<br><br>This verb will appear in parts B (i) and C (i) of the EBQ.<br><br>• Part B (i) Question Stem: **Support** your claim **using at least one piece of specific and relevant evidence** from one of the sources.<br><br>• Part C (i) Question Stem: **Support** your claim **using an additional piece of specific and relevant evidence** from a different source than the one that was used in Part B (i). |
| **Cite Your Evidence** | Mention the source your evidence came from.<br><br>• **Cite** your sources in parentheses after the evidence. "For example, .... (Source 2)."<br><br>• **Cite** your source by incorporating it into the sentence directly. For example, "According to Source 2..." |
| **Explain** | Give enough of a description or information to make something easy to understand.<br><br>This verb will appear in parts B (ii) and C (ii) of the EBQ.<br><br>• Part B (ii) Question Stem: **Explain** how the evidence from Part B (i) supports your claim using a psychological perspective, theory, concept, or research finding learned in AP® Psychology.<br><br>• Part C (ii) Question Stem: **Explain** how the evidence from Part C (i) supports your claim using a different psychological perspective, theory, concept, or research finding learned in AP® Psychology than the one that was used in Part B (ii). |

*(continued)*

| FRQ Verb | Question Stem |
|----------|---------------|
| **Apply** | Make use of a psychological concept. |
|  | This verb will appear in part B (ii) and part C (ii) of the EBQ. |
|  | • Part B (ii) Question Stem: Explain how the evidence from Part B (i) supports your claim **using** a psychological perspective, theory, concept, or research finding learned in AP® Psychology. |
|  | • Part C (ii) Question Stem: Explain how the evidence from Part C (i) supports your claim **using** a different psychological perspective, theory, concept, or research finding learned in AP® Psychology than the one that was used in Part B (ii). |

**Test Tip**

The readers who will be evaluating your free-response questions are "gatherers," not "hunters." They will be glad to pick up the points that are apparent in your answer, but they will not infer your meaning.

## V. SCORING OF THE TWO TYPES OF FRQs

A. Section II of the exam consists of two distinct types of free-response questions that are all weighted the same in terms of your overall exam score.

B. **Article Analysis Question (AAQ):** The article analysis question involves examining one summarized peer-reviewed study.

1. **Part A: Research Method (1 point)**

   i. This part of the question will ask you to accurately **identify** the research method in the study.

   ii. You WILL be assessed on Science Practice 2.A. Determine the type of research design(s) in a given study.

   iii. Your answer options WILL be the following: experiment, correlation, case study, naturalistic observation, and meta-analysis.

2. **Part B: Operationally Define the Research Variable (1 point)**

   i. This part of the question will ask you to **state** a measurable or quantifiable definition of the identified variable as used in the study.

   ii. DO NOT define the identified word; instead, make it measurable or quantifiable (an operational definition).

   > Happiness is being content WILL NOT score.

   > Happiness is the score on the Likert scale WILL score.

3. **Part C: Statistic Interpretation (1 point)**

   i. This part of the question will ask you to accurately **describe** the identified statistic in relation to the study.

   ii. You WILL be assessed on Science Practice 3: Data Interpretation.

   iii. You WILL need to interpret the statistic rather than restate it.

   > The mean for group 1 is 5 and the mean for group 2 is 6 WILL NOT score.

   > The mean is the average score of the group WILL NOT score.

   > The means show the experimental group had better recall WILL score.

4. **Part D: Ethical Guideline (1 point)**

   i. This part of the question will ask you to accurately **identify** at least one ethical guideline applied by the researchers in the study.

   ii. You WILL be assessed on Science Practice 2.D. Ethical guidelines include: institutional review, informed consent/assent, protection from harm, confidentiality, anonymity, and debriefing.

   iii. You MUST provide an ethical guideline specifically indicated in the study.

   iv. You CANNOT use informed consent if it was not discussed in the study.

   v. Your answer MUST be related to ethics, not the research design (e.g., double-blind technique, random assignment).

   vi. Use the term *informed consent/assent* rather than an element of informed consent such as voluntary participation or the right to withdraw.

5. **Part E: Generalizability (1 point)**

   i. This part of the question will ask you to **explain** the extent to which the study is generalizable using **specific and relevant evidence** referencing participant variables from the study.

   ii. You MUST reference a population relevant to the study's participants.

   iii. You MUST describe the specific sample used in the study and whether it does or does not match the relevant population.

   ➤ Consider using the phrase, "The study is generalizable to . . . [relevant population] . . . because . . . the specific sample used was. . . .

   iv. Reminder: To be generalizable, your sample should be representative of the relevant population.

   v. Reminder: Generalizability is the goal of all research methods and is made possible by using a representative sampling process. It is not directly related to random assignment in experiments!

   vi. Reminder: Sample size will often not score, so have an additional example related to how the sample is representative of the population.

6. **Part F: Argumentation (2 points)**

   i. This part of the question will ask you to use a **specific** result from the study to bold the phrase **explain how** the results **support or refute** the psychological concept or hypothesis presented in the question.

   ii. You MUST interpret the results accurately.

   iii. Your answer MUST provide the results (1 point) AND explain how those results support or refute the psychological concept or hypothesis (1 point).

**Test Tip**

Remember to pay attention to task verbs. If you are asked to identify or state, your response will likely be shorter. However, if you are asked to describe or explain, your response will likely be longer.

**C. Evidence-Based Question (EBQ):** The evidence-based question involves forming a well-reasoned argument that is supported by evidence from two of the three summarized peer-reviewed source studies on a common topic.

1. **Part A: Claim (1 point)**

   i. This part of the question will ask you to propose a defensible claim based on psychological science that is relevant to the question.

   ii. The question is located in the stem right above part A. You MUST make sure your claim responds to this question being asked.

   iii. Your claim MUST meet the following criteria:

      ➤ It is clear.

      ➤ It takes a firm position.

      ➤ It addresses the prompt and can be supported with evidence.

      ➤ Do not start supporting or explaining your claim in the answer box for part A.

2. **Part B (i): Evidence (1 point)**

   i. This part of the question will ask you to use one piece of correctly cited, specific, and relevant evidence from one of the provided articles.

      ➤ Provide a specific AND relevant statistic, fact, example, description, or quotation to support your claim.

      ➤ Evidence is NOT opinion-based.

   ii. The evidence MUST be correctly cited.

      ➤ For example, "The mean number of reported symptoms was lower in the experimental group than in the control group (Source 2)."

      ➤ Text prior to the citation will be considered evidence. Using the method above will completely separate the evidence from the explanation and application for the AP® exam reader.

3. **Part B (ii): Explanation and Application (2 points)**

   i. This part of the question will ask you to explain how the evidence supports your claim (1 point) AND correctly apply a psychological perspective, theory, concept, or research finding (1 point).

   ➤ Clearly and explicitly make connections to explain how the evidence you have presented supports your claim.

   – For example, "This evidence supports the claim that... (repeat your claim) because..."

   – Clearly explain the relationship between the evidence and your claim by making an inference. Do not simply restate the evidence.

   ➤ You MUST correctly apply a psychological perspective, theory, concept, or research finding that is explicitly identified in the AP® Psychology Course and Exam Description.

   – Underline the <u>concept</u>, to point it out to the AP® exam reader. It must be clear that you understand the concept and that it applies to your claim. You cannot just use the concept in a sentence or "term drop."

   – The psychological perspective, theory, or concept should NOT already be found in the article.

   – Applying a psychological perspective is a great "reserve player" to add to your answer.

4. **Part C (i): Evidence (1 point)**

   i. This part of the question will ask you to support your claim with a different piece of correctly cited, specific, and relevant evidence from either of the other two provided sources.

   ➤ Provide a specific AND relevant statistic, fact, example, description, or quotation to support your claim.

   ➤ Evidence is NOT opinion-based.

   ii. The evidence MUST be correctly cited.

   ➤ For example, "Distributed studying led to increased test scores for high school students (Source 3)."

   ➤ Text prior to the citation will be considered evidence. Using the method above will clearly separate the evidence from the explanation and application for the AP® exam reader.

5. **Part C (ii): Explanation and Application (2 points)**

   i.  This part of the question will ask you to explain how the evidence supports your claim (1 point) AND correctly apply a different psychological perspective, theory, concept, or research finding (1 point).

   ➤ Clearly and explicitly, make connections to explain how the evidence you have presented supports your argument.

   – For example, "This evidence supports the claim that... (repeat your claim) because..."

   – Clearly explain the relationship between the evidence and your claim by making an inference. Do not simply restate the evidence.

   ➤ You MUST correctly apply a different psychological perspective, theory, concept, or research finding that is explicitly identified in the AP® Psychology Course and Exam Description.

   – Underline the <u>concept</u>, to point it out to the AP® exam reader. It must be clear that you understand the concept and that it applies to your claim. You cannot just use the concept in a sentence or "term drop."

   – The psychological perspective, theory, or concept should NOT already be found in the article.

   – Applying a psychological perspective is a great "reserve player" to add to your answer.

6. For parts B and C, there should be three total items in each answer box. Consider using this organization to guarantee you do all three.

   i.  State your evidence **before** the citation (Source number).

   ii. **After** the citation explain the evidence with the sentence stem, "This evidence supports the claim that...(repeat your claim) because..."

   iii. Finally, apply a psychological perspective, theory, concept, or research finding to explain how the evidence supports the claim. **Underline** this concept to point it out to the AP® exam reader.

**Test Tip** **Use the Digital Tools:** Practice using the Bluebook app's annotation tools (highlighting, underlining, and notes) to organize your thoughts while reading and answering free-response questions.

## VI. SAMPLES

### Question 1: Article Analysis Question (AAQ)

Your response should be presented in six parts: A, B, C, D, E, and F. Write the response to each part of the question in complete sentences. Use appropriate psychological terminology in your response.

Using the source provided, respond to all parts of the question.

(A) Identify the research method used in the study.

(B) State the operational definition of the dependent variable.

(C) Describe what the differences in the means indicates for the common and uncommon conceptual category groups in the third section of the list.

(D) Identify at least one ethical guideline applied by the researchers.

(E) Explain the extent to which the research findings may or may not be generalizable using specific and relevant evidence from the study.

(F) Explain how a finding from the study supports the researchers' hypothesis that the placement of a word in a list influences recall, consistent with previous findings on the primacy and recency effects.

### Source

| Introduction |
|---|
| Previous research has shown that words at the beginning and end of a list are more readily recalled than those in the middle due to the primacy and recency effects. This study aimed to explore this effect further using a list with a common conceptual category and one without to determine the impact of list composition on recall. |

| Participants |
|---|
| The study involved 20 University of Western Ontario students, ten from the university and ten from affiliate schools. The participants consisted of 14 females and 6 males between the ages of 18 and 22, majoring mainly in psychology, with a few in philosophy or political science. Participants were selected based on their availability and willingness to engage in the study. Before beginning the experiment, each participant was given a detailed letter outlining the study's purpose, procedures, and potential risks. Participants were required to sign a form acknowledging that they understood the information provided and agreed voluntarily to be in the study. |

*(continued)*

## Method

The study exposed the same group of participants to two different conditions to see how they performed under each. This approach allowed researchers to directly compare the effects of different types of word lists on memory recall. Participants were presented with two types of word lists. One list contained words belonging to a common conceptual category—animals. This meant that all the words in this list were names of animals, which share a thematic connection. The second type of list was composed of words that did not share any common conceptual theme; these words were randomly selected without any thematic linkage.

The words for both lists were nouns and chosen based on their concreteness, imagery, and meaningfulness values. Concreteness refers to how tangible or sensory a word is, imagery involves how easily a word can evoke a mental picture, and meaningfulness measures how many associations a person can make with a word. These characteristics were controlled to ensure that any differences in recall could be attributed more likely to the type of list (common conceptual category or not) rather than differences in how easily the words could be visualized or their relevance to the participants.

Each participant was read one list at a time, with a brief pause between the presentation of each word. This allowed participants time to process each word individually. After the reading session, participants were given a sheet of paper numbered 1 to 18 and asked to write down as many words from the list as they could recall in any order. This measure of recall was used to assess their memory performance.

To analyze the data, the researchers calculated the average number of words recalled from each third of the list (first six, middle six, and last six) for each list type. These averages were then compared to see if there were differences in recall depending on the list type and the position of the words in the list. This analysis helped in understanding how the organization of words and their thematic connections influenced memory recall.

## Results and Discussion

Results showed a typical serial position effect in both lists, with higher recall rates for the first and last six than for the middle six words. In the common conceptual category, the difference in recall between the last six and middle six words is less pronounced than the uncommon category. In the common category, the average recall for the last six words is 2.6, while for the middle six, it's 2.4. In the uncommon category, the average recall for the last six words is 3.6, while for the middle six words, it's 1.3. Overall, the average recall for each section, except for the final six words, is higher for the common

*(continued)*

category list compared to the uncommon list. The third section of the uncommon list has a higher recall than the third section of the common list.

| Mean words correctly recalled for common and uncommon concept lists | | | |
|---|---|---|---|
| List Type | Mean Recall for First 6 Words | Mean Recall for Second 6 Words | Mean Recall for Third 6 Words |
| Common | 3.6 | 2.4 | 2.6 |
| Uncommon | 2.5 | 1.3 | 3.6 |

The study confirmed the serial position effect and that the results have statistical significance. However, the study did not find that a common conceptual category significantly improved overall recall.

*Adapted from The Huron University College Journal of Learning and Motivation.*
*Lowe, A. (2012). A special place in our minds: Examining the serial position*
*effect. The Huron University College Journal of Learning and Motivation,*
*50 (1), Article 6. https://ir.lib.uwo.ca/hucjlm/vol50/iss1/6*

**Sample Response**

(A) The research method is an experiment.

(B) The operational definition of the dependent variable is the average number of words recalled from the list.

(C) The means indicates that the uncommon group had better recall than the common group for the third part of the list.

(D) The researchers obtained informed consent from participants.

(E) The study is generalizable to college students majoring in psychology, philosophy, or political science ONLY because that is the only group the researchers used in the sample.

(F) The mean recall for the first six words (3.6) and last six words (2.6) was higher than the mean recall for the second six words (2.4) for the common group. The mean recall for the first six words (2.5) and last six words (3.6) was higher than the mean recall for the second six words (1.3) for the uncommon group. This study shows that recall is higher in both groups for words located at the beginning or end of a list, which is consistent with previous findings on primacy and recency effects.

## Scoring Guidelines for the Article Analysis Question (AAQ)

| Part A | 0 Points | 1 Point |
|---|---|---|
| Research Method | Does not accurately identify the research method used in the study. | Accurately identifies the research method used in the study. |
| Example | The research method is a correlational study. | The research method is an experiment. |
| **Part B** | **0 Points** | **1 Point** |
| Research Variable | Does not state a measurable or quantifiable definition of the identified variable used in the study. | States a measurable or quantifiable definition of the identified variable used in the study. |
| Example | • The dependent variable was the word list. [The response was the independent variable and was not operationally defined.] <br><br> • The dependent variable was memory. [The response was not operationally defined.] | The operational definition of the dependent variable is the average number of words recalled from the list. |
| **Part C** | **0 Points** | **1 Point** |
| Statistic Interpretation | Does not accurately describe the identified statistic in relation to the study. | Accurately describes the identified statistic in relation to the study. |
| Example | • The difference in the means indicates they were different. [The response does not describe what this difference means.] <br><br> • The mean for the common group was 2.6 and the mean for the uncommon group was 3.6. [The response does not describe what this difference means.] | The means show that the uncommon group had better recall than the common group for the third part of the list. |
| **Part D** | **0 Points** | **1 Point** |
| Ethical Guidelines | Does not accurately identify at least one ethical guideline applied by researchers in the study. | Accurately identifies at least one ethical guideline applied by researchers in the study. |

*(continued)*

| Example | • The researchers used a convenience sample. [The response indicates a research design element, not an ethical guideline.]<br>• The researchers made sure participation was voluntary. | • The researchers obtained informed consent from participants. |
|---|---|---|
| **Part E**<br>**Generalizability** | **0 Points**<br>Does not propose a claim regarding the generalizability of the study to a population (general or specific).<br>**OR**<br>Does not use specific and relevant evidence that references participant variables, which would impact the generalizability of the study. | **1 Point**<br>Explains the extent to which the study is generalizable using specific and relevant evidence referencing participant variables from the study. |
| Example | • The study is generalizable.<br>• The study is generalizable to the larger population. | • The use of a convenience sample, consisting of University of Western Ontario students mainly majoring in psychology, philosophy, or political science, may limit the generalizability of the results to a population of all college students.<br>• The study is generalizable to college students majoring in psychology, philosophy, or political science ONLY because that is the only group the researchers used. |

*(continued)*

| Part F | 0 Points | 1 Point | 2 Points |
|---|---|---|---|
| **Argumentation** | Does not accurately explain how the results of the study support or refute the psychological concept or hypothesis presented in the question. | Uses the results of the study but does not explain how the psychological concept or hypothesis is supported or refuted.<br><br>**OR**<br><br>Explains that the psychological concept or hypothesis is supported or refuted but does not use any results from the study. | Uses a specific result from the study to explain how the results support or refute the psychological concept or hypothesis presented in the question. The results are accurately interpreted. |
| **Example** | • The study shows that word order impacts memory. | • The mean recall for the first (3.6) and last six words (2.6) was higher than the mean recall for the second six words (2.4) for the common group. The mean recall for the first (2.5) and last six words (3.6) was higher than the mean recall for the second six words (1.3) for the uncommon group. [The response uses results from the study without further explanation.]<br><br>• Words are better recalled based on where they are located on a list. [The response provides an explanation without using results.] | • The mean recall for the first (3.6) and last six words (2.6) was higher than the mean recall for the second six words (2.4) for the common group. The mean recall for the first (2.5) and last six words (3.6) was higher than the mean recall for the second six words (1.3) for the uncommon group. This study shows that recall for words is higher in both groups if they are located at the beginning or end of a list, which is consistent with previous findings on primacy and recency effects. |

### Question 2: Evidence-Based Question (EBQ)

This question has three parts: Part A, Part B, and Part C. Use the three sources provided to answer all parts of the question.

For Part B and Part C, you must cite the source that you used to answer the question. You can do this in two different ways.

- Parenthetical Citation:

  For example: ". . . (Source 1)"

- Embedded Citation:

  For example: "According to Source 1, . . ."

Write the response to each part of the question in complete sentences. Use appropriate psychological terminology.

Using the sources provided, develop and justify an argument about the role of expectations in performance.

   A. Propose a specific and defensible claim based in psychological science that responds to the question.

   B. (i) Support your claim using at least one piece of specific and relevant evidence from one of the sources.

      (ii) Explain how the evidence from Part B (i) supports your claim using a psychological perspective, theory, concept, or research finding learned in AP® Psychology.

   C. (i) Support your claim using an additional piece of specific and relevant evidence from a different source than the one that was used in Part B (i).

      (ii) Explain how the evidence from Part C (i) supports your claim using a different psychological perspective, theory, concept, or research finding learned in AP® Psychology than the one that was used in Part B (ii).

### Source 1

| Introduction |
|---|
| Expectations about a person can lead to behaviors that make these expectations come true. This idea was inspired by earlier psychological research, notably the case of "Clever Hans," a horse thought to possess human-like intelligence. However, it was found that his owner unintentionally was signaling the animal due to his expectations. This |

*(continued)*

led to the identification of how a researcher's biases and expectations could influence the outcomes of their experiments. Rosenthal and his team studied how experimenter expectations affected behavior in lab settings. They divided rats into "bright" and "dull" groups despite no actual differences. "Bright" rats performed better, attributed to unintentional cues and different treatments by experimenter expectations. Based on these results, a new study was conducted. This study focused on how these biases could extend beyond laboratories to everyday interactions, particularly in educational settings.

## Participants

The study was conducted at Oak School, located in a predominantly lower-middle-class neighborhood of a large town. It involved all students from grades one through six, totaling several hundred children. The participants included 18 teachers, 16 of whom were women and two were men. This reflects the typical gender distribution in elementary education at the time. The student body was diverse in terms of academic abilities, providing a broad spectrum for assessing the impact of teacher expectations.

## Method

The method involved administering the Test of General Ability (TOGA) to all students at the start of the school year. The TOGA is a nonverbal IQ test designed to assess cognitive abilities without relying on academic skills like reading or arithmetic. Teachers were falsely informed that the test was the "Harvard Test of Inflected Acquisition," which they were told could predict which students would likely experience a bloom in academic growth in the coming year. Based on random assignment, teachers were given a list of students purported to be the top 20% scorers, labeled as potential "academic bloomers." This deception was critical to establish expectations without any actual academic basis. At the end of the year, all students were measured again with the TOGA. The degree of IQ change was calculated for each student. The differences between the groups could be examined to see if there was an expectancy effect in a real-world setting.

## Results and Discussion

The study's primary findings revealed significant differences in IQ gains between students randomly designated "academic bloomers" and those not. Notably, based on fictitious test results, the students labeled as potential bloomers showed greater increases in their IQ scores (12.2 points) by the end of the school year compared to their peers in the control group (8.2 points). The most significant effects were observed in the youngest students, particularly those in the first and second grades, where the IQ score increases were statistically significant.

*(continued)*

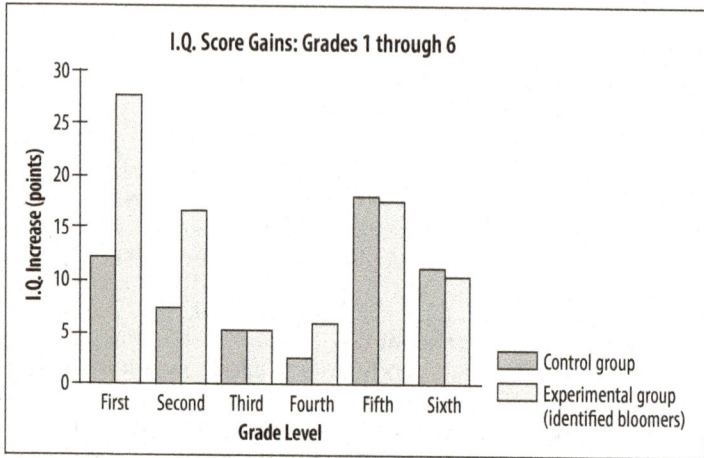

I.Q. Score Gains: Grades 1 through 6

Rosenthal and Jacobson's study highlighted the powerful role of teacher expectations in influencing student performance. It called for a reevaluation of educational practices and teacher training programs to address the potential impacts of these expectations on student outcomes, especially in the formative years of education.

Adapted from Psychological Reports. Rosenthal, R., & Jacobsen, L. (1966). Teachers' expectancies: Determinants of pupils' IQ gains. Psychological Reports, 19, 115–118.

## Source 2

### Introduction

Recent academic discussions challenge the notion that simply having high aspirations* directly leads to better academic performance. Studies indicate that just because students aim high doesn't automatically mean they will achieve high grades. Khattab's research aimed to expand this understanding by examining how different combinations of aspirations, expectations, and achievements can predict students' future educational behavior, particularly their likelihood of applying to university.

### Participants

The study utilized data from the Longitudinal Study of Young People in England (LSYPE), involving a sample of young people from various socioeconomic, ethnic, and educational backgrounds. The data were collected in multiple waves. Most of the data on aspirations and expectations came from the first wave, which had 15,770 students aged 13–14 from 647 schools.

*(continued)*

---

* What an individual hopes will happen in the future

| Method |
| --- |
| The achievement data was completed by age 15–16. The dependent variable was the General Certificate of Secondary Education (GCSE) at grade A–C. It is a set of exams taken by students in the required education, usually at age 15 or 16. GCSE results are important as they influence further educational and career opportunities for students. |

### Results and Discussion

A majority of students (58%) held both high aspirations and high expectations. Of these students, 68% were able to translate this into high achievement on their GCSEs. They achieved an average of 8.39 GCSE at grade A–C, whereas the other 32% only had an average of 1.6 GCSE at grade A–C. Approximately 14% of students held both low aspirations and low expectations and had the lowest number of GCSEs at grade A–C. Of these students, 17% of them achieved five or more GCSEs at grade A–C despite having low aspirations and low expectations.

This means having high aspirations and high expectations does not always guarantee high achievement. Also, low aspirations and low expectations do not guarantee a lack of success. The two remaining groups, 25% of students with high aspirations and low expectations and 3% of students with low aspirations and high expectations, seem to achieve similar numbers of GCSEs at grade A–C. This suggests that holding misaligned aspirations and expectations will likely result in low achievement. Changing them to both be high could make a big difference.

| | % with each category | Students with less than 5 GCSEs at A–C | Students achieved 5 GCSEs at A–C or more |
| --- | --- | --- | --- |
| High aspirations-High expectations | 58% | 32% | 68% |
| Low aspirations-High expectations | 3% | 65% | 35% |
| High aspirations-Low expectations | 25% | 64% | 36% |
| Low aspirations-Low expectations | 14% | 83% | 17% |

*Adapted from the British Educational Research Journal. Khattab, N. (2015). Students' aspirations, expectations and school achievement: what really matters? British Educational Research Journal, 41(5), 731–748. https://doi.org/10.1002/berj.3171*

**Source 3**

| Introduction |
| --- |
| This study examined the role of family involvement in schools, highlighting how parents actively work with schools to support their children's social, emotional, and academic growth. It reviewed previous research to understand how different ways parents engage can affect their children's school success. |

| Participants |
| --- |
| Data from 37 studies conducted between 2000–2013 were collected and statistically analyzed. These studies involved a wide range of participants, totaling approximately 80,580 students and their families. The students represented diverse age groups and socioeconomic and ethnic backgrounds. The studies used had been published in scientific journals, which adds credibility to the results. By examining such a large and diverse group of data, the researchers could make broader conclusions about how parental involvement impacts student success. |

| Method |
| --- |
| The researchers combined data from various studies to find overall trends. These studies were selected using keywords related to parental involvement and academic achievement from major research databases. There were four inclusion criteria included. First, they had to be published between 2000–2013. Second, they had to include parent participation in their child's education that is not defined as part of a special program. Third, it had to be a study with school children. Finally, the relationship between parent participation and academic achievement had to be studied by calculating the correlation coefficient or estimates of regression models. |

| Results and Discussion |
| --- |
| The results suggest that parents playing an active role in education generally leads to better school performance among students, though the impact is moderate. The effect size, which measures the strength of this impact, varied depending on factors like what aspect of performance was measured, how family involvement was defined, and at what school level the students were. For instance, when parents had high expectations and engaged in specific activities like discussing school topics or reading with their children, these actions were strongly linked to better academic results. The analysis showed that having supportive and involved parents could make a significant difference, especially when it involved high expectations and concrete support in learning activities. |

*(continued)*

The table below shows various types of family participation and their corresponding effect sizes, which measure the impact on academic performance. Parental expectations have the highest positive impact, while homework supervision has a minimal effect. This breakdown helps in understanding which activities are most beneficial for student achievement.

| Type of Family Participation | Effect Size | Notes |
|---|---|---|
| General Description of Participation | 0.167 | Strongly positive effect |
| Communication on School Matters | 0.200 | Strongly positive impact |
| Homework Supervision | 0.024 | Very small positive effect |
| Parental Expectations | 0.224 | Strongest positive impact noted |
| Reading with Children | 0.168 | Strongly positive effect |
| Attendance and Participation in School Activities | 0.010 | Negligible impact |
| Parental Style | 0.137 | Noticeable positive effect |
| Other | 0.125 | Positive effect |

*Adapted from Educational Research Review. Castro, M., Expósito-Casas, E., López-Martín, E., Lizasoain, L., Navarro-Asencio, E., & Gaviria, J.L. (2015). Parental involvement on student academic achievement: A meta-analysis. Educational Research Review (14), 33–46. https://doi.org/10.1016/j.edurev.2015.01.002*

**Sample Response**

(A) High expectations lead to better performance.

(B) When teachers have high expectations, students have IQ gains of 12.2 points (Source 1). This supports the claim that high expectations lead to better performance because it will allow students to live up to a <u>self-fulfilling prophecy</u> that their teachers have for them.

(C) When students have high expectations and high aspirations, they have more GCSEs at grade A–C (Source 2). This supports the claim that high expectations (along with high aspirations) lead to better performance. So it is important for the 25% of students with high aspirations but low expectations to improve study strategies to increase their expectations. By incorporating <u>metacognition</u>, or reflection, in their studies, students will feel more confident, which translates into higher expectations. With both high expectations and high aspirations, they will now be more successful.

For parts B (ii) and C (ii), the psychological perspective, theory, concept, or research finding must be explicitly identified in the AP® Psychology Course and Exam Description (2024). Possible connections for each source are provided below.

### Source 1

- Cognitive perspective is the belief that behavior and mental processes result from thought processes (e.g., memory, attention, problem-solving, perception, language).

- Self-fulfilling prophecy is the tendency for our beliefs about ourselves or another person to lead us or them to act in a way that brings about the behaviors we expect and confirms our original impression.

- Self-efficacy is the level of confidence an individual has regarding their ability to perform a specific task or skill.

### Source 2

- Harness the motivation that comes with high aspirations and high expectations by using strategies such as metacognition, spacing effect, and retrieval practice.

- If expectations are too high and unrealistic, then this can lead to an increase in stress and anxiety.

- Having high aspirations but being unable to achieve them may lead to student resentment, frustration, and social withdrawal. May result in learned helplessness.

### Source 3

- Overall, the authoritative parenting style in the United States has been found to be the most strongly correlated to positive self-esteem and high levels of self-reliance.

- Meta-analysis is the statistical technique for combining effect size estimates (results) from numerous studies on the same topic into a single effect size.

- Social learning theory is the theory that gender roles may be acquired through the observation of models and operant conditioning. Children imitate individuals in their family or culture of the same sex, especially in regard to behaviors that are reinforced or punished.

## Scoring Guidelines for the Evidence-Based Question (EBQ)

| Part A | 0 Points | 1 Point |
|---|---|---|
| Claim | Does not propose a claim that is relevant to the question. | Proposes a claim that is relevant to the question. |
| Example | • Expectations are important.<br>• Students should have expectations. | • High expectations lead to better performance.<br>• Low expectations lead to lower performance. |

| Part B (i) | 0 Points | 1 Point |
|---|---|---|
| Evidence | Does not identify nor correctly cite one piece of evidence from one of the provided sources to support the claim. Any evidence provided is not relevant to the question. | Uses one piece of correctly cited, specific, and relevant evidence from one of the provided sources to support the claim. |
| Example | • Sources say high expectations lead to high IQ gains. [The response has no citation.] | • When teachers have high expectations, students have IQ gains of 12.2 points (Source 1). |

| Part B (ii) | 0 Points | 1 Point | 2 Points |
|---|---|---|---|
| Explanation and Application | Does not explain the relationship between the evidence and the claim. | Explains the relationship between the evidence and the claim. | Applies a psychological perspective, theory, concept, or research finding to explain how the evidence supports the claim. |
| Example | • There should be high expectations because I believe this is the best for students. | • This supports the claim that high expectations lead to better performance because it will allow students to do better in first and fifth grades. | • This supports the claim that high expectations lead to better performance because it will allow students to live up to a self-fulfilling prophecy that their teachers have for them. |

| Part C (i) | 0 Points | 1 Point |
|---|---|---|
| Evidence | Does not identify nor correctly cite a **different** piece of specific evidence from either of the other two provided sources to support the claim. | Uses a **different** piece of correctly cited, specific, and relevant evidence from either of the other two provided sources to support the claim. |

*(continued)*

| Example | • When students have high expectations and high aspirations, they have more GCSEs at grade A–C. [This response does not list a source.] | • When students have high expectations and high aspirations, they have more GCSEs at grade A–C (Source 2). |
|---|---|---|
| **Part C (ii)** | **0 Points** | **1 Point** | **2 Points** |
| **Explanation and Application** | Does not explain the relationship between the evidence and the claim. | Explains the relationship between the evidence and the claim. | Applies a **different** psychological perspective, theory, concept, or research finding to explain how the evidence supports the claim. The psychological perspective, theory, concept, or research finding is **different** from the one used in Part B (ii). |
| Example | • Students should have high expectations because it is good for them.<br>• This evidence clearly supports my claim. | • This supports my claim because high expectations can increase performance. | • When students have high expectations and high aspirations, they have more GCSEs at grade A–C (Source 2). This supports the claim that high expectations (along with high aspirations) lead to better performance. So it is important for the 25% of students with high aspirations but low expectations to improve study strategies to increase their expectations. By incorporating metacognition, or reflection, in their studies, students will feel more confident, which translates into higher expectations. With both high expectations and high aspirations, they will now be more successful. |